W9-AOX-522

Embattled Democracy

EMBATTLED DEMOCRACY

Missouri Democratic Politics, 1919–1932

Franklin D. Mitchell

University of Missouri Studies Volume XLVII
University of Missouri Press
Columbia • Missouri

54581

Copyright © 1968 by

THE CURATORS OF THE
UNIVERSITY OF MISSOURI

*Library of Congress Catalog
Card Number 68–11347*

Printed and bound in the United States of America

for

Laura Schreck Mitchell (1892–1955)

and

Worth Sprott Mitchell

ACKNOWLEDGMENTS

THE DEBTS A SCHOLAR ACCUMULATES in the writing of a book are many — especially if it is a first book. I am happy to acknowledge my indebtedness to my professors at the University of Missouri: Professor Richard S. Kirkendall introduced me to the fascinating realm of the recent American past and guided the first version of this study, which served as my doctoral dissertation; Professors Lewis E. Atherton, James L. Bugg, Jr., Lloyd E. Jorgenson, Charles F. Mullett, and Walter V. Scholes provided instruction and intellectual stimulation that must be reflected in this study; Professors Atherton and Richard A. Watson read the manuscript in dissertation form and made several useful suggestions for its improvement. I have also benefited greatly from the incisive suggestions of Professors Richard O. Davies of Northern Arizona University and Lyle W. Dorsett of the University of Southern California. The responsibility for all errors of fact and interpretation, of course, is solely mine.

Several other individuals and institutions rendered valuable assistance. Dr. Richard S. Brownlee, Mr. Kenneth Holmes, and Mrs. Nancy Prewitt cooperated fully in making available material in the joint collections of the State Historical Society of Missouri and the Western Historical Manuscripts Collection of the University of Missouri. The staffs in charge of manuscripts at the Franklin D. Roosevelt Library, the Library of Congress, Missouri Historical Society, New York Public Library, and Yale University Library courteously and efficiently aided my research in their respective collections. Mrs. Lan Nielson of Aurora, Missouri, loaned several annual reports of the Missouri Women's Christian Temperance Union from her library. Mrs. James A. Reed graciously consented to an examination of the papers of her late husband, and Mr. and Mrs. David Q. Reed made me welcome in the Reed residence, where the papers are housed. Grants from the University of Missouri and from Washburn University of Topeka enabled me to research in these various libraries. I am grateful to Mrs. Virginia Wade, Mrs. Lucille Ross, and Theodore Palm for typing the final draft of the manuscript.

Much of Chapter IV of this work has appeared in the *Missouri Historical Review*. I wish to thank Dr. Richard S. Brownlee, editor of the *Review*, for permission to include it in this book.

I express one measure of my appreciation to my parents in dedicating my work to them.

F.D.M.

Washburn University of Topeka
July, 1967

CONTENTS

INTRODUCTION

A FEW YEARS AGO a leading scholar of recent United States history called the 1920's "the exciting new frontier of American historical research."[1] This characterization is substantiated by the interest scholars are showing in the decade and by the rapidly growing body of historical literature on the twenties.[2] Historical studies of the politics of the period are, however, still few. The explanation is well recognized: Historians of twentieth-century American politics have found the Progressive and New Deal eras more exciting and significant than the intervening years.

This study of the Democratic party in Missouri, 1919–1932, attempts to contribute to a fuller understanding of one aspect of our political past that hitherto has been related largely in the perspective of one man — Franklin Delano Roosevelt. As illustration, Frank Freidel's biography of Roosevelt contains the best scholarly account of the Democratic party in the years of Harding, Coolidge, and Hoover.[3] The ultimate synthesis of national Democratic politics during the twenties, however, must draw not only upon the biographies of the party's leading politicians, but also upon a number of monographs that probe the nature of politics at the state and local levels.[4]

Proceeding upon the general assumption that political histories of states can contribute to an understanding of the political life of the nation, this study rests upon the particular assumption that a history of one major party — the Democratic — in one state can provide considerable insight into the political behavior of the entire electorate, because Democrats contested for the votes of all citizens. The study confirms an observation offered recently by a student of Democratic politics of the 1920's: The traditional division of national Democracy along geographical lines into eastern, western, and southern wings is too rigid and ignores the influence of subtle subdivisions and personal followings.[5] Although the sectional interpretation of politics has not been discarded in this investigation of the Missouri Democracy, equally if not more useful tools of analysis have been the rural-urban, ethnic, and the "great man" hypotheses of politics.[6]

All of these factors — sectional rivalries, rural-urban antagonisms, ethnic differences, and charismatic leaders — influenced, in varying degree, Democratic politics in Missouri. Sectional rivalries did not influence Missouri politics in the manner they did elsewhere, because the state was a geographical and demographical composite of neighboring sections. The cotton farmer of the southeast counties, in many instances, shared the economic interests and social outlook of the Deep South's cotton planter; the grain and livestock producer of the northern counties differed little in his views from other farmers of the Midwest's corn-hog farm belt; the St. Louis and Kansas City industrialists and their eastern counterparts dealt with many similar problems, and the workers in both sections experienced common grievances.

The tensions that existed nationally between rural and urban Democrats during the 1920's, however, clearly manifested themselves in clashes between country and city Democrats of Missouri. The rural-urban clash fed, in part, on the antagonistic, contrasting values of rural Anglo-Saxon Protestants and urban immigrant Catholics. Finally, the presence in the national legislature of Missouri's Senator James A. Reed, the chief Democratic opponent of the League of Nations, a major critic of President Wilson's leadership, and three times a contender for his party's presidential nomination, gave added significance to both Missouri and national politics.

But to focus upon the internal dissension that split the Democracy on the state and national levels is to miss half the story. The decade of the twenties was also the seedtime of new political attitudes and developments designed to unite old factions and recruit new voters to the Democratic party. The major new ethnic element to be drawn into Missouri's Democratic coalition — the Negro voter — was wooed long before the Depression shattered the national economy. White Democrats of the state, reversing their historical practice of excluding the Negro in politics, began formulating and implementing their new deal for colored citizens at the local and state level several years before the administration of Franklin D. Roosevelt inaugurated a New Deal for the nation. At the same time, Missouri's Negroes examined their traditional ties to the Republican party and found them ineffective. The Republicans by their apathy and indifference to the needs of Negroes unwittingly assisted the transition of colored voters from the G.O.P. to the Democratic party.

The story of the dissension, division, and reconstruction of the Missouri Democracy is an important part of the larger drama within the Democratic party that was acted on the national stage during the years of Woodrow Wilson's decline and continuing to Franklin D. Roosevelt's election. Its telling will clarify not only the reasons for the Republicans' ascendancy in the twenties, but also the bases for the Democrats' restoration to power in the thirties.

CHAPTER 1

MISSOURI AND MISSOURIANS

IN 1920 a proud Missouri, secure within the American Union, stood on the threshold of her centennial year. A century earlier the question of slavery's existence in the territory of the trans-Mississippi West had fed the flames of sectional controversy and had stayed for a time the granting of Missourians' impatient petitions for statehood. Compromises between North and South paved the way in 1821 for Missouri's admission into the Union as a slave state. The star of the twenty-fourth state was never to be officially represented in the Confederate constellation, however, for the antebellum migration that brought pro-Union settlers to Missouri altered the state's once predominantly southern character. At the celebration of her centenary many Missourians could agree that the state defied sectional classification: She was neither southern, nor northern, nor western. Missouri, her citizens believed, was a microcosm of America.[1]

During the 1920's Missouri's Democrats made a further claim that the state's electorate embodied all of the diversity residing in the national Democracy. A letter addressed to the principals of the deadlocked National Democratic Convention of 1924, William G. McAdoo and Alfred E. Smith, by the Democratic state legislators of Missouri described Missouri's heterogeneity:

> We are farmers and manufacturers. We are of the city and the country. We live in the mountains and the plains. We have among us the rich and the poor, Protestant and Catholic, wet and dry. With our native born we include German and French, Irish and Italians, and emigrants from all other nations and

states. Our fathers came here from the North and the South;
tens of thousands fought for the Confederacy and as many or
more for the Union.

From this variety of ideals, interests, loyalties, and passions
in the state's conglomerate society, the solons concluded,
sprang the diversity operating within Missouri's Democratic
party.[2]

The legislators' appeal to history for an explanation of Missouri's people and politics was appropriate, for the electorate
and the party systems of the twenties bore distinct inheritances from the past. Many Missourians could trace both their
ancestry and politics to the state's early residents — southerners and westerners who had migrated from Kentucky,
Tennessee, Virginia, North Carolina, and Maryland. Until
1850, pioneers from the Upper South and New West poured
into Missouri in larger numbers than any other group of
westward-moving migrants. Although these first settlers
brought with them the tenets of both Democracy and Whiggery, a majority professed the Democratic creed. In the
decade before the Civil War, however, German immigrants
and northerners from Ohio, Indiana, Illinois, Pennsylvania,
and New York swept into Missouri to give the state's society
a more diverse character. When the bonds of the Union
broke and the states aligned themselves in civil war, the pro-Union newcomers had more than counterbalanced Missouri's
once preponderant southern and Democratic orientation.
Missouri remained within the Union and Republicans controlled state politics during the decade of the sixties.[3]

By 1872 Union Democrats and former Whigs had combined forces in a revived Democracy that, after a bitter
struggle, wrested control of the state from the rule of Radical Republicans. Party membership had broadened with the
refranchisement of former Confederates in 1871 and with
the collapse of the Liberal Republican movement in 1872,
but the resulting union was unstable. Hatred of the Radicals

had provided the one major cohesive force in an era in which lingering war animosities and conflicting agrarian, commercial, and industrial interests threatened every coalition. During the last three decades of the nineteenth century, whenever the different factions within the Democracy failed to shape a unifying stand on such issues as redemption of county bonds, regulation of railroads, reduction of tariffs, state finances, and monetary policies, the dissatisfied elements either deserted to the Republicans or to a third party.[4] The one-party Democracy of the Deep South was not to be fixed upon Missouri.

At the same time, the tides of migration and immigration worked against Democratic supremacy in Missouri. The ante-bellum movement of northerners into the state continued after the Civil War at a rate approximately four times that of southerners. The flood of Yankees, together with the steady stream of Germans immigrating to Missouri, swelled the ranks of the Republican party. The incoming Irish contributed some strength to the Democratic party, but the days of this large movement into Missouri as well as to the nation ended as the nineteenth century drew to a close. Immigration from Germany, on the other hand, continued unabated into the twentieth century. By 1900 Germans composed half of the total foreign influx into the state, while the Irish constituted only one seventh. Of course, not all the immigrants from Germany and from the northern states were Republicans, nor were all the Irish and the southern migrants Democrats, but the evidence tends toward this generalization.[5]

With their ranks augmented by new residents, Missouri Republicans began demonstrating their political power with convincing victories during the 1880's. St. Louis shifted back to the Republicans in 1888 for the first time since 1870; four years later the G.O.P. elected several candidates for state administrative offices, a majority of the Missouri House of

Representatives, and ten of the state's fifteen representatives in Congress. In 1904 Missouri's electoral votes went to Theodore Roosevelt, and in 1908 Herbert S. Hadley, a Republican, became governor. The political pendulum swung back to the Democratic party in 1912 and 1916, when Democrats carried the state for Woodrow Wilson and their gubernatorial candidates. Democrats continued their victories into 1918 by capturing eleven of the sixteen congressional seats that year, but Republican Selden Spencer won the contest for the unexpired term of the late Democratic senator, William J. Stone.[6] The state's strong two-party system reasserted itself with impressive Republican victories in the 1920's.

Reinforcing the Republican party's ability to win at the polls was the gradual induction of Negro migrants into the state's political order. A decline in colored population during the first decade of the twentieth century proved to be an exception to the historic trend, for a continuing movement of Negroes into Missouri after the outbreak of the European War in 1914 more than offset the emigration of colored citizens to other states. Wartime opportunities in expanding commerce and industry attracted Negroes to St. Louis and Kansas City from both outstate and the Deep South; still others were attracted to the developing cotton culture of southeast Missouri.[7] A small number of Negroes had been won over to the Democratic party as early as 1880, but an overwhelming majority of the state's colored voters supported the G.O.P. in 1920. Although numbering only 178,241 when the nation returned to "normalcy" with the election of Warren G. Harding to the Presidency that year, Negroes were one of the most dynamic new elements in the state's electorate.[8]

A principal catalyst of cultural, social, and political ferment elsewhere in the nation in the decade after the First World War — the so-called "new" immigrant from southern and eastern Europe — was not an important factor in Missouri. The reason is simple: Few new immigrants came to Missouri in the late nineteenth and early twentieth centuries. Although large numbers of southern and eastern Europeans emigrated to America during this period, most of the newcomers to the Show-Me State were northern Europeans. True, during the first two decades of the twentieth century Russians and Italians ranked second and third in numbers, respectively, behind the traditionally first-place Germans, as the number of Irish immigrants in the same period slipped from second to fourth place. Proportionately, though, the new immigrants were outnumbered by northern Europeans two to one, and when all recent arrivals were compared to second-generation immigrants and native-born citizens, they were outnumbered nineteen to one.[9] The relative political insignificance of all foreign-born Missourians during the postwar decade is borne out by voter registrations in the state's two largest cities, home of almost all of the newcomers. In 1924 only 6 per cent of Kansas City's registered voters were foreign-born, while in St. Louis the figure was slightly less than 10 per cent.[10]

The prevailing pattern of Missouri's people and politics, then, was clearly discernible as the state began a second century of statehood. An overwhelming majority of the state's citizens were old-stock whites; 74 per cent of the population were born of parents native to America. Only 5.5 per cent of the population were foreign-born whites, and the remaining white citizens were either of foreign parentage or of mixed parentage. Negroes, constituting a mere 5.5 per cent of the total population, rounded out the picture. Both major political parties drew heavily upon the old Anglo-Saxon elements. Republicans gained ethnic diversity by adding Germans and Negroes to their primary old-stock core, while Democrats gathered into the party fold Anglo-Saxon and Irish-Americans. Generally, both parties embraced an electorate of old-stock Protestants of rural Missouri and urban Catholic immigrants.[11]

The demographic design that provided the foundation for a rural-urban political structure also constituted the basis for a diversified, but balanced, agricultural and industrial economy. According to the *Fourteenth Census*, 53.4 per cent of the state's 3,404,055 citizens were rural dwellers and 46.6 per cent urbanites. Actually, Missouri was much more rural than the percentages indicate. Of the state's 114 counties, 66 had no urban population in 1920; that is, there were no villages, towns, or cities of 2,500 or more inhabitants in these counties; of the remaining 48 counties, 41 had rural majorities.[12] Agriculture provided more jobs for the state's residents than any other enterprise; almost 400,000 persons were engaged in farming and forestry and annually produced commodities that totaled nearly one billion dollars in value, ranking Missouri fourth among the states, behind Iowa, Texas, and Illinois.[13]

Complementing and yet contrasting with this rural and agricultural pattern was the urban and industrial concentration shared principally by the state's two major cities, St. Louis and Kansas City. Approximately 70 per cent of Missouri's 1,586,903 urban population resided in these cities in 1920. Of the other Missouri cities, only St. Joseph, with a population of 77,939, had more than 50,000 persons, and only 7 counties had urban majorities.[14] Although St. Joseph and other towns eagerly campaigned for industries to be located in their communities, most of the state's manufacturing plants and commerce centered in St. Louis and Kansas City. In all, the 330,883 workers employed in manufacturing and mechanical industries in 1920 numbered nearly 70,000 less than those engaged in agriculture, but the value of manufactured products amounted to $1,594,208,338 that year, surpassing the value of farm and forest products by more than a half billion dollars to place Missouri in eleventh position among the manufacturing states. Moreover, the residents of the state's two largest cities constituted a majority of the half million Missourians employed in transportation and trade, professional, clerical, public, and domestic services. Only mining, employing 21,516 persons and dominating the economy in several southern counties, altered this picture.[15] To a high degree, then, the economic pursuits of Missourians mirrored the division of the population into rural and urban dwellers.

Of the state's two metropolitan centers, St. Louis was the older, larger, and more truly cosmopolitan; her society and politics were, therefore, less representative of the state. St. Louis' large immigrant and Negro population held a small majority over the city's old-stock native whites — 53.5 to 46.5 per cent, to be exact.[16] And although Protestants constituted 62.8 per cent of the state's church membership, the population of St. Louis comprised almost as many Catholics and Jews as Protestants.[17] St. Louis German-Americans had played a major role in placing the city in the Republican camp before the turn of the century, but during most of the 1920's neither they nor other old-stock St. Louisans held major leadership positions within Missouri's G.O.P. The social strains of the World War had dealt severe blows to German-American leadership in the party, but the refusal of most St. Louisans to accept prohibition was a more potent factor in shifting power to antiprohibitionists outstate and in Kansas City during the dry decade. Not until the election of 1928 did the Republican leadership of St. Louis regain its position within the party through the governor-elect, St. Louisan Henry S. Caulfield.[18]

Democratic leaders of St. Louis commanded no larger voice in the Missouri Democracy than did their counterparts in Republican politics. Since the destruction of "Boss" Ed Butler's machine by Joseph W. Folk's progressive Democratic organization in 1902, the St. Louis Democracy had lacked effective leadership. Nominally, J. Joseph Mestres, chairman of the City Central Democratic Committee during the 1920's, was the leader of St. Louis Democrats, but in practice the ward committeemen did as they pleased. In fact, leadership was fractionalized among the twenty-eight ward chairmen and influential Democrats of the city. The latter included Congressman (later, United States Senator) Harry B. Hawes, senatorial aspirants Breckinridge Long, Charles M. Hay, and Bennett Champ Clark, State Senator Michael J. Kinney, former Governor Frederick Gardner, National Committeeman Edward J. Goltra, and mayoralty candidates William Igoe, Lawrence McDaniels, and Bernard Dickmann.[19]

On the state's western border, sprawled on the bottoms and bluffs of the Kaw and the Missouri rivers, lay Kansas City. In 1920 Missouri's second city was a relatively young and growing metropolis, lacking the staid sophistication and cosmopolitan culture of St. Louis. A majority of her 324,410 residents — 64.5 per cent — were classified by the census as "native whites of native-white parentage." Of the nation's twenty largest cities, none had a higher percentage of old-stock whites than Kansas City. Like rural Missouri — source of many of the city's residents — Kansas City was predominantly Protestant.[20] Understandably, the cultural values of most Kansas Citians were characteristically more rural than urban. It is not surprising, then, that both Republican and Democratic politicians there could more readily establish rapport with outstate Missourians than could their counterparts in St. Louis. Kansas City Democrats, moreover, were more skillful in these matters than their Republican opponents — an advantage gained perhaps from integrating old-stock Protestants and Irish Catholics of Kansas City and rural Jackson County into an effective political organization.

That advantage, however, was fully realized only after Kansas City's Irish bosses Thomas J. Pendergast and Joseph B. Shannon could agree on a division of the spoils. Until Pendergast could establish his organization's clear ascendancy in the mid-twenties, his Democratic rival made every effort to gain the upper hand for his machine in the Kansas City-Jackson County Democracy. Much earlier in the city's history, supporters of the two chieftains became known as "Goats" and "Rabbits." The Goat label had been pinned on the Pendergast faction because poor Irish families residing in the city's West Bottoms kept goats for their milk supply. Across town and over the bluffs the homes of Shannon's followers bordered on the wooded haunts of rabbits. "When we come over the hill like goats," Alderman Jim Pendergast once promised his friends, the Shannon forces would "run like rabbits."[21] The labels stuck.

The Pendergast label stuck, too, and for many Missourians, especially for Republicans, the Pendergast organization became the Kansas City version of New York City's Tammany Hall. The House of Pendergast had its beginning in the 1880's when Jim Pendergast, Tom's older brother, welded together an efficient organization of discordant factions in the city's West Bottoms. Pendergast brought both leadership and organization into Kansas City Democratic politics, but these skills were worth little without support by the voters. The support came, however, when a grateful lower-class constituency reciprocated at the polls for the personal favors Jim generously dispensed from his popular saloon in the First Ward. After his election to the Board of Aldermen in 1892, Pendergast, with more favors to bestow, extended his power to the city's slum-ridden North End. By 1900 Alderman Jim was ready to challenge old-stock Republicans for the mayoralty of Kansas City.[22] The Irish boss's candidate was an old-stock Protestant of Scotch-Irish descent, James Alexander Reed.

Jim Reed, born in Ohio in 1862 and reared in Iowa, had moved to Kansas City during the 1880's, at the time Jim Pendergast was introducing his order into the unorganized wards of the West Bottoms. Reed's high intelligence, fine speaking voice, eloquence, and courage to express his convictions brought him rapid success in the rugged politics of Kansas City. This stormy petrel of the Missouri Democracy made his political debut in 1887 by delivering a blistering attack upon the intolerant Catholic-baiting American Protective Association. From that time on, the paths of the two Jims converged, and in 1898 Jackson Countians elected the young lawyer to the office of prosecuting attorney, on the Pendergast slate. Two years later, with Pendergast's backing, Reed won the Kansas City mayoralty contest; continued support enabled him to secure re-election in 1902.[23] This alliance of Pendergast and Reed, William M. Reddig has observed, was a mutually valuable arrangement: Reed used the mayoralty as a position from which to bid for state and national office, while Pendergast benefited from Reed's command of patronage and his campaigning abilities. Jim Pendergast died in 1911; that same year Jim Reed began his first term in the United States Senate.[24]

It fell to Alderman Jim's younger brother, Thomas J. Pendergast, to expand the machine he had inherited from Jim and, ultimately, to transform Kansas City into "Tom's town." In many ways Tom continued the policies of his popular and resourceful brother, but he widened the machine's circle of influence by providing services to the city's middle-class as well as to its lower-class citizens. The Irish boss was well equipped to deal with both groups. Endowed with a shrewd intellect and a powerful frame, Tom could, when the occasion demanded, perform with the finesse of a diplomat or the ferocity of a saloon bouncer. But while the pudgy Irishman was equally at home at a political bargaining session or a Donnybrook, he usually remained behind the scenes, the reins of power firmly in his hands.[25]

Joe Shannon, Pendergast's rival, wanted both the glare of the public spotlight and the power that accompanied control of a successful political organization. A handsome appearance and modest oratorical skills adequately fitted the Rabbits' leader for his self-styled role as a politician-statesman, but his talents as a political broker could not match those of Tom Pendergast. After losses to the Pendergast organization in the elections of 1924 and 1925, Shannon wisely settled for a junior partnership in Tom's machine. Under Pendergast's leadership, a united Kansas City and Jackson County Democracy commanded unprecedented power locally as well as within the Missouri Democracy for a decade and a half.[26]

Many of the factors that shaped the politics of the cities were reflected in the outstate political map for 1920. The political cartographer could easily designate seven areas of strength for either the Democratic or the Republican party; only the state's newest frontier, the southeast counties, retained a politically marginal character after the First World War.[27] Political maps, however, fail to illustrate what Charles Sellers, Jr., has called the "dynamics of the political situation — the elements of leadership, impetus, financing, and propaganda."[28] Some areas, richer than others in these political resources, were correspondingly more important in Missouri politics.

The oldest and most important rural Democratic region proudly called itself Little Dixie. Embracing thirteen north and northeast counties lying north and south of the Missouri River, Little Dixie possessed a distinct southern culture and tradition inherited from the Kentuckians and Virginians who, with their slaves, first settled the river counties. Although a two-party system had flourished there during the ante-bellum years, after the Civil War the area became the hard core of the Missouri Democracy. No one immediately assumed the leadership of the district that became vacant upon the death of Champ Clark in 1921; however, young Clarence Cannon from Lincoln County was destined to exercise much power in both state and nation after he began, in 1923, his congressional career of forty-one continuous years.[29] Because the area turned out Democratic majorities with undeviating regularity, the city bosses respected the wishes of Little Dixie's courthouse politicians and country editors, even if they did not always comply with them.

The rugged south central Ozarks, ranging from Maries County in the north to Oregon County on the Arkansas border, constituted a second Democratic stronghold. Although sparsely populated, the area's influence was carried into state legislative circles and Democratic politics through the commanding person of Frank H. Farris of Rolla. Farris, an exceptionally able leader and polished orator, began his public career as a state senator in 1898 and for the next thirty years sat in one or the other house of the General Assembly, serving almost always in a major position of leadership. The legislator from Rolla gained leadership within the Democratic party also, including the chairmanship of the State Central Committee during the mid-twenties. Until his death in 1926, Farris was known in the Missouri Democracy as a legislative leader and party general without peer.[30] The farmers and town dwellers in the Ozark area who regularly returned Farris to the General Assembly, election after election, were loyal to the Democratic ticket also, thus placing these south central counties among the most consistently Democratic counties of the state.

The third rural Democratic area embraced several Osage Plains counties that surround Kansas City and are adjacent to the Kansas-Missouri line. The border wars between proslavery Missourians and abolitionist Jayhawkers and the forced evacuation effected by Union General Thomas E. Ewing's Order No. 11 of 1862 had reinforced and hardened the Democratic proclivities of the area's first settlers. Harriet Louisa Young's memories of the turbulent fifties and sixties remained vivid throughout her lifetime, so much so that when her grandson Harry S Truman visited her, dressed in his bright blue National Guard uniform, she told young Harry firmly that Union blue was an unwelcome sight in her home. Harry never forgot his grandmother's rebuke or the attitudes within the state that it reflected.[31] The Youngs and other pioneers of the Osage Plains passed on to their children and their children's children a durable inheritance that favored the Democratic party.

While old-stock Americans of British descent predominated in all three outstate Democratic areas, the same was true in only three of the four major Republican strongholds. The heavily German Missouri and Mississippi river counties constituted the major exception. The "German belt" extended from Lafayette and Carroll counties in the central west, east along the Missouri River, and then downward from St. Louis as far south as Cape Girardeau. The German farmers of these river counties had retained many of the customs and ways of the old country. Both Lutheran and Catholic Germans drank their dark beer with gusto and regarded prohibition a perversion of democracy. Consequently, wet Republican candidates during the twenties were almost automatically assured of a large vote from the German counties.

The other three Republican areas of the state, peopled largely by old-stock Protestants, were as dry as the German counties were wet. Further, none of these areas looked to the cities for leadership; their own leaders were successful candidates for governor and United States senator during the dry decade. The first of the Republican governors of the twenties, Arthur M. Hyde, was reared in Shelby County, center of the traditionally Republican northwest and a pioneer prohibitionist stronghold. Shelby County voters had exercised the privilege of local option to outlaw the saloon in 1887, ten years after Hyde was born. After the prohibitionist and businessman-lawyer secured the governorship in 1921, he used the power of his office to extend the influence of rural Republicans in the state G.O.P. organization. And since state law empowered the governor to appoint the election and police boards in the state's three largest cities, Hyde, with varying degrees of success, brought rural standards of morality to bear on the politics of St. Louis, Kansas City, and St. Joseph.[32]

Although political leadership within the G.O.P. shifted south to the Republican-dominated southeastern Ozarks after the election of Wayne Countian Sam A. Baker to the governor's chair in 1924, the rural-oriented policies of Governor Hyde were continued in Baker's Administration. In many ways Baker's background paralleled that of other pioneers of the southeast hill country. During the Civil War the Baker family had divided their loyalties between the North and the South. Two Baker brothers fought for the Confederacy; a third, Samuel Baker, father of the Governor, sided with a majority of the region's residents and supported the Union and the party of Abraham Lincoln. Sam A. Baker and his generation kept the Republican faith of their fathers.[33]

The Ozark southwest constituted the fourth traditionally Republican region. This timber- and mineral-rich country was like the eastern Ozarks and had consistently returned Republican majorities since its settlement by pro-Union, non-slaveholding people of the Upper South and, in more recent times, by Yankee farmers from the North. The most influential Republican of the district, Roscoe Conkling Patterson, born in Springfield in 1876 when Reconstruction was ending, shared the spiritual and cultural values of the Ozark people, and they helped elect the dry, Protestant stalwart to the United States Senate in 1928.[34]

Completing the political map of Missouri in 1920 was the state's newest agricultural frontier, the southeast "Bootheel" area, so named because its configuration in relation to the rest of the state suggested the heel of a boot. At one time the wooded swamp counties were also called "swampeast" Missouri, but major lumbering and drainage projects undertaken during the early twentieth century rendered the label inaccurate. Further, although some Bootheel counties had been unfailingly Democratic, the influx of northern Republicans into the area after 1900 made their designation as Democratic inappropriate in 1920. In fact, the population and the political trend seemed to indicate that the southernmost part of the state would become a stronghold of the Republican party.[35]

The present and future of political parties, however, flow only in part from the durable patterns of the past; as Professor V. O. Key, Jr., once observed, parties must also cope successfully with changing realities in order to survive.[36] The realities of the postwar decade, involving the clash of old and new cultural, economic, and social forces, were especially challenging to both the Democratic and the Republican parties. Missouri Republicans, like their national counterparts, were generally sucessful in either submerging or surmounting the troublesome problems that arose after the First World War. Missouri Democrats, however, fell victim to all of the antagonistic issues that plagued the national Democracy. Unable to resolve differences over such diverse matters as the League of Nations, philosophies of government, cultural liberalism, prohibition, agricultural relief, and other economic and social issues, Democrats in Missouri split into quarreling factions. As a consequence, the party declined to minority status, and the twenties, for Missouri and the nation, was a time of Republican ascendancy.

The first of the troublesome postwar issues, the League of Nations, did more than introduce dissension into the ranks of the Democratic party; it furthered the breakup of the Democratic coalition that had elected Woodrow Wilson to a second term as President in 1916 and evoked a durable ethnic and emotional alignment outside party affiliation that survived several years after enthusiasm for the League had waned. Ironically, one of the first casualties of Democratic President Woodrow Wilson's peace plan was the Democratic party.

CHAPTER 2

THE DISRUPTION OF
MISSOURI DEMOCRACY

A HARMONIOUS MISSOURI DEMOCRACY and a gracious St. Louis played host to the Democratic National Convention of 1916. Missing from the meeting in St. Louis was the acrimony that had marred the convention at Baltimore four years earlier, when Missouri's favorite son, Champ Clark, lost the presidential nomination to Woodrow Wilson. Even the ruffled relations between President Wilson and Missouri's Senator Reed had been smoothed over in order to unify the campaign effort, and the delegates, in a mood of harmony and accord, renominated Wilson by acclamation. In the election, James A. Reed won a second term in the Senate, and the state cast her electoral votes for Woodrow Wilson.[1] Four years later, however, the state and the national Democracy were dissension-ridden and divided, Irish Democrats were at odds with party leadership, and Reed and Wilson were implacable foes.

At the core of the controversies was the League of Nations. Pro- and anti-League Democrats were quarreling in every state of the Union in 1919 and 1920, but in no state did the League question provoke so much bitterness and dissension as it did in Missouri. The fundamentally different political philosophies of President Wilson and Senator Reed, brought into full opposition by the League issue, accentuated the dispute that plunged the party into a maelstrom of controversy. Moreover, Wilson's peace program evoked a deeply rooted emotional and ethnic response that aligned old-stock Democrats outstate behind the League and the Irish of the cities against it. This division of the Missouri Democracy's rural and urban coalition, sustained by the continuing question of America's role in world affairs and reinforced by controversial domestic issues, survived to plague the party for more than a decade.

To a remarkable degree the clear-cut division within the Democracy caused by differences over the League reflected the rigid positions taken on that issue by President Wilson and the party's leading irreconcilable, Senator Reed. Indeed, the intransigence of the two leaders on the question accounts in large measure for the factionalization of the Democratic party in Missouri. No simple explanations exist for Wilson's inflexible advocacy of the League and for Reed's equally adamant opposition to America's entrance into the world organization. In the President's case, Arthur S. Link has written, the historian can provide no final explanation for Wilson's uncompromising promotion of the League. "The sympathetic biographer," Link explains, "would like to believe that it was his illness, which aggravated his bitterness and his sense of self-righteousness." But at the same time, Link adds, Wilson might have acted thus even had he not suffered his breakdown, "for it was not in his nature to compromise away the principles in which he believed."[2]

Reed opposed the League with the same unwavering determination that marked Wilson's fight for his peace program. His motives were varied and complex, but antipathy to collective security and devotion to unfettered nationalism were primary causes of the Missourian's refusal to support the League; important supporting factors were Reed's deep-seated Anglophobia, his disagreement with the President's liberal domestic policies, and an apparent personal dislike of Wilson. In short, Reed's opposition to Wilson's League combined many of the major motives of other irreconcilables.[3]

Of greatest significance for the Democratic party's fortunes in state and nation during the controversy over the League, however, were the contrasting concepts of party and government held by President Wilson and Senator Reed. In fact, the means Wilson either suggested or employed to gain the Senate's and the nation's approval of the peace covenant were as repugnant to the Democrat from Missouri as the League itself. Consequently, Reed emerged not only as a leading opponent of the League, but also as a major critic of Wilson's presidential leadership.

Wilson brought to the White House a profound admiration for the British parliamentary system and a conviction that he should provide the country with strong executive leadership.[4] "The President," Wilson wrote in 1913, "must be prime minister, as much concerned with the guidance of legislation as with the just and orderly execution of law, and he is spokesman of the nation in everything, even in . . . dealings . . . with foreign nations."[5] Through active leadership of Congress and development of the caucus to promote party regularity, and by carrying his case on major issues directly to the people, Wilson added greatly to the power of the Presidency. The enactment of the New Freedom in the first two years of his administration stands as a model of Wilson's political theories translated into action; the fight Wilson waged for the League in the last two years of his second administration points up his tragic failure as President of the people and leader of his party.[6]

Reed's determination to act independently of both President and party is best explained by his concept of the legislator's role. The lawmaker, Reed believed, should rely upon his "highest judgment" and "conscience" in legislating.[7] In contradiction to Wilson's political theory, then, Reed did not seek his guiding principles in the will of the Chief Executive, as President of the nation and party leader; nor did he submit himself to the party caucus in Congress. Even more important, as a review of the controversy over the League shows, Reed rejected the notion that the legislator should make himself obedient to the wishes of the majority of his constituents. "The majority," Reed once said, "has been wrong oftener than it has been right in all the course of time."[8]

As an influential member of Senate committees on manufacturers and banking and currency, and as a skilled, forceful orator, Jim Reed contributed in an important way to the successes and failures of the President. Until America entered the First World War, he generally supported the Administration on major legislation. On the declaration of war, Reed broke with Missouri's senior Democratic United States senator, William J. Stone, casting his vote with the Administration forces. But after the country's entrance into war and with the attendant increase of presidential and governmental powers, the Democrat from Missouri began to move away from the President.[9]

Reed's refusal to back numerous wartime measures drew quick fire from the Administration's supporters in Missouri. In the summer of 1917 the *St. Louis Republic*, the only Democratic metropolitan newspaper in the state, blasted Reed's failure to "stand behind the President."[10] At the same time, the Republican *Kansas City Star* reprinted excerpts of articles appearing in various newspapers, openly critical of Missouri's Senator. One opinion, expressed in the *Ohio State Journal* (Columbus), summed up a sentiment held by many Wilson Democrats of Missouri: "Probably the two most unpopular men in America are Senator Reed of Missouri and Senator La Follette of Wisconsin."[11] In the spring of 1918 the *New Republic*, still supporting the President but soon to oppose him on the League issue, charged that "Reed has been doing his best to block an approach to war efficiency."[12]

Independent on matters pertaining to the war, Reed indicated soon after the Armistice that he would pursue a similar course in matters pertaining to the peace. In November,

1918, nearly three months before the Senate received the published peace treaty, the militant nationalist advanced four closely related reasons for opposing the League: the nation's participation in the international order would threaten the sovereignty of the United States; the integrity of the Monroe Doctrine would be challenged; the Constitution would be violated; and the life of the Republic would be endangered.[13]

The idealism bound up in the League also came under strong attack from Reed. Speaking in January, 1919, before a convention of St. Louis businessmen in his first speech against the League in Missouri, Reed scoffed at the bright hopes many Americans held for the League. What had not been accomplished in nearly two thousand years, he declared, would certainly not be accomplished "within the next sixty days through the instrumentality of a League of Nations. . . . Sensible men deal with conditions as they are. They do not build castles in Spain or search for pots of gold at the end of the rainbow."[14]

Since pro-League sentiment apparently dominated the state in the early months of 1919, Reed's opposition to the international organization increased his wartime unpopularity with the rank and file of his party, if not with a majority of the voters.[15] Perhaps mirroring Missourians' initial enthusiasm for the League, Selden Spencer, Reed's Republican colleague in the Senate, disclosed on March 11 that, while he considered the proposed Covenant of the League "unacceptable in its present form," he was "heart and soul" in favor of a league of nations.[16] A few days later, Speaker of the House Champ Clark, one of the most reticent of the state's Democratic congressmen on the subject of the League and reportedly opposed to the United States' membership in the organization, angrily denied reports that he had ridiculed the League.[17] Apparently, the strong pro-League feeling throughout the state made politicians of both major parties wary of any forthright denunciation, such as that propounded by Senator Reed. The Senator, however, seemed confident that Missourians would ultimately approve of his course, once they were informed of the dangers he believed to be inherent in the League.

Reed's opportunity to enlighten his constituents came in March, 1919, when the Democrats of Missouri's state legislature invited him to address the lawmakers in joint assembly. At the outset of his three-hour speech Reed asserted that his conscience and judgment, not the judgment of others, had led him to his present stand of opposition to the League. "Wide public misconception of the League," Reed told the legislators, stemmed from the fact that a majority of Americans had not read its proposed constitution. While the American people had been told that the League had been conceived by American representatives, "the entire scheme," Reed charged, was "the product of British statesmanship." This authorship explained, he said, why, in the League's councils, Great Britain would outvote the United States five to one and would be allowed to retain her entire fleet. Reiterating the arguments he had advanced in debates in the Senate, Reed asserted that the United States' entrance into the League would constitute a threat to the sovereignty of the country, impair the Monroe Doctrine, violate the Constitution, and imperil the life of the nation.[18] Frankly asserting his belief that President Wilson was wrong in advocating the League, Reed evoked angry cries of "No! No! You're wrong!" from the Democratic side of the assembly. And with this outburst sixteen Democratic representatives, led by Speaker of the House Frank H. Farris, left their seats and stormed from the hall.[19]

The chain of events that quickly followed Reed's appearance in the State Capitol gave further evidence that his address had generated more heat than light. Fifty rural old-stock Democratic representatives, at a hastily arranged meeting that evening, vented their anger in the adoption of a stiff resolution severely censuring Reed. The Senator, the lawmakers charged, had spoken of the President "in a most sneering, sarcastic, and disrespectful manner." Further, Reed had spoken "sneeringly and disrespectfully" of such fundamental ideas as the "brotherhood of man" and other tenets of democracy. In all, these Democrats read Reed out of the party, challenged him to submit his course — opposition to the League — to Democrats in a primary contest, and soundly condemned him for opposing President Wilson.[20] Significantly, and indicative of the frame of mind of many old-stock supporters of Wilson, the Democratic lawmakers did not take issue with Reed's analysis of the League's constitution or challenge the interpretation he placed on the nation's participation in the world order. It was enough for them that the Senator from Missouri, a Democrat, had differed with the Democratic President.

The developing controversy not only left Reed unruffled, but also elicited from the skeptical Senator a masterly bit of sarcasm:

> When a crowd of gentlemen gets together and decides that human nature has changed, that ill feeling is dead, and that universal love is the rule, and then proceeds to demonstrate the belief by calling those who do not agree with them anarchists, by demanding that they resign from office, and by indulging in talk that those who do not hold their views ought to be hanged, it leads to the conclusion that the world is much the same as it has been for a number of years.
>
> As an ordinary, unregenerated sinner, old-fashioned enough to believe in the Constitution of the United States and not sufficiently informed as to be willing to turn over the control of our country to European governments, I can extend that old-fashioned sympathy to these excited individuals who adopted the resolution.[21]

While Reed rejected the charges and demands of the rural representatives,[22] Irish Democrats began to voice their views on Reed's opposition to the League. Kansas City's Irish leaders Thomas J. Pendergast and Joseph B. Shannon had heard Reed's address to the legislators. "I'm not fool enough to think that I know anything about the League of Nations," Pendergast declared, "but men like Senator Reed and Mr. Wilson have made a study of the subject and are competent to give opinions. I know Jim Reed would not attack the proposed League until he honestly believed he was right." Reed would continue to receive his personal support, Pendergast announced, and the Goat faction of the Kansas City Democracy that he headed would also back the Senator.[23] Shannon, boss of the Rabbit Democrats of Kansas City, asserted that he would have been against the League, regardless of Reed's position.[24] Professing sincere hopes for the Irish independence movement, Shannon expressed his conviction that Article X of the League would work against a free Ireland. Nevertheless, Shannon insisted, he had listened to both sides of the controversy over the League before arriving at his decision. He urged other Missourians to do the same: "Every public forum should be opened to a discussion of the question — in the schools, the churches — and every humble citizen should not miss an opportunity to hear a discussion on both sides."[25]

An educational campaign got under way in April with both pro- and anti-League orators stumping the state. Senator Reed headed up the anti-League speakers; his articulate antagonist was Charles M. Hay, a leading prohibitionist, former state legislator, and erstwhile small-town lawyer turned successful partner in a St. Louis law firm. Sponsored by the League to Enforce the Peace, Hay's addresses represented the first significant attempt of Wilson Democrats of Missouri to advance the League in other than emotional, idealistic terms.[26]

The educative efforts of Senator Reed apparently had little immediate success in swinging popular sentiment to his side on the League issue or in lessening the faith of many Missourians in the League. In fact, a more discernible effect was a heightening of hostility between supporters of Wilson and supporters of Reed. Rumored about were reports that the Wilson men had brought pressure on the state's Democratic Committee chairman, Ben M. Neale, to call a meeting of the committee for the express purpose of repudiating Reed's anti-League activities. These rumors were verified when the state committeemen assembled at St. Louis in late May.[27]

The presence of National Democratic Chairman Homer S. Cummings and the President's secretary, Joseph Tumulty, at the St. Louis meeting attested to the national party's and the Wilson Administration's concern over the growing dissension in Missouri. Although the two emissaries engineered an agreement that restrained the state committee from an explicit condemnation of Senator Reed, this action was counteracted by the committee's resolution that strongly endorsed President Wilson and the League. Kansas Citian R. Emmett O'Malley, who held the proxy for Tom Pendergast and spoke for many discontented Irish Democrats, warned the committee that any pro-League resolution would be considered by friends of Reed as a direct insult to the Senator. O'Malley's displeasure was compounded when the state committee adjourned to permit Wilson supporters to convene the first session of a new state Democratic club.[28]

This new and frankly pro-League organization, which styled itself "The Missouri State Democratic Club," made its first order of business the chastising of the irreconcilable Senator. "If Senator Reed really wants to represent the people of Missouri," declared Charles M. Hay, "he will want to know how the people of Missouri stand." The Senator had not been moved by "the orphan's cries and the widow's tears," Hay concluded; "perhaps he will be moved by the voice of his constituents."[29] For the next several minutes Wilson men from every section of the state testified for Wilson and the League. Finally, after informally censuring Reed, the group approved resolutions commending Wilson's advocacy of the League and expressing "the earnest wish that the Senate . . . will speedily ratify the proposed treaty of peace including the League of Nations."[30]

Despite an accompanying resolution that "urged the President to see that the rights of the Irish race for self-determination be recognized," an enraged O'Malley refused to believe that Cummings and Tumulty had visited Missouri to secure party harmony. Their real purpose, the fiery Irishman charged, was to discredit Reed through the instrumentality of the newly formed Missouri State Democratic Club.[31]

O'Malley's analysis had, in fact, hit upon the truth. Since early 1919 several members of the Wilson Administration had lent advice and encouragement to Missourians in their efforts to repudiate Senator Reed. Presidential Secretary Tumulty, in addition to his visit to Missouri to co-ordinate anti-Reed strategy, had arranged for Bainbridge Colby, then a minor figure in Washington but later Wilson's last Secretary of State, to deliver a pro-League address in St. Louis in late March. This activity, Tumulty happily wired Wilson in Versailles, had "Reed worried."[32] Additional reports reached Wilson from National Committeeman Edward J. Goltra of St. Louis and brought the President's blessings to the pro-League maneuvers in Missouri. He was confident, Wilson cabled Goltra, that Missouri would not sustain Reed's "extraordinary course."[33]

For a while in early June, Wilson even contemplated making St. Louis the scene of his first major appeal in the United States for the League, upon his return from the Versailles Peace Conference. The opportunity arose from a grandiose scheme promoted by Goltra and supported by a number of Wilson's followers in Missouri. Goltra insisted that he could assemble in St. Louis' Forest Park an audience of several million people that would constitute, in his words, "a

mass meeting of the nation on the banks of the Mississippi."
An address before this symbolic congress of the American
people in the home state of the major Democratic foe of the
League, Goltra predicted, would arouse strong support from
the public and thereby force the recalcitrant senators — except the obstinate Reed — into line.[34]

Wilson dismissed this proposal at first, primarily because
the affair was decidedly too partisan,[35] but a new bipartisan
appeal from a group that included even Missouri's Republican United States senator, Selden Spencer, caused him to
give the scheme a second thought. The President eventually
ruled out the St. Louis meeting, but the urgent appeal of his
friends had made an impression upon him. The devotion of
adherents of the League in the home state of the party's leading opponent helped to firm the President's resolve to tour
the country in an effort to rally support behind his peace
program.[36]

Meanwhile, the Democratic State Committee proceeded
with its own plans to repudiate reports that Reed's influence
was growing in the party's chief governing body. Despite
the clear-cut resolutions in support of Wilson and the League
adopted by the group in its May meeting, committeemen
planned to assemble in St. Louis for a mid-August meeting
in order to consider the whole matter further.[37] This meeting,
designed to make official the committee's commitment to the
League, won Wilson's approval: "I applaud the purpose of
the State Committee," he wrote Goltra, "and hope with all
of my heart that everything will work out as you plan."[38]

Looming as the only major threat to the state committee's
endorsement of the League was the increase in vocal protests
from anti-League Irish groups that were disillusioned with
Wilson's failure to press for Ireland's self-determination at
Versailles.[39] Both the Irish in the Pendergast and Shannon
organizations of Kansas City and the St. Louis societies of
the national Friends of Irish Freedom indicated that they

would oppose any action to make a pro-League stand the official Democratic policy. On August 9, two days before the state committee meeting, the St. Louis Irish societies adopted a resolution aimed at heading off an apparent endorsement of the League:

> We earnestly urge the members of the Democratic State Committee not to ignore and disregard the rights of the Democrats of the State by indorsing the League of Nations. We believe that such action will be regarded as an unwarrantable attempt to choke off and suppress the full and free discussion which the tremendous import of this question requires.

Should the League be endorsed, the resolution concluded, the action would "entail strife and confusion in Democratic ranks and finally end in disastrous Democratic defeat at the polls."[40] Even at that moment, Peter Barnett, an Irish leader in St. Louis, boasted that the Friends of Irish Freedom were stronger in St. Louis than the Democratic party. "Within sixty days," Barnett claimed, "this condition will prevail over the entire state."[41] R. Emmett O'Malley of Kansas City predicted that 95 per cent of the Irish voters would bolt the party if it adopted a pro-League stand. O'Malley expressed his belief, which was probably the belief of Tom Pendergast as well, that a pro-League plank would cost the party Kansas City's usual ten thousand to fourteen thousand Democratic majority in the 1920 election.[42]

But neither the protests and threats of anti-League Irish nor Reed's plea that the committee take no action which "might divide our party" could stay the committee's hand.[43] The question facing Democrats, according to Burris Jenkins, an editor and pastor in Kansas City, was uncomplicated and clear: "We are here to accept or reject Woodrow Wilson — the greatest man that walked the earth — the prime minister of mankind." In quick order the pro-League Democrats approved a resolution that combined a strong endorsement of

Wilson and the League with an equally strong condemnation of Reed's opposition to the international order. Reed was bluntly instructed to vote in the Senate for the League of Nations "without modification or reservation."[44]

For National Committeeman Edward Goltra, the committee's action had finally settled the wrangling over the League in Missouri. In a letter to former Governor David R. Francis, Goltra gleefully explained that Wilson's supporters had had a "lively time in executing on Jim Reed a *coup de grâce*. I verily believe Jim could not now be elected constable in any precinct in the state." And, he added, "it is useless for him to shout 'no authority' to the State Committee."[45] Goltra's analysis, however, was hardly accurate. A United States senator was not bound by the action of his party's state committee. Moreover, with Irish Democrats predominating in many precincts throughout the state, it would have been more pertinent to question the success of a pro-League Democrat ticket without Irish support. Nor could the pro-League Democrat take heart in the growing opposition to the League among the state's German and Italian population, who for reasons of their own were as unhappy with Wilson's League as the Irish. The Germans complained that the Versailles Treaty had fixed a Carthaginian peace upon their homeland, and Italians expressed disappointment over President Wilson's failure to support Italy's claim to the port of Fiume.[46] Although Missouri's Italians were few in number and the Germans of the state were predominantly Republican, the anti-League sentiment of both groups precluded a Democratic appeal to them based primarily upon the League.

The reaction of Senator Reed and anti-League Democrats to the committee's resolution was based upon these realities. "The Democrats of this state need no boss," Reed snapped. "I was not elected to office by the State Committee, but by the people of Missouri. I hold myself responsible to the people of Missouri, when they have spoken in a convention regularly called, as provided by law."[47] And Irish Democrats, true to their threats and undeterred by the committee's weak resolution expressing sympathy for Ireland's independence efforts, immediately expressed their dissatisfaction with the turn of events. Resolutions adopted by the St. Louis Friends of Irish Freedom societies bluntly served notice that Irish Democrats would bolt the party if the League became a plank in the Democratic platform.[48] Reed remained confident that this would not happen. "Public sentiment is swinging our way," he wrote an Irish supporter in St. Louis. "Let the fight over the League of Nations proceed to the end."[49]

In Washington, meanwhile, a weary President was completing his plans to carry the fight for his peace program to the people. With popular support for the League in noticeable decline nearly everywhere, Wilson decided that the time for rallying the public to his cause had arrived. On September 3 he began his ill-fated western tour, arriving two days later in Missouri for major speaking appearances in St. Louis and Kansas City.[50]

St. Louisans gave the President an especially warm greeting in a morning parade through the city's streets, and in the evening twelve thousand persons packed the Coliseum to hear his address. Despite the President's desire to make a nonpartisan appeal, a partisan flavor permeated the occasion. In a song session before the President's arrival at the Coliseum an irreverent group persistently parodied one line of the solemn "Battle Hymn of the Republic," singing: "And we'll hang Jim Reed on a sour apple tree." The Coliseum crowd seemed to call for fighting words, and Wilson did not disappoint them. He characterized the League's opponents as "absolute, contemptible quitters," incapable of "constructive opposition." He was no quitter: "My ancestors were troublesome Scotchmen and among them were some of that famous group that were known as Covenanters. Very well, here is the covenant of the League of Nations. I am a covenanter." A storm of applause swept the hall after these concluding remarks.[51]

The following day Wilson carried his fight to Reed's home town. In an evening address before fifteen thousand in Kansas City's Convention Hall, Wilson argued that "a minority was obstructing the majority's desire to enter the League. . . . If we do not want little groups of selfish men to plot the future of Europe," he advised tactlessly, "we must not allow little groups of selfish men to plot the future of America." Then, perhaps sensing the impact his words would have upon Reed's friends, Wilson added: "I am not here to fight anybody." He hesitated, and then slowly repeated with emphasis, "a-n-y b-o-d-y."[52]

The President's two major addresses in Missouri did little to alter the alignment on the League question and nothing to ameliorate the growing rift in the dissension-ridden Democratic party. In fact, a few days after the President's visit, Republican Senator Selden Spencer, under pressure from the Republican State Committee, announced that he would join the opposition forces of Henry Cabot Lodge.[53] Reed, angered by the President's words, bitterly assailed the President, calling him an autocrat.[54] Wilson's venture into the state had only worsened the friction within the party.

The ensuing events of 1919 turned the bright dreams of Wilson's supporters everywhere into a horrible nightmare. The denouement began in late September with the collapse of the President on his western tour; next came the stroke on October 2 that partially paralyzed him; finally, in November, the President's uncompromising strategy that forced loyal pro-League senators to vote against the altered covenant presented to the Senate by the Republican leadership ended the drive for the League that year.[55] A prediction made in August by Missourian Breckinridge Long, third assistant secretary of state, that the President's tour would compel ratification of an unreserved and unamended League by September 20, had fallen far short of the mark.[56] Instead, at the year's end, the possibility of the United States' remaining outside the League seemed much more realistic.

As 1919 drew to a close, the situation within the Missouri Democracy typified the contentious conditions manifested elsewhere in the nation. Controversy over the League had split the party into two cohesive factions — old-stock pro-League Wilson Democrats and the anti-League Irish. Supporters of Wilson, imbued with a spirit of idealism, outraged over Senator Reed's flouting of the wishes of an apparent majority of the party, and increasingly suspicious of the "Americanism" of the Irish and their German and Italian sympathizers, entered the new year pledged to support the nation's entrance into the League without amendments or reservations. But with Reed's Democratic followers convinced of the wisdom of their opposition to the League, the disaster many foresaw for the party, especially in view of the threatened bolt of the Irish, seemed a safe prognosis.

CHAPTER 3

THE GREAT AND SOLEMN REFERENDUM

THE DOUBLE DEFEATS of the League in the Senate in November, 1919, and March, 1920, did not end the nation's debate on the question of the United States' entrance into the new world order. Even before the Senate's second adverse vote President Wilson had indicated that he would make an ultimate appeal to the American people. In his now familiar letter to Democrats at the annual mid-January Jackson Day dinner in Washington, Wilson insisted that his assertions about the popular approval of the League were not being credited. "If there is any doubt as to the views of the people," Wilson wrote, "the clear way out is to submit the treaty issue to the voters [and] give the next election the form of a great and solemn referendum." [1]

This challenge in an election year simply delighted Wilson's proponents in Missouri, for throughout 1919 they had tried repeatedly and unsuccessfully to subject Senator Reed to a referendum. But no Missourian was more pleased with the prospect of a campaign on the League issue than senatorial aspirant Breckinridge Long. Around his candidacy, Long advised prospective supporters in an early January announcement, Missouri Democrats could center their fight for Wilson and the League. [2]

Although Breckinridge Long had never held an elective office, his family background and administrative experience in Wilson's Administration helped qualify him as the senatorial candidate most likely to win votes from Wilson's supporters. Scion of the Longs of Virginia and the Breckinridges of Kentucky, Long sought to make his mark in law and politics, as had his patrician forebears. Woodrow Wilson had first won his loyalty when, at the turn of the century, the young Missourian sat as a student in Professor Wilson's political science classes at Princeton. Educated with a specialty in international law at St. Louis University, Long established a practice in his native St. Louis in 1906. Six years later, he married Christine Graham, heiress to the Graham paper fortune. Independently wealthy, Long furthered his ambitions in politics with generous contributions and loans to the Democratic party, such as underwriting a sizable portion of the expenses of Wilson's campaign for re-election in 1916. The following year Wilson rewarded Long with the position of Third Assistant Secretary of State. In this post in the State Department Long gave loyal and enthusiastic support to Wilson and to the League.[3]

Shortly after Reed raised a storm of controversy in Missouri over the League, during the early months of 1919, Long began to lay the groundwork for his entrance into the senatorial primary to contest for the seat currently held by Republican Selden Spencer.[4] "I think," he confided to his diary in March, 1919, "it will be necessary to disown Reed and his followers and to annex to the party Republicans in sufficient number to offset their numerical strength." On the basis of this strategy Long and Wilson's supporters in Missouri prepared to wage their part of the national referendum.[5]

The first phase of the movement — disowning Reed — proceeded at first along lines strikingly similar to the plan formulated privately in December of 1919 by President Wilson.[6] The ailing and uncompromising President, unconvinced that public opinion had shifted to disapproval of his peace program, wanted to challenge all senators who opposed the League to resign and stand for re-election on the basis of that record. If the voters returned all of these senators or a majority of them, so the proposal went, Wilson and the Vice-President would resign, presumably preparing the way for a

Republican chief executive. Thomas Bailey has correctly labeled Wilson's plan "utterly fantastic," for it stood little chance of succeeding with the senators and ran afoul of the constitutional provisions that governed special elections in many states.[7]

Although some mystery still surrounds the entire proposal, the action of Wilson men in Missouri offers new insight into why Wilson, doggedly persistent in such matters, decided to drop the unworkable scheme. For on January 13, W. R. Hollister, the retiring secretary of the Democratic National Committee and Breckinridge Long's campaign manager, renewed the demand Democratic legislators had issued in March, 1919, that Reed resign and submit his anti-League record to the voters.[8] Two days later Reed brushed off this challenge with disdain, thus killing the plan at its first stage; with more than two years remaining in his term, Reed had no intention of seeking a vote of confidence in 1920.[9] The timing of this latest challenge suggests that Hollister, through his close association with the Democratic National Committee, had knowledge of the President's comprehensive scheme and wished to implement it at once against Reed. Further, Reed's swift refusal to submit his course to the voters made evident one of the many flaws in the President's scheme. It seems reasonable that Wilson knew about the mid-January rebuff and realized this defect in his proposal. In any event, Wilson abandoned the plan in late January without revealing it to the general public.[10]

Adherents of Wilson in Missouri, however, persisted in their efforts to demonstrate that Reed's course ran counter to majority opinion. In the first place, they believed that the party's repudiation of Reed would help the President secure the necessary support in the Senate for his peace program. Secondly, they confidently expected pro-League Republicans and independents to offset the defection of Reed and his anti-League partisans in an election show-down. Consequently, the President's supporters simply turned to new tactics to isolate Reed. The same day that the Senator rejected Hollister's demand that he resign, a group of Wilson men in St. Louis announced that a state-wide campaign would be made to keep Reed off the delegation to the Democratic National Convention.[11]

Since custom dictated that the party send her United States senators as delegates-at-large to the national convention, this new challenge confronted Reed and his supporters with a contest from which they could neither escape nor expect to emerge victorious. Indeed, evidence of Wilson's strength outstate came from every section as county after county adopted resolutions opposing Reed's selection as a delegate to the national convention. And when the Democrats in the Fifth Congressional District — Kansas City and Jackson County — announced their plan to send Reed to the national convention in San Francisco as their representative, thus bypassing the state convention, Wilson's supporters countered with an announcement that all district delegates would be subject to the approval of the convention. Both Tom Pendergast and Joe Shannon replied to this declaration with a cryptic warning that "action at the state convention on the League or Senator Reed" might cause the Democrats of Kansas City to bolt the ticket in the fall.[12] St. Louis' Democratic City Committee, dominated by anti-League Irish and old-stock conservatives, now revealed that it would support the Fifth District's selection of Reed as delegate from that area.[13]

In combining their support for Reed, the St. Louis and Kansas City Democrats indicated that the fight at the state convention would proceed along both ethnic and rural-urban lines. In terms of delegate strength, the old-stock country Democrats were numerically superior — St. Louis' 296 delegates and Kansas City's 178 totaled only 474 to outstate's 1,109. Nevertheless, the big-city delegates, united under

Irish leadership, hoped to achieve through unity what a larger number of uncoordinated delegates could not. The Reed, anti-League Democrats of the two urban centers hoped also to capture all or parts of still undeclared county delegations around the state.[14]

Outstate, however, county conventions in every section elected Wilson Democrats as delegates to the state convention. Only Knox County in northeast Missouri went on record for Reed and against the League. In all, Democrats in 111 of Missouri's 114 counties were in the pro-League camp. Almost as many counties — 107 — refused to support Reed's bid for a delegateship.[15]

In light of the preconvention activity, the state convention itself presented few surprises. A few contested delegations were seated in favor of the Wilson men, and the Democrats from the Fifth District, true to their promise, designated Senator Reed their delegate to the national convention. Perhaps the utter confusion and disorder of the sessions and the staying power of the women delegates in the convention's one all-night meeting provided the most unexpected developments. By a vote of 1,074 to 490 — an indication of the rural-urban line of battle — the convention rejected the Fifth District's selection of Reed as a delegate to San Francisco. By a voice vote delegates endorsed the League of Nations "without reservations which tend to weaken the provisions of the covenant and the purposes of the League." In addition, the delegation to the national convention was instructed to vote as a unit for the adoption of a platform approving the League of Nations.[16] The rural Democracy, loyal to the President, carried the day.

Reed, confident that his friends would secure a seat for him at the San Francisco convention, refused to comment publicly on his censure by the state convention. But in May, when President Wilson appealed to Democrats for "a League without reservations" plank in the national platform, Reed took sharp issue with the President. That advice, Reed asserted, constituted "the finest scheme of premeditated political suicide yet devised." If the national convention heeded the President's recommendation, the Missouri Democrat warned, the party would lose every state north of the Mason and Dixon line, and the Solid South would be broken.[17]

Pro-League sentiment, however, was not to be denied at San Francisco. Although Wilson's adherents could not unite behind a single presidential candidate — rural Missourians favored William G. McAdoo and A. Mitchell Palmer, while the urban delegates supported James M. Cox — they stood firm on a pro-League plank.[18] Further, despite the fight made by Joe Shannon and other anti-League Democrats to seat Reed, the Credentials Committee upheld the action of the state convention. It was a bitter, dejected, and yet unbending Senator who gave a short explanation of his repudiation to the press:

> In a word, I was excluded because I refused to support the League of Nations. . . . The action taken will in no respect affect my lifelong Democracy, neither will it change my course in the Senate. I am still a Democrat. I am still opposed to the League of Nations.[19]

Back in Missouri, Reed opened yet another round in his anti-League campaign. At the Senator's urging and on the last day for filing for office, ex-judge Henry S. Priest, an avowed opponent of the League and prominent antiprohibitionist, entered the race for United States senator. On the same day, Charles M. Hay, disregarding his earlier statements that he would not file for office, announced his candidacy on a platform of support for the League and for prohibition. Up to this time Breckenridge Long had had a clear field as "the Administration's candidate for the League." As a moderate wet, Long was acceptable to drys such as Charles Hay until Priest, an out-and-out wet, announced his candidacy.

In spite of the late injection of the question of prohibition into the primary contest, Senator Reed probably correctly assessed the importance of the wet-dry issue: Forget about prohibition, he advised, "because it is a dead issue. The great question is settled and the thing is going to be tried out whether you and I like it or not." The vital issue, Reed believed, was the nation's membership in the League.[20]

In the Democratic primary contest for United States senator, pro-League candidates Long and Hay polled 65,825 and 44,504 votes, respectively, to anti-League candidate Priest's 40,637. The St. Louis Democracy split its votes between Long and Priest, while Jackson County and Kansas City gave 11,906 of their 16,783 votes to Reed's candidate, Judge Priest. Rural Democrats threw the bulk of their votes to the League candidates. Although the League issue figured only incidentally in other contests, the prevailing pattern matched the vote in the senatorial race: Anti-League candidates won backing in the cities, while pro-League Democrats performed best outstate.[21]

Although Long's nomination and the G.O.P.'s renomination of anti-League Senator Selden Spencer seemed to assure the League issue a paramount place in the fall senatorial election, Senator Reed made a last desperate attempt to divert the party from a course he considered utter folly. When Democrats from around the nation traveled to Ohio in early August for the traditional ceremonies notifying James M. Cox of his presidential nomination, Reed as well as Breckinridge Long attended. The Senator from Missouri made a passionate appeal to Cox that the League be abandoned as an issue in the campaign. Cox, when writing his autobiography in 1946, recalled telling Reed that he would be happy if he could find a plank upon which the Senator "could walk back into the councils of the Democratic party." At the same time, Cox added, he would be mindful of neither the self-respect of the Democratic party nor his own self-respect if he followed Reed's advice.[22] According to Breckinridge Long, Reed coupled a threat to his plea: If Cox refused to abandon the League in the campaign, Long wrote in his diary at the time, Reed would use his position and influence on the Senate Subcommittee on Campaign Expenditures to investigate and disbar Long, should Long win the election.[23]

Subsequent events lend plausibility to Long's account. In October the Senate Subcommittee on Campaign Expenditures summoned Long to St. Louis for the announced purpose of questioning the candidate on his campaign expenditures. Both senators from Missouri, Reed and Selden Spencer, were on the committee. Reed announced that he would not participate in the hearing; his presence, he said, served only to make a quorum to enable the committee to meet. Senator Spencer, Long's Republican opponent in the general election and chairman of the hearings, observed that, since Long was the only senatorial candidate in the nation to be called before the committee, it seemed unfair to single out the Missourian; therefore, Spencer requested that Long be excused. Reed concurred and the committee adjourned.[24] The incident remained closed after Long's defeat by Spencer in the November election, but the episode raises questions about the lengths to which Reed would go to discredit the pro-League candidate for the Senate.

As Long resumed his outstate speaking tour, he refused to refer to his activity as a campaign; it was, he told an audience at Versailles in Morgan County, a crusade for the League.[25] Even in Kansas City there were indications that Joe Shannon would catch the spirit and fall into line. In a mid-October speech to Democrats of the Ninth Ward, Shannon criticized Reed for failing to come to the aid of the ticket. Shortly after Shannon's criticism the entire Kansas City-Jackson County Democratic ticket came out for the League of Nations. Newspaper reports stated that many of Reed's friends in Kansas City were angered by the Senator's intentional absence from the city when Cox appeared there for a speech on October 2.[26]

Reed made only one campaign speech in Missouri, an address arranged under his own auspices in Kansas City's Convention Hall in late October. Before an unruly crowd of 12,000 the irreconcilable opposer of the League endorsed the party's state, city, and county ticket amid a chorus of catcalls from the Republicans in the assemblage. Democrats in the audience howled their objection to Reed's call for a vote against the League by "voting for the senatorial candidate who is opposed to the League." This advice constituted an indirect but clear endorsement of Republican Selden Spencer and a rejection of Democrat Breckinridge Long. Reed refused to endorse either Cox or his Republican opponent, Warren G. Harding, explaining that in Cox's case Wilson might exercise undue influence for the League while the pro-League former President, William H. Taft, might persuade Harding to a similar position.[27]

Reed's final blast at the League in Missouri before the election served further to swing the Shannon faction into line behind Cox. "I have come to realize," Shannon told Kansas Citians, "that the League of Nations is the only salvation for mankind — and if you want to know, for the Irish people."[28] Boss Pendergast, on record for the entire ticket, did not attribute any virtues to the League. He simply recognized that outstate Missouri harbored strong sympathy for the League. "It has been created largely by propaganda," Pendergast said, "but it's there."[29]

While the Irish Democrats in Kansas City began to rally behind the ticket, the situation in St. Louis remained bleak. Apparently, few Irish of that city experienced Shannon's late conversion to the League. Important Irish leaders did announce support for Harry B. Hawes, candidate for Congress from the Eleventh Congressional District. Hawes's pro-League stand had all but disappeared during the campaign.[30]

But the sentiment of the rank-and-file Irish in St. Louis was expressed by Dr. R. Emmett Kane, a leader of the Friends of Irish Freedom, in a mass meeting October 13. The state and national Democratic conventions had erred in endorsing the League and repudiating Reed, he declared, and were mistaken to think that the Irish voters' traditional support for the Democratic party would prevail in the coming election. "We'll show you on election day," Kane asserted, "whether you can 'make something' but a Democrat out of an Irishman."[31]

On election day the Irish, as well as a good number of other Democrats, rural and urban, deserted the party either by staying away from the polls or by casting ballots to make the Republican landslide in Missouri as spectacular as the Harding-Coolidge sweep in the nation.[32] The Republican victory extended from the national ticket down to the state legislature, where the Democrats lost control for the first time since the Civil War. Long might have gained some consolation from the fact that he outpolled all others on the Democratic ticket while going down to defeat; he ran nearly 150,000 votes behind Selden Spencer. Champ Clark was the best-known casualty among the incumbent Democratic congresmen as Republicans swept to victory in fourteen of the state's sixteen congressional districts. Incumbent W. W. Rucker of the Second District, drawing upon a record in the House that extended back to 1896 and upon traditional support from the Democrats of north central Missouri, weathered the Republican storm. The Eleventh District, lying within St. Louis City and County, sent Harry B. Hawes to his first term in the House. Hawes had essentially disassociated himself from Wilson and the League in his campaign and thus appealed to enough of the disaffected Democrats to win.[33]

More important to the Missouri Democracy than the succession of Republicans to state and national offices, however, was the debilitated, factionalized state of the party, brought on by the bitter struggle over the League. The two-year-long controversy had clearly established Senator Reed as the champion of the urban Democrats — especially the backbone of urban Democracy, the Irish — and as spokesman for the isolationists, both city and country. Internationalist old-stock rural Democrats looked to Breckinridge Long and Charles M. Hay for leadership. The viability of these two factions depended in part upon the interpretation each placed on the election's outcome.

Reluctantly, Wilson's supporters began to realize that the election simply could not be a true referendum on any one single issue, because other issues — particularly the high cost of living, low farm prices, and a general disillusionment with idealistic causes — though less talked about, were involved.[34] Consequently, ardent pro-League Democrats like Breckinridge Long remained convinced that a majority of Missourians actually favored the United States' participation in the League. Senator Reed, on the other hand, expressed the irreconcilable interpretation of the election as the reason for the Democrats' defeat: "The League of Nations did it. . . . It was the policies of Washington against the policies of Wilson."[35]

These contrasting views meant that the League would survive as an issue in the nation's politics. Furthermore, the overwhelming defeat of the Wilson men by the Republicans raised the question as to which of the two contending Democratic factions deserved control of their party. That question was never to be resolved; instead, it would eventually disappear. For the moment, debate of the question was deferred, awaiting 1922, when Senator Reed would either retire from politics or seek a third term in the Senate.

CHAPTER 4

THE TRIUMPH OF SENATOR REED

THE MISSOURI DEMOCRACY emerged from the 1920 election a dispirited, divided party, out of power in state government, heavily in debt, and holding little promise of unifying its warring factions. Supporters of Wilson, bent upon forcing Reed's retirement in 1922, issued postelection statements that bore no harmonious sentiments. Reed, on the other hand, in the first indication that he would seek re-election, issued an appeal in late November, 1920, for a cessation of party bickering and dissension. "Speaking for myself," the Senator said, "I have no enemies to punish."[1] The feeling of Wilson men toward Reed, however, needed no expression. Because the Senator had opposed the League of Nations, had assailed Wilson's party leadership, and had failed to compaign in behalf of Democratic pro-League candidates in 1920, most of them considered Reed guilty of party treason and therefore not entitled to renomination.

Few supporters of Reed agreed with the Wilson adherents' interpretation of the Senator's differences with the former President and with the party in the state and nation. Most realized, however, that party sentiment prevailed against Reed. The Senator's repudiation at the state and national conventions had demonstrated that an overwhelming majority of the party rejected Reed's opposition to Wilson and to the League. On the eve of the 1920 election, Boss Tom Pendergast spoke frankly about Reed's political future: "I haven't talked with Reed about his plans, but I'm certain he's not such a fool as to think he ever can get anything again in this state with feeling toward him like it is in the rural districts."[2] For several months following the 1920 election, it seemed a foregone conclusion to Reed and Wilson Democrats alike that, should Senator Reed seek the Democratic nomination in 1922 for a third term, he would be soundly defeated.[3]

At the same time, most supporters of Wilson discounted reports that Reed would retire from active politics in 1922 and would return to the private practice of law. They believed that Reed, in spite of overwhelming opposition, would seek renomination. Indeed, many Wilson men hoped that he would enter the Democratic primary so they might administer a humiliating defeat upon the independent-minded Senator. Accordingly, anti-Reed Democrats, such as St. Louis lawyer Charles M. Hay, the Reverend Burris Jenkins, editor of the *Kansas City Post*, and banker William T. Kemper of Kansas City, privately began casting about in the fall of 1921 for a suitable candidate to oppose Reed.[4]

Anxious to demonstrate their unswerving faith in both the leadership of Woodrow Wilson and the League of Nations, Wilson men in Missouri gave major consideration in their search for a candidate to a Democrat closely identified with the former President and the League. Another requirement, unexpressed but nevertheless important, considering the large debt still burdening the party from the last election, was that the candidate possess the means to finance a large part of his campaign. Most important of all, the Wilson men wanted a candidate who, in contrast to the independent Reed, would adhere to the party's platform.[5] Breckinridge Long, the party's defeated senatorial aspirant of 1920, came closest to meeting these requirements.

The forty-one-year-old Long had gained valuable experience in his unsuccessful candidacy for a seat in the Senate in 1920, but he was virtually a novice in the rough-and-tumble politics of Missouri. Moreover, several other Democrats in the Wilson camp, notably ex-Governors Joseph Folk and Frederick Gardner and former State Representative Charles M. Hay, were all better qualified in terms of ability and legislative experience than Long. Only Hay, however, was strongly inclined to make a race for the nomination, and his finances would not permit the waging of a costly primary battle.[6] Despite Long's limitations, Hay advised friends, "he has consistently been with Wilson and the things Wilson has stood for . . . not an ideal candidate . . . [but] a clean, honest, level-headed and sensible fellow, who will make a faithful and acceptable Senator."[7]

The conviction of Wilson partisans that they could count on Long's loyalty to the party rested upon Long's uncritical acceptance of Wilson's concept of responsible party government. That doctrine, fashioned by President Wilson after the British parliamentary system, rejected the Burkean concept of government by independent legislators with responsibility of each lawmaker based on the individual's conscience and judgment. It postulated, instead, that responsible legislators function as members of political parties, binding themselves to the will of the party as expressed in caucuses, conventions, and primary elections.[8] Breckinridge Long had conducted his 1920 senatorial campaign around the Wilson doctrine; to a remarkable degree that philosophy was to guide him in the 1922 senatorial primary.

On January 8, 1922, Long, in the fashion of the responsible Democrat, announced his acceptance of the draft by a citizens' committee to enter the senatorial primary race. Looking ahead to 1924, when the party might elect a Democratic President, Long sounded the theme that became the keynote of his campaign: "I want an opportunity to serve in the Senate under that President that I might aid him in the fulfillment of the wishes of the people by rendering him my full support."[9] This indirect slap at Reed's record of opposition to President Wilson drew the Senator's fire when Reed, to the surprise of no one, announced his candidacy for re-nomination on March 21.

In contrast to the "grass-roots" draft of Long, Reed simply announced that a personal sense of duty compelled him to seek a third term in the Senate. Flatly rejecting the doctrine of responsible party government, Reed reasserted his loyalty to the concept of the independent legislator. A senator who failed to exercise personal judgment on legislation, he explained, deprived the people of the representation due them. Not once did Reed mention the word "Democratic" in his announcement. Moreover, he declined to name the issues on which he would base his campaign.[10]

The major issue, however, was clear: Would Missouri Democrats endorse Reed's Burkean philosophy or Long's Wilsonian doctrine of responsible party government? In the words of one old Wilson supporter, the most vital question confronting the Democrats of Missouri was the "elimination of this Old Man of the Sea who has misrepresented his constituency for six years." The pro-League *St. Louis Star* agreed and, further, asserted that "the overwhelming issue . . . is Mr. Reed's attitude toward Wilson and the League of Nations."[11]

Breckinridge Long lost little time in establishing himself as the only candidate of the Wilson branch of the party. Recalling that Wilson had previously "intimated" a desire to be kept informed of the senatorial race in Missouri, Long initiated correspondence with the former President and requested that Wilson endorse no other senatorial hopefuls.[12] Wilson complied with this request and advised other would-be entrants to keep the senatorial primary a two-man race between Reed and Long.[13] Long may have persuaded Wilson to this position by informing his former chief in late March:

> Unless Senator Reed and his adherents succeed in getting someone else in the race . . . it will remain a contest between your adherents and your opponents. I represent the former,

Reed the latter. And you will win easily. And I shall be nominated by a large majority.[14]

In the same letter Long sounded a warning note: Some Wilson men, including owner-publisher John C. Roberts of the *St. Louis Star*, were receiving an impression from Reed and his supporters that the Senator had gained Wilson's backing. Long asked the former President to write Roberts to assure him that Reed did not enjoy his support.

Wilson replied to publisher Roberts through Long. In perhaps his most scathing denunciation of Reed, Wilson wrote:

> I consider Reed my implacable opponent in everything that is honorable and enlightened. He has been false to his own character on the few occasions when he has affected to support me, and has generally opposed me. I regard him as a discredit to the party to which he pretends to belong but to which he has no true allegiance. He can indeed have no true allegiance to anything, for he is essentially false. I have never dealt with a man who more thoroughly and completely earned my distrust, and I should consider it a discredit to the party and an unhappy omen for the country if he should be returned to the Senate.[15]

These were strong words, Wilson admitted, but "it is high time to put on our war paint and fight for the right things, and I for one mean to do so without compromise of any kind or degree."[16]

Wilson's deeds, however, did not match his words; he permitted Long to show his letter to the *Star*'s publisher, Roberts, but withheld permission to make it public.[17] Disappointed, Long sent still another letter to Wilson to request the use of the recent correspondence as well as of a letter he had received from the former President in February, 1919, in which Wilson condemned Reed for attacking the League and commended Long for supporting the world organization. Both letters, Long explained, would greatly support his candidacy "against the man who has to his discredit violent and wilful opposition to you in person, to you as the Chief of our party, and to you as the representative of . . . humanitarian and peaceful policies."[18] Wilson, through his secretary, authorized the use of the 1919 correspondence, [19] but personally advised Long that use of his recent letter denouncing Reed would be discounted by the opposition, on the grounds that it was addressed to the rival candidate. It would be better, Wilson believed, to have someone other than Long write Wilson for an opinion of Reed.[20] The need to exercise this formula, however, did not arise. A letter by a Reed supporter, Lee Meriwether, to the editor of the *St. Louis Globe-Democrat* on April 12 gave Wilson his opportunity.

Meriwether, in his letter, took issue with a publicity release from Long's campaign manager that asserted that Long enjoyed the support of an overwhelming number of Missouri Democrats because he represented the principles and ideals of Woodrow Wilson. Meriwether disputed this claim and challenged the implication that Reed did not represent the ideals of democracy. "In so far as Wilson stood for the fundamental principles of democracy, he had the support of Senator Reed," insisted Meriwether. Meriwether offered for proof his recollection of a letter President Wilson had written to Reed "warmly thanking him for the great service which the Senator rendered in perfecting and passing the Federal Reserve bill."[21]

Wilson responded to the Meriwether letter by penning a reply intended for publication in the *St. Louis Globe Democrat*. The former President's letter made front-page news under the headline, "Woodrow Wilson Curtly Repudiates Senator Reed." Wilson did not remember having written any letter "warmly thanking" Reed for services connected with the Federal Reserve bill, as Meriwether had claimed; rather, he recalled Reed's interposing every possible objection to the completion and adoption of the bill. Moreover, Wilson charged that Meriwether's letter appeared to convey the impression that Wilson and Reed held the same principles, advocated the same policies, and therefore entitled Reed to Wilson's endorsement as a candidate for re-election to the Senate. This, the former President declared, was not the case: "Reed has shown himself incapable of sustained allegiance to any person or cause. I shall never willingly consent to any further association with him." [22]

While Long's supporters delighted in Wilson's public denunciation of Reed, the Senator sought to clarify his earlier relationship to the former Chief Executive; he produced for publication in the *Globe-Democrat* a letter in which Wilson, during the 1913 Senate hearings on the Federal Reserve bill, had in fact thanked Reed for the Senator's expression of satisfaction with an amended bill. But, as the *St. Louis Star* suggested, Wilson's 1913 letter to Reed had little significance in light of Reed's later course of opposition to Wilson's policies. [23] "The real gist of Mr. Wilson's criticism," Reed told reporters, "is that I do not yield a personal allegiance. I have never subscribed to the doctrine that a Senator elected by a great state owes allegiance to any man." [24] In this episode, as on other occasions, Reed mixed arguments that he had often supported the former President with reaffirmations of his belief in the doctrine of the independent legislator.

Intent on keeping the incumbent senator on the defensive, Breckinridge Long began his formal campaign in late April at Poplar Bluff, eight days in advance of Reed's opening. Arguing that the rejection of Wilson's peace program had cost the nation more than the war, Long called for the lowering of the tariff and the abandonment of economic isolationism. Concluding his speech with a plea for responsible party government, he asked the voters to send him to the Senate so he might serve a Democratic President — obviously an internationally minded Chief Executive to be elected in 1924. It was an inauspicious opening; some Democrats were disappointed that Long had failed to wage a direct attack upon

Jim Reed and to mention the League of Nations by name. Still, Long was clearly the favorite with the party's rank and file as the campaign got under way.[25]

Fully realizing the difficulties that faced him in his bid for renomination, Reed and his managers had planned for weeks the opening event in the Senator's campaign, at Moberly on May 5. On that Saturday in the spring of 1922 Reed's followers transformed the small seat of Randolph County into a center of excited political activity. In the morning a band greeted nearly two thousand of the Senator's supporters as they discharged from excursion trains that brought them to Moberly from St. Louis and Kansas City. These enthusiastic city followers of Reed, mingling on the streets with the townfolk and area farmers, turned a basically neutral setting into a definite pro-Reed community. In midafternoon, the focal point shifted from the spontaneous street parades to a large circus tent, decked out with bunting and flags and furnished with five thousand seats, where Reed was to deliver the first formal speech of his campaign. All together, nearly ten thousand Missourians were in Moberly to see and hear Reed; hundreds more could hear the radio broadcast of his speech.[26]

Reed's oratory that afternoon was as dramatic and forceful as any he had used to oppose the League during the Senate debates. "Where comes the doctrine that the President may dictate to Congress what laws shall be passed?" Reed asked. "If Missouri wants a rubber stamp in the United States Senate," he shouted, in reference to his opponent, "it can find one without searching far or long." Refusing to be measured by the yardstick of responsible party government, the independent-minded Senator asserted: "The test to be applied to my public acts is not whether I agreed or disagreed with the President, but whether my votes and acts were in accordance with sound public policy." The record would show, Reed insisted, that his differences with Wilson arose not from disagreements over patronage, but from differences on principles. Now that the former President was a sick man, Reed explained, "my sentiments toward him are not those of animosity but of profound sympathy. I believe the people of Missouri in the coming campaign will not permit a former President to tell them how to vote, and they will not punish a Senator for declining a President to tell him how to vote."[27]

Reed's opener was a credit to the old campaigner, but the Long camp regained its momentum a few days later with the timely release of another letter from the former President to ex-Governor Lon Stephens. "I hope, and confidently believe," Wilson wrote Stephens, "[that Reed] will be repudiated by the Democrats in the primary. Missouri cannot afford to be represented by such a marplot, and it might check enthusiasm of Democrats throughout the country if their comrades in Missouri fail to substitute for Reed a man of true breed of Democratic principles."[28]

At first Reed refrained from commenting on Wilson's latest denunciation, but a few weeks later he rebuked the former President, telling an audience at Boonville that he "refused to take orders from a resident of New Jersey," regardless of "how many letters he writes to political 'has-beens'." Reiterating a familiar phrase, Reed advised: "If you want a rubber-stamp Senator, don't elect me, for I will take orders from no man at Washington."[29] This ridicule and analysis of Wilson's and Long's beliefs in responsible party government effectively placed Long on the defensive as the first month of the three-month campaign ended.

If Long were to recapture the offensive, the voters needed a clearer concept of his political beliefs as well as a refutation of Reed's creed of political independence. Long made his move in a speech at Columbia, charging by implication that Reed's independence had degenerated into "mere obstinacy and . . . obstruction." Rather than advocating a "one-man government," as Reed would have Missourians believe, Long supported loyalty to party; he elaborated the doctrine on which he was waging his campaign:

> This is a government by political parties. Responsibility rests upon the political party in control. The policies of political parties are determined — not by presidents — not by the senate — but by the rank and file of the party. . . .
>
> Platforms . . . represent the combined wisdom of party leadership . . . the ultimate decision of the rank and file of the party. Opposition by a party leader to a party platform is of vastly more significance than the independent opposition of a senator who disagrees with the president or disagrees with his party colleagues in the senate. If a senator sets his judgment above the judgment of his party it becomes a serious matter.

As for himself, Long concluded, quoting from one of Reed's own speeches in his first race for the Senate in 1910, "I have not claimed to be wiser than the combined wisdom of our party as expressed in its platform regularly adopted." [30]

Long was mistaken, of course, in assuming that the American political system embodied the doctrine of responsible party government, but his primary campaign faithfully followed the essentials of the doctrine formulated in the writings of his mentor Woodrow Wilson.[31] In spite of the invalid assumptions in Long's and Wilson's political creed, however, Democrats who shared these same assumptions drew the easy conclusion: Reed's refusal to be bound by the will of the party rank and file made the Senator an unfit representative of Missouri Democrats.

Supporters of Long also exploited the theme of party loyalty to advance their campaign of opposition to Reed. The "Volunteer Association of St. Louis Democrats" and the "Rid-Us-Of-Reed" organization — the informal name of "Missouri Women Opposed to Senator James A. Reed" — emphasized the Senator's record of opposition to Wilson's policies in their literature. The St. Louis League of Women Voters, avowedly nonpartisan, called upon voters to defeat Reed. The Missouri Women's Christian Temperance Union urged the voters to end Reed's "misrepresentation of Missouri." These organizations opposed Reed for his refusal to support causes dear to their membership — woman suffrage, prohibition, the child-labor amendment, and the Sheppard-Towner Maternity bill.[32]

Reed countered this opposition from women's organizations by an appeal to the individual woman voter. He heaped ridicule upon St. Louis "lady bosses" who "were attempting to tell the good women of Missouri how to vote." He explained that his opposition to woman suffrage had been based on states' rights principles rather than on hostility to the participation of women in politics. He amused his listeners while attacking the Sheppard-Towner Maternity bill, claiming that under its provisions, "maiden ladies in Washington" would tell mothers how to rear their children. He climaxed his appeal for votes with an emotional tribute to mother love, so effective that many men and women were moved to tears![33]

Reed also persuasively promoted himself as the farmer's friend. Speaking to the men as farmers and not as Democrats, Reed castigated Herbert Hoover, charging that Wilson's food administrator was responsible for their economic plight. Recalling his attacks on Hoover during the war, Reed interpreted his own actions then as attempts to secure a fair deal for the farmers. "If I could have succeeded," Reed claimed, "the farmers of Missouri might have had balances in the bank in their credit to carry them over the slump in prices which inevitably followed the war."[34] William Hirth, editor of the *Missouri Farmer*, biweekly publication of the Missouri Farmers' Association, printed in full one of Reed's anti-Hoover speeches and editorially endorsed Reed's candidacy.[35] Reaching into several thousand farm homes, the

MFA journal no doubt helped Reed to reduce Long's lead in several traditionally Democratic counties.

Long deplored the tactics Reed used to snare the farm vote; he persisted in his belief that the rural Democracy would not be swayed by "a sordid appeal . . . directed at the avarice, greed, selfishness, unpatriotism, and prejudice of the American citizen." The country Democrat, Long insisted, placed loyalty to his party above personal interests; indeed, the rural voter constituted the "real Democrat," the "bone and sinew" of the party.[36] Under this romantic conviction Long could do little more than offer a weak defense of the Wilson Administration's wartime food control program and proclaim the legislator's responsibility to adhere to the party platform.[37]

While Reed hoped to cut heavily into Long's support out in the state, he placed even greater emphasis upon his hopes for building a large vote in the cities. Irish, German, and Italian Americans in St. Louis and Kansas City, hostile to Wilson and the League in 1919 and 1920, could be counted on to support Reed's bid for renomination. It was no surprise that, soon after Reed announced his candidacy, the Irish bosses of Kansas City, Tom Pendergast and Joseph Shannon, as well as twenty-four of St. Louis' twenty-eight Democratic ward leaders came out for the anti-League Senator as they had when Wilson men attacked Reed during the fight for ratification of the League. Similar support, however, had been unable to prevent Reed's repudiation in 1920 at the Democratic State Convention.[38] Reed needed an issue that could broaden the basis of his appeal and add to his urban vote. He found the issue in prohibition.

Reed's call for the restoration of beer and light wine to the nation's permitted pleasures, in contrast with Long's undeclared position on the prohibition issue, improved his chances in St. Louis and the heavily German counties of eastern Missouri, where an appreciative beer-drinking populace chafed under the drys' social experiment. St. Louisans probably disliked prohibition in 1922 even more than they did in 1918, when they voted 7 to 1 against a state prohibition enforcement law.[39] Indirectly, all residents of Missouri's largest city felt the economic effects of the dry laws: The closing of the city's several breweries upon the enactment of prohibition had thrown thousands out of work and represented a sizable economic loss to the city.[40] With the Anti-Saloon League, Women's Christian Temperance Union, and other dry forces already committed against him, Reed had little to lose and much to gain in advocating a modification of the prohibition-enforcing Volstead Act.[41] Nevertheless, he attempted to mollify the drys by declaring for the enforcement of the Eighteenth Amendment. At the same time, Reed sought to discredit Long with both drys and wets, branding his opponent "the dryest man in the country and the wettest man in St. Louis" — a position that certainly came close to representing his own stand![42] Long remained silent on prohibition, neither repudiating nor cultivating the support of the Anti-Saloon League and the W.C.T.U.[43]

The Reed-Long campaign also affected the seven-man race for the Republican senatorial nomination as the front-running candidates made frantic efforts to be more anti-League and anti-Wilson than Senator Reed. R. R. Brewster, the eventual winner, angrily denied he had once supported the League and had called Wilson "another Lincoln." Indeed, Brewster asserted, he was "one of the most outspoken and bitter opponents the League of Nations ever had."[44]

The Republican most important to the plans of Senator Reed was the "light wine and beer" candidate, William G. Sacks of St. Louis, whose platform threatened to draw the wets' support away from Reed. Could wets depend upon Sacks to work for a modification of the Volstead Act? Reed implied that Sacks would make deals with the drys and charged that the wet Republican had given rent-free office space to the Anti-Saloon League in exchange for political support in the past.[45] The *St. Louis Star* correctly interpreted Reed's attack on Sacks as an attempt to draw wet Republicans into the Democratic primary in his own behalf. Sacks agreed with this interpretation, and in a public letter to Reed he predicted that the Senator's effort would boomerang.[46]

But Reed's stratagem with the wets was to redound in his favor. In fact, his over-all strategy, aimed at bringing independents and Republicans into the Democratic primary to offset the vote of "loyal" Democrats, exposed the vital flaw in Long's campaign. Under Missouri law, there simply was no effective way of maintaining a closed primary. A voter might call for a ballot of any political party, regardless of his previous party affiliation; should election judges challenge any voter, the challenged citizen could still receive the ballot he requested by taking an oath to support the same party in the general election. In other words, future intention rather than past or present allegiance was the criterion for participation in the August 1 primary election. Long's manager hoped that the appointment of "old-time" Democratic election judges who would challenge all Republicans and require the necessary oath might prevent a strong invasion of the Democratic primary. No one in the Long camp had taken concrete steps, however, to secure the appointment of Wilson Democrats to the election boards.[47]

Long personally refused to take seriously the idea that Republicans might vote in the Democratic primary, until late in the campaign. Finally, with the election less than two weeks in the offing, Long issued a public letter to Reed requesting the Senator to join him in an appeal for an election along party lines, thus preserving the integrity of the Democratic primary.[48]

Reed refused Long's request and countered with an appeal of his own: Would Long require Republican members of the Anti-Saloon League to take a pledge to stay out of the Democratic primary, and would Wilson Democrats support Reed in the general election should Long lose the primary contest?[49] This maneuver to checkmate Long presented the prospect of a wide-open primary. The whole structure of the Wilson candidate's appeal, based on a foundation of responsible party government and a primary election along previous party affiliation, began to collapse as the campaign closed.

On August 1 Missourians voted in numbers approximating the turnout for the presidential election of 1920. Reed, clearly the underdog at the beginning of the campaign, emerged the victor, but with a scant margin of 6,000 votes. In his victory Reed carried only 24 of Missouri's 114 counties, half of which traditionally voted Republican; in the Republican stronghold of St. Louis he garnered slightly more votes than the front-running Republican candidate there, William G. Sacks. Outpolling Long approximately 3 to 1 in St. Louis, Reed received a 5-to-1 margin in Kansas City. Unquestionably, the large urban vote pulled Reed through. Even in the rural areas, however, Reed's vote, though a definite minority, was large enough to prevent Long's victory.[50]

A stunned, disbelieving Breckinridge Long, vainly hoping that the slow returns from the country would establish him as winner, waited nearly a week before conceding the victory to Reed. Friends of the defeated candidate urged a recount of the ballots, but as Long bitterly admitted in his conceding statement, "a recount would not affect the Republican ballots." In Long's opinion, between 40,000 and 50,000 Republicans had voted in the Democratic primary and thus "circumvented the expressed will of the great majority of the Democrats who voted."[51] The evidence, although not clearcut, tends to support Long's charge.[52]

What is quite clear is that Long counted too heavily on the doctrine of responsible party government as the main

campaign issue and upon the primary election as a valid
means of testing that doctrine against Reed's belief in the
independent legislator. Neither Wilson in theory nor Long
in practice appreciated the relationship of a closed primary
to the waging of a contest between a political independent
and a "loyal" party member. While Long appealed to the
Democrats of Missouri in general and to "loyal" Democrats
in particular, Reed went after the bloc voters without party
labels — the anti-League Irish, Italians, and Germans, farmers, laborers, veterans, wets, and women. In addition, Reed
solicited the support of Missourians who shared his Burkean
political philosophy.[53]

There were other reasons for Long's defeat. The incumbent Reed skillfully combined old and new campaign tech-
niques that far surpassed in effectiveness the ambitious but
unimaginative campaign of his opponent. On the speaker's
platform, too, Reed's oratory exceeded the best efforts of
the relatively inexperienced Long. Many Wilson supporters,
including the former President himself, regarded Long's refusal to resort to personal attacks on his opponent as a sign
of weakness.[54]

Ironically, Long's major weakness in the primary — his
slavish devotion to the doctrine of responsible party government — became Reed's strength in the general election campaign. It would have been difficult, even in the face of the
Republicans' participation in the Democratic primary, for
Long to break his pledge to support Reed should the Senator win the nomination.[55] Nevertheless, many other Democrats, as much anti-Reed as pro-Wilson, indicated they
would not be bound by the primary returns. Former Governor Lon Stephens and former Congressman W. D. Van-
diver lent their names and energies to a "League of Loyal
Democrats," pledged to work for the defeat of Jim Reed.
The "Rid-Us-Of-Reed" women also swung back into action
after the primary, calling for the election of Reed's Republi-

can opponent. Other anti-Reed Democrats such as Charles M. Hay proposed to sit back and "let real Democrats knife Reed" in the general election.[56]

Still, the Republican senatorial nominee, R. R. Brewster, a successful and popular Kansas City lawyer, faced a hard campaign in spite of the dissension within the Democratic ranks. Although he might gather the disaffected Democratic vote, as a dry he faced the prospect of losing the vote of the wet Republicans of St. Louis and the eastern counties to Reed. Sacks, the wet Republican candidate in the primary, had polled 43,000 votes in St. Louis and 24,000 outstate votes to finish second behind Brewster. The Republican candidate hoped to demonstrate to wets that Reed could not bring back beer and light wines and to frighten drys into thinking that the Senator could. Even before the election, though, it became apparent that Brewster's tactics were failing as a group of St. Louis wet Republicans, taking the name "Liberal Republicans," urged the election of Senator Reed.[57]

Brewster's efforts to draw the support of Wilson Democrats proved no more effective than his attempts to halt the disaffection of wet Republicans. Although he constantly reminded anti-Reed Democrats that the Democratic campaign platform, written entirely by the Senator, contained no mention of Woodrow Wilson, Reed met these thrusts as well as those of the League of Loyal Democrats by enlisting the aid of his Democratic colleagues in the Senate.[58] Senators David Walsh of Massachusetts and Joseph T. Robinson of Arkansas spent several days with Reed during the fall campaign. Senator A. Owsley Stanley of Kentucky also came into the state several times in Reed's behalf, delivering "wet" speeches in St. Louis and "party regularity" addresses in outstate Missouri, telling rural voters that Woodrow Wilson would rather cut off his arm than fail to support the ticket.[59]

Wilson, however, chose to maintain the policy of silence he had adopted back in June, when he left Long and his admirers to their own devices.[60] The ailing former President who had resolved to "fight without compromise" had, in effect, left the political battleground before the primary contest was well under way. Considering Long's strategy of making party loyalty and responsible party government the dominant theme of the campaign, a more active role by Wilson, even if limited to timely letters to the press, might have aided Long enough to provide the margin of victory. No evidence can be found, however, that Long personally tried to secure additional aid from Wilson after his extensive correspondence of March and April. Long, confident of victory, evidently was satisfied with Wilson's unequivocal, though limited, repudiation of Reed.[61]

It was with considerable embarrassment, therefore, that Long wrote Wilson in mid-October to explain what had gone wrong with his preprimary estimate of a 100,000-vote margin over Reed. The official returns showed that over 81,000 more votes had been cast in the senatorial contest than in the other contested places on the ticket, Long informed Wilson. That number of votes, Long believed — revising upward his first postprimary estimate — represented the extent of the Republicans' participation in the Democratic primary. Because public pledges of support had been exchanged between himself and Reed at the end of the primary campaign, Long added, he was now calling upon all Democrats to support the entire ticket in the general election.[62]

On the surface, the November returns suggested that enough Wilson Democrats heeded Long's call for help to boost Reed to a 506,267 to 462,009 triumph over Brewster. A closer examination of the election results, however, reveals that the wet vote played a crucial role in Reed's re-election. The traditionally Republican city of St. Louis, going Democratic in the senatorial race for the first time in eighteen years, gave Reed an impressive 104,680 to 60,878 victory over his dry opponent; other Democratic candidates lost the city to Republicans by nearly 20,000 votes.

A similar pattern prevailed outstate. While other Republicans carried the wet counties of Cole, Perry, Osage, St. Charles, Ste. Genevieve, and St. Louis, Brewster lost every one of them to Reed. The dry Republican carried 71 of the state's 114 counties, but Reed received a slightly larger outstate vote, outpolling Brewster 342,705 to 341,228.[63] In Kansas City, where dry supporters had prevailed over anti-prohibitionists in a dry-law referendum in 1918, Reed achieved a narrow 52,005 to 51,642 victory. Reed had been expected to do much better there; evidently, dry Democrats either voted for Brewster or stayed away from the polls.[64] Over all, the urban Democracy, strengthened by an infusion of support from wet Republicans, gave Reed a third term in the Senate.

Contrary to the fears of both Wilson Democrats and Reed Democrats at the start of the campaign, the bitterness of the senatorial race did not adversely affect the party's chances in the congressional and state contests. Democrats won eleven of the sixteen House seats, regained a majority in both houses of the state legislature, and captured all of the state administrative and judicial offices. Several factors contributed to the Democratic victories, but economic considerations probably played a major role in the election of Democrats to congressional and state offices. In congressional races the economic recession of 1921 worked to the disadvantage of the incumbent Republicans, while on the state level many Missourians were dissatisfied with the taxing policies of the state Republican administration.[65]

Reed's re-election clearly represented a personal triumph, for to his core of urban, anti-League Irish Democrats and rural opponents of Wilson, Reed added the votes of independents and wet Republicans. This coalition returned him to the Senate, but it did not give the Senator and his supporters control of the party. Ardent Wilson Democrats, it will be remembered, had favored Breckinridge Long over Reed in 90 of the state's 114 counties in the primary and still dominated the state Democratic organization. In a real sense, Long's close primary vote was a personal tribute of Missouri Democrats to the leadership and ideals of Woodrow Wilson.[66]

Some contemporary political observers regarded Reed's triumph as a decisive defeat for internationalism and a victory for isolationism.[67] Certainly, Reed's re-election was to allow him to continue to speak forcefully against an internationalist course for America during the 1920's, but too many other issues were involved in the 1922 campaign to regard its outcome as an outright endorsement of isolationism. Moreover, the primary and general elections were devices too imperfect to constitute a valid test of any one issue.

Reed's victory greatly enhanced his standing in the Senate. More significantly, his remarkable political comeback elevated him in the eyes of many Democrats around the country to consideration as possible presidential timber. As a consequence, in 1924 Reed was to make an active bid for his party's presidential nomination.

CHAPTER 5

STATE AND NATIONAL POLITICS
IN THE KU KLUX YEARS

AS THE DECADE OF THE TWENTIES neared its mid-point, cultural and social forces that had long influenced Missouri politics — immigration and migration, urbanization, nativism, religious ferment, and even political loyalties themselves — were undergoing change. By 1924 restrictive federal immigration laws had stemmed the flood of Europeans coming to America, but sectional migration continued unimpeded, gradually introducing out-of-staters into Missouri society. Within the borders of the state the seemingly inexorable forces working for urbanization continued unabated, much to the distress of farm leaders and agrarian romantics. Economic and social realities underlay the decline of the countryside and the attendant rise of the cities, but not everyone could fully comprehend them, thus evoking a nativist response from some of the more bewildered old-stock Protestants. Regardless of the rate and nature of these changes, powerful old and new forces affected in significant ways the political behavior of all Missourians.

The most important change in the state's electorate of immediate political significance was a twofold development involving Negroes: the urbanization of many outstate Negroes, and the movement into the state of over 90,000 colored persons in the two decades from 1910 to 1930. During this period, 102 of Missouri's 114 counties experienced an absolute decline in colored population as Negroes left the farms and small towns outstate to seek better opportunities in Kansas City and St. Louis. Migrating Negroes swelled St. Louis' colored population from 43,960 in 1910 to 82,214 in 1925 and in the same period pushed Kansas City's Negro population upward from 23,566 to 34,226. At the end of the twenties the state's two major cities contained approximately 60 per cent of Missouri's 223,830 Negroes.[1]

An exception to Negro urbanization and settlement of out-of-staters in either St. Louis or Kansas City was southeast Missouri — the seven-county area embracing Butler, Dunklin, Mississippi, New Madrid, Pemiscot, Scott, and Stoddard counties. Extensive drainage and land-clearing programs, fertile delta soil, a long growing season, and boll weevil infestation of cotton lands farther south had contributed to the rapid and extensive spread of cotton farming in these southeast counties. In the 1920's the area's Negro population, employed largely on the farms of white cotton farmers, spurted from 9,111 to 26,809.[2]

The traditional tie of colored people to the Republican party and the political implications of a burgeoning bloc of Negro Republicans soon aroused Democrats to action. The Democratic party's responses varied from the skillful recruitment of Kansas City Negroes into the ranks of the Democratic machines of Pendergast, Shannon, and Casimer J. Welch[3] to callous campaigns of intimidation and terror in rural Missouri that were frankly designed to eliminate the Negro from participation in Missouri's politics. In the Bootheel's Pemiscot County, 1,500 Negroes were effectively kept from the polls in the 1922 congressional elections by the distribution of leaflets warning: "There is going to be an election, Tuesday, Nov. 7th. For White Voters only. Nigger — you are not wanted." The leaflets carried the forbidding symbol of the skull and crossbones and were signed "K.K.K."[4] Republicans were convinced that Democrats were the instigators of the intimidating dodgers, and Governor Hyde advanced this view in a letter to United States Attorney General Harry M. Daugherty. Hyde requested that federal protection be afforded the Negroes in the southeast counties and charged that Democratic county officers, unwilling to guarantee Negroes their voting rights, had distributed the scurrilous sheets.[5]

There is no direct evidence that either Democrats or the Klan were responsible for the leaflets, but it is quite clear that Democrats in the Bootheel opposed the Negro's participation in politics. Democratic newspaper editors of the area wrote blatantly racist editorials that called for the maintenance of a "white man's government" while chiding white Republicans for soliciting "nigger" votes.[6] Democrats in all sections of the state voiced fears that the "Negro problem" posed a serious obstacle to the party's hopes of recapturing or retaining state offices and several congressional seats in 1924. "A little zero weather in January may send them back to the Sunny South," Breckinridge Long wrote Edward M. House, "but unless it does we have 40,000 additional votes to overcome."[7]

While white G.O.P. leaders seemed to take the colored vote for granted, Negro Republican C. A. Franklin, editor of the *Kansas City Call,* refused to believe that the newcomers to the state would automatically support the party. "Remember," he advised Governor Hyde, "they have no experience in voting. They have fled from the intolerable conditions created in the South by the Democratic party."[8] Research in Kansas City and St. Louis, Franklin informed the Governor, revealed an appalling degree of apathy among the colored voters. The challenge confronting the Republicans of Missouri, he advised, was twofold: First, Negro citizens must be accorded "good treatment" and shown that a vote for the G.O.P. would "help defeat the party that sponsored peonage, lynching, injustice in the courts, and all the other evils in the South"; second, the party must finance an ambitious voter registration drive in the cities.[9] Franklin's analysis convincingly pointed up the political apathy and inexperience existing in the colored communities and the opportunity awaiting the Missouri G.O.P. Indeed, given the traditional tie of Negroes to the Republican party, the inability of Republicans to poll the full Negro vote during the twenties worked to the advantage of the Democratic party.

Even more damaging, potentially, to the Republican party in Missouri than the apathy of the Negro rank and file was the apathy of white G.O.P. leaders to the needs of colored citizens. Although Governor Hyde gave limited support to policies suggested by C. A. Franklin and other spokesmen for the race,[10] Negroes grew restless in view of the lack of Republican support for their programs. Evidence of this restlessness came to light at an organizational meeting of the Missouri Negro Republican League in Jefferson City on Lincoln's Birthday in 1924: "We . . . are a real contingent of the great Republican party," the organization's president asserted, "who . . . can no longer be hoodwinked into the acceptance of a five-dollar bill upon election day, a groundhog dinner or an opossum supper, as a reward for our efforts to advance the Republican cause."[11] As the assertion makes clear, political discontent among Negroes stirred within the framework of Republican politics.

With the Republican rolls continuously augmented by Negro newcomers to the state, harmony within the strife-torn Democratic party became all the more imperative if Democrats were to achieve any degree of success in the congressional and state elections of 1924. On the surface, the prospects of reuniting the party appeared better in late 1923 than at any time since the party split into Reed and Wilson factions in 1919. This situation resulted largely from the changed political status of the Democrats who had given leadership to their respective factions, and to altered sentiment for the League of Nations. On the one hand, Reed's reelection to the Senate for another six-year term placed him beyond the reach of his enemies; on the other, former President Wilson's declining health seemed to parallel the waning enthusiasm among his supporters in Missouri for the League of Nations.[12]

Yet the Reed-Wilson controversy, because of the dominating personalities of the two men and the intense feeling evoked by the League of Nations, partially obscured the more fundamental party cleavage that separated rural, old-stock Protestants from urban, Irish, Roman Catholic Democrats. The postwar intraparty fight over the League made Irish power evident, and the triumph of Senator Reed in 1922, due in large measure to the support of hyphenated Americans of the cities, seemed to underscore the declining influence of "loyal" old-stock Democrats of rural Missouri.

It is not surprising, then, that hostility of the rural Democrats toward the urban wing of the party began to intensify and to find illiberal expression in 1923 and 1924. Ewing Y. Mitchell, a Democrat in Springfield, voiced a sentiment shared by many old-stock Democrats when he described the main body of Senator Reed's supporters as the "underworld of the cities, the sports, gamblers, bootleggers, wets, and the riff-raff of society generally."[13] Other Democrats were doing more than voicing derogatory sentiments about the party's urban, Irish Catholic wing. In the fall and winter of 1923–1924, many old-stock rural citizens and small-town residents found an outlet for their cultural, social, and political frustrations by joining the Ku Klux Klan.

Appropriately, from the standpoint of many old-stock Protestants, the Klan of the twenties, as had the American Protective Association of the 1890's, featured anti-Catholicism as its dominant nativist attitude. Anti-Negro and anti-Semitic prejudices, too, were harbored by the Klan and figured in the secret order's exaltation of the native, white, Protestant, "100 per cent American." Many Missourians, Democrat and Republican, applauded the Klan's "positive" program of upholding law and order, especially the enforcement of prohibition. Most political observers, however, believed that the Klan, in 1924, counted more Democrats than Republicans in its membership of approximately 100,000.[14] Unquestionably, the Klan proved more disruptive to Democratic than to Republican politics.

Before the Klan gained enough members to make itself noticeable on the political scene, the Democratic party's first significant movement toward harmony since the intraparty fight over the League got under way in the summer of 1923. The sponsors of the movement, members of the Democratic Editorial Association, hoped to please urban supporters of Senator Reed and rural backers of Breckinridge Long by naming both men delegates-at-large to the 1924 National Democratic Convention. In order to avoid a fight for Missouri's votes for the presidential nomination, the editors urged that former Governor Frederick D. Gardner be put forward as the state's favorite son candidate for President.[15]

On December 1 the editorial association met in St. Louis to reveal their plan for harmony. Although Governor Gardner had not sanctioned the movement in any way, he nevertheless was on hand to deliver the major address. Gardner's speech, however, hardly furthered the unification of the party's warring factions. Rather, his calls for the United States' entrance into the World Court and for the creation of a large federal organization to enforce prohibition seemed intended more to resurrect the bones of controversy than to bury them.[16]

If any hopes for the success of the harmony movement remained after Gardner's speech, they were abruptly removed on December 10, when Senator Reed viciously assailed the ex-Governor's address. Reed, lashed into a fury by the key proposals of the speech, characterized Gardner's call for the United States' entrance into the World Court and increased federal enforcement of prohibition as a dangerous promotion of national and international centralization and an ominous threat to individual liberties. When rural Democrats responded to Reed's severe criticism of Gardner's address with a vigorous condemnation of the Senator, Reed explained that his criticism was not prompted by ill will but simply reflected a difference of opinion.[17]

Subsequent events, however, proved that Reed had more in mind than an expression of differences when he assailed Gardner on December 10. The truth was that the move to present Gardner as the Missouri Democracy's "favorite son" frustrated Reed's own desire for that honor and his plans to win the presidential nomination for himself. Furthermore, though the editorial association's scheme was at the outset a genuine movement for harmony, supporters of William G. McAdoo hoped to use Gardner's nomination as a cloak for their efforts to secure Missouri's convention votes for McAdoo. Reed may have sensed this device and therefore criticized Gardner's address in order to force the hand of McAdoo's group. When Gardner announced on January 15 that he was withdrawing from the presidential race and would personally support the candidacy of McAdoo, Reed may have felt, as his supporters charged, that "harmony" had been a McAdoo movement all along.[18] In any case, Gardner's withdrawal paved the way for Reed's announcement on January 27 that he would campaign in Missouri for an endorsement by the state convention of his candidacy for the Presidency. A day later Walter K. Chorn, state manager for McAdoo, informed the press that friends of McAdoo would seek an instructed delegation from Missouri for Woodrow Wilson's son-in-law.[19]

Since the contest in Missouri was crucial to both presidential aspirants, each announcement from either camp signaled the beginning of another round in the Democrats' continuing intraparty battle. On the one hand, Reed could not expect to receive consideration at the Democratic National Convention unless he could line up his own state behind his candidacy; on the other, the state's thirty-six convention votes were important to McAdoo, who needed all the southern and western states he could muster in order to attain the two-thirds majority necessary for nomination. The prospect of capturing Missouri's votes looked good to the dry progressive, since most old-stock Wilson men had swung to his standard at the outset of the 1924 campaign; Reed, however, seemed assured only of the support of wets and the anti-League Irish and Germans.[20]

Why, in the face of strong opposition within his own state and with little apparent outside support, did Senator Reed believe he had a chance to gain the Democratic presidential nomination? It would seem that Reed, with other presidential hopefuls, felt that McAdoo, though leading the field in the preconvention campaigning, would be unable to secure the necessary two-thirds vote for nomination in convention. A deadlocked convention in 1924, Reed thought, could very possibly turn to him as the "most available" candidate. Indeed, Reed and his supporters believed that he, better than any other candidate, could unite the warring eastern and southern-western wings of the national party. They argued that the wet urban organizations of the East and the dry Democrats of the South and West could, without compromising their positions, nominate Reed, since he favored modification of the Volstead Act while sharing the conviction of many dry Democrats that enforcement of prohibition was a matter that belonged properly to each state rather than to the federal government. In addition, Reed believed his candidacy would bring back to the party those voters of Irish and German extraction who bolted Cox and the Democratic ticket in 1920 because they opposed the League of Nations. Finally, Reed's supporters reasoned, the Senator's attacks on monopolies and plutocrats would draw the radical element to the Democratic standard, yet conservatives would not be alienated, since the Missourian favored little governmental interference in private business.[21]

However dubious some of these arguments were, Reed's opportunity for testing them in the national arena depended first upon a victory over McAdoo in Missouri. At the outset, the Senator suffered reverses in maneuvers designed to wrest the Missouri delegation away from the Californian. The State Democratic Committee, meeting in St. Louis on January 28, voted down an attempt by Bennett C. Clark, son of the late Speaker and key Reed lieutenant in that city, to fix the appointment of delegates to the state convention on the basis of the 1922 senatorial election rather than of the 1920 presidential election. A motion that only "known Democrats" be allowed to participate in ward and township conventions won over Clark's motion, which would have permitted anyone to vote in those conventions who voted the Democratic ticket in 1922 and who would declare his intention to support the ticket in 1924.[22] Wilson Democrats thus retained the upper hand.

Then, on February 1, the high-flying McAdoo campaign went into a tailspin in Missouri and throughout the nation. A Senate investigating committee learned from E. L. Doheny, an oil magnate who was involved in the Teapot Dome scandals, that McAdoo was on his payroll. At the same time, newspapers revealed that Senator Reed, on the floor of the Senate the day before, had demanded that Doheny be called before the committee to answer questions designed to bring out the fact of McAdoo's employment. Official Washington knew before the public disclosure that McAdoo's legal services had been engaged by Doheny. Nevertheless, the revelation of this fact in connection with the Senate hearings had the effect of linking the California presidential hopeful to the notorious Teapot Dome affair.[23] It is difficult to escape the conclusion that this was precisely the purpose Reed had in mind. This shrewd stratagem offered Reed the possibility of switching Democratic backing from McAdoo to himself. The bold move severely crippled the Californian's chances for winning the nomination,[24] but it subsequently proved to be equally damaging to Reed's presidential ambitions that year.

The death of President Wilson on February 3 delayed by only a day the unfavorable reaction of many McAdoo supporters to Doheny's disclosure. Frank H. Farris, Democratic State Committee chairman and member of the McAdoo executive committee in Missouri, declared that McAdoo had become "an impossible candidate" and called for an uninstructed delegation to the national convention. Congressmen Sam Major, J. C. Milligan, and J. F. Fulbright, hitherto silent on both McAdoo's and Reed's candidacies, asserted that McAdoo was now eliminated from the presidential race. The *St. Louis Globe-Democrat*'s sampling of grass-roots sentiment showed that many Democrats believed McAdoo no longer available as a candidate.[25]

Breckinridge Long came at once to his candidate's defense with an offensive directed against Reed. The same day Doheny told Senate investigators of McAdoo's relation to his organization, Long wired the *Kansas City Star* with the charge that "the same men who fought Woodrow Wilson and harassed him to his present sad plight are the same ones now seeking to discredit McAdoo. . . . Republicans are trying to bring in the names of some prominent Democrats to relieve them of the odium," Long added, "and Reed is helping them as usual."[26] Long was responsible also for the release of a story revealing Reed's employment as counsel and special attorney for the Universal Oil Company of North Dakota, thus implying that the Senator from Missouri had a connection with oil interests similar to that of McAdoo's.[27] Both Long and Charles M. Hay kept up a drumfire of criticism of Reed until after February 18, when a meeting of McAdoo's supporters in Chicago absolved the Californian of any wrongdoing. According to Long and Hay, McAdoo still deserved Missouri's convention votes.[28]

Ten days before the election of state convention delegates, Senator Reed returned to Missouri from Washington to wage an all-out attack on McAdoo. In his whirlwind tour of the state, Reed told Missourians that the oil-splattered McAdoo could not carry a single state. Reed ridiculed the idea that Doheny had hired McAdoo for his legal ability; rather, he charged, it was McAdoo's political connections that made him useful to Doheny. And while he flayed McAdoo for not extending to him the political courtesy given to other presidential aspirants in their home states, he challenged the Californian to come to Missouri for a debate on the oil scandals.[29]

The vitriolic character of Reed's attack upon his rival convinced McAdoo's strategists in Missouri and in the rest of the nation that a personal visit to the state was imperative. They agreed unanimously that a victory over Reed in the Senator's home state would give the McAdoo campaign a badly needed impetus.[30] McAdoo, however, rejected this urgent advice of his managers. Instead, he explained to Breckinridge Long, a strong dignified statement would be more effective "than for me to rush into the state as though Reed had a chance." If he went to Missouri, McAdoo argued, other states would demand the same treatment, "and I cannot make a tour of the country."[31] This explanation, however, as well as the protest that time did not permit a visit to Missouri, is unconvincing.[32] At that juncture in McAdoo's campaign Missouri was the major battleground, and Reed's cutting attacks were front-page news across the nation. Moreover, ten days elapsed between the first urgent appeals of McAdoo's advisers and the Democratic county conventions in Missouri, which were held on March 7. Apparently McAdoo, having no stomach for the rough personal campaigning in which Reed excelled, feared further humiliation at the hands of the wily Missourian. In any event, his decision to remain away was a fateful one; a potential turning point was missed, and McAdoo supporters began to shift to other candidates.[33]

Instead of coming to Missouri, from the safety of his California home McAdoo wired a blistering reply to Reed's charges that conveyed the idea that his imbroglio with the Senator had developed from a willingness to contest Reed for Missouri's convention votes. The Californian claimed that Sam Fordyce, a St. Louis Democrat who represented the Senator, conveyed to McAdoo's strategist Daniel Roper the information that, should McAdoo enter Missouri, Reed would enter primaries in Georgia and California against McAdoo.[34] When he refused to stay out of Missouri, McAdoo explained, Reed took further action "for the sole purpose of dragging my name, without justification, into the oil inquiry." If Senator Reed wanted to know why he had made an exception in the case of Missouri to his announced policy of not contesting a state against a bona fide candidate. McAdoo concluded, "he will find my explanation in his own record."[35]

The brief but bitter contest between Reed and McAdoo ended March 7 as Democrats met in county conventions to elect delegates to the state convention. In an overwhelming fashion rural Democracy rejected Reed's candidacy by giving him the delegations of only thirteen counties. The 70 votes of these counties, added to the Senator's sweep of St. Louis and Kansas City, gave Reed only 359 of 1,158 delegates. But the 518 votes McAdoo received from his outstate supporters fell 62 short of a majority. The balance of the votes went to a large number of uncommitted delegates, probably reflecting the attitude of many Missourians that McAdoo was unavailable because of the disclosures in the Senate oil hearings.[36] Still, the prospect of a McAdoo-dominated delegation to the Democratic National Convention appeared likely, while Reed's presidential aspirations were shattered beyond hope. Reed acknowledged this end to his ambitions on March 24 when he asked his supporters not to "endorse his candidacy or to confer upon him any honors whatsoever." [37]

Although the McAdoo-Reed campaign for state convention delegates did not touch on the controversy over the Klan, that organization may nevertheless have influenced the outcome of that contest in McAdoo's favor. Reed's opposition to the Klan was well known, since he had vigorously condemned the secret order in 1922. McAdoo, on the other hand, maintained a policy of silence on the Klan while endorsing civil and religious liberty for all Americans. A clear-cut case of active Klan influence against Reed was evident in Pike County, home of Reed's campaign manager Ed Glenn and of his supporter Bennett Clark. In 1922 the county gave primary and general election majorities to Reed, but in 1924 the county elected pro-McAdoo convention delegates to the state convention. In all, 13 of the 24 counties that voted for Reed in the 1922 primary election sent McAdoo, anti-Reed, or uninstructed delegations to the state convention of 1924. In every county of the thirteen, membership in the Klan was reportedly strong.[38]

When Democrats assembled in convention at Springfield on April 15, the Reed-McAdoo controversy of the previous three months gave way to a Klan–anti-Klan fight. The convention elected with relative ease a McAdoo-dominated, though uninstructed, delegation to the Democratic National Convention, but when delegates from Kansas City and St. Louis pressed for the adoption of an anti-Klan plank, the convention erupted in a near riot. Although the plank had little chance of passing, rural delegates refused to permit a reading of the anti-Klan resolution, and speakers who took opposing sides of the Klan controversy had difficulty in being heard. Order returned to the convention only after the adoption of a compromise plank that upheld civil and religious liberty without mentioning the Klan by name.[39]

The dissension over the Klan that marked the Springfield convention was re-enacted in midsummer at the National Democratic Convention in New York City, with Missourians in the thick of the battle. Representative Harry B. Hawes of St. Louis, who claimed the distinction of being the first congressman to condemn the Klan, played a prominent part in carrying the fight to denounce the hooded order to the floor of the convention after the platform committee failed to write an anti-Klan plank. But on the roll call the Missouri delegation, dividing along rural and urban lines, voted 25½ to 10½ against the resolution that would have mentioned the Klan by name.[40]

The vote on the Klan issue also gave an approximate indication of the delegation's sentiment for McAdoo. So long as the McAdoo delegates could maintain a majority, under the unit rule the state's entire 36 votes would be cast for the Californian. Yet the pro-Smith delegates from Kansas City and St. Louis, by requesting time-consuming polling of the state's delegation in the early balloting, exasperated enough McAdoo supporters to effect a switch of the delegation away from the Californian to John W. Davis on the 20th ballot. Then, on the 39th ballot the majority swayed back to McAdoo and remained with him until the 80th roll call. After several rounds of voting for Carter Glass and Samuel Ralston, the delegation moved back to Davis on the 95th roll call and stayed with the West Virginian until he gained the nomination on the 103rd ballot.[41] Although Davis had some ardent supporters in Missouri before the convention,[42] the true Missouri sentiment for him represented little more than lukewarm acceptance of a compromise candidate by the rural McAdoo delegates and the urban Smith supporters.

In many respects, the primary race of the four Democratic gubernatorial contestants resembled the clash of city and country, Klan and anti-Klan factions at the New York City convention.[43] St. Louis candidates George Moore and Henry

S. Priest, waging their contests on anti-Klan platforms, tried without success to get Arthur W. Nelson, a favorite before the primaries, to state his views on the Klan. Nelson, the only gubernatorial candidate from rural Missouri, contended that, since the Klan was not a valid issue, he would not comment on the secret order. A similar policy was followed by Kansas City lawyer Floyd Jacobs, the candidate backed by the Rabbit boss of that city, Joseph Shannon. When the Klan published its election choices before the August primary, Nelson rather than Jacobs, however, received its nod.

If the Klan knew that Nelson was the leading candidate and if it wanted to back a winner, as some newspapers observed, the same could be said of Tom Pendergast, who also endorsed Nelson's candidacy. Nelson's 171,180 votes placed him far ahead of second-running candidate Jacobs' 91,097 total. The rural Democrat received enough votes outstate alone to win the nomination and, because of Pendergast's support, carried Kansas City over Jacobs by a vote of 19,796 to 18,204. In St. Louis, however, Nelson received only 3,446 votes. The winner of the wet city's vote was antiprohibitionist Henry S. Priest, who amassed nearly half of his 50,000 votes there.[44]

The Klan's choice for governor on the Republican ticket was State Superintendent of Schools Sam A. Baker, who also defeated his anti-Klan, big-city opponents. The prospect of the Klan being eliminated entirely from the campaign appeared a possibility after both parties adopted specific anti-Klan planks in their platforms that fall. Baker, however, issued a personal denunciation of the Klan, a move prompted no doubt by the belief that Nelson would be reluctant to do the same for fear of alienating the rural Klansmen who, most observers agreed, were more numerous in the Democratic than in the Republican party. At the same time, Nelson could ill afford to be less anti-Klan than Baker and to risk losing the support of the urban Irish Catholic Democrats.

For nearly a month the Klan issue lay dormant as Baker and Nelson campaigned on almost identical platforms of better schools, improved roads, and lower agricultural land tax. Since both men were drys, prohibition did not figure in their campaigns. Then, on September 28, outgoing Governor Arthur M. Hyde, chief campaigner for Baker, issued the first of several challenges to Nelson in an effort to get the Democrat to state his past and present affiliation with the Klan. Hyde climaxed his badgering of Nelson on the latter's connection with the Klan by releasing to the press on October 21 affidavits obtained from two Cooper County farmers that alleged that Nelson's name was on the roster of the Tipton Klan.

This allegation threw Democrats into a turmoil. Representative Harry B. Hawes, waging an uphill fight for re-election in St. Louis, called upon Nelson to clear himself if he expected to receive the support of anti-Klan Democrats. Nelson admitted that he had once attended a Klan ceremony, but denied membership in the Klan. When Baker made an affidavit to the effect that he had no past or present connection with the Klan, Nelson weakly responded that anyone who wished to consider the Klan an issue would have to regard as adequate his oral statements denying Klan affiliations. Anti-Klan Democrats such as Harry Hawes, who were faced with the alternatives of either disassociating themselves from Nelson or staying with the gubernatorial candidate, expressed satisfaction with Nelson's oral denials.[45] Senator Reed, ill since June, fulfilled the requests of urban, anti-Klan Democrats by making three speeches in behalf of the entire state ticket. Reed asserted that Nelson's denial of affiliation with the Klan satisfied him; otherwise, he could not speak in behalf of the gubernatorial candidate. Although Reed assailed the Klan at length, he softened his denunciation somewhat by declaring that he "preferred the Klan to Governor Hyde."[46]

In spite of the efforts of Hawes, Reed, and Tom Pendergast's machine, Irish Democrats in Kansas City and St. Louis were all but publicly opposing Nelson and showing little enthusiasm for the presidential candidate, John W. Davis. Too, Senator Reed found it difficult to support Davis. In fact the Senator refused to speak in Davis' behalf until the candidate satisfied him that he would adhere to the party's weak plank on the League.[47] Joe Shannon actually made a speech endorsing the Progessives' presidential candidate Robert M. La Follette, and rumors circulated that the disgruntled Irishman had ordered his Rabbit supporters to bolt Davis, Nelson, and the rest of the Pendergast slate.[48] Privately, Democrats admitted that the prospects for the state and national ticket were bleak.[49]

The balloting on November 4 confirmed many of the rumors and predictions that had been current during the campaign. Republicans carried the state for Coolidge, elected Baker governor, captured all of the state offices, and regained a majority in the state's House of Representatives. Davis ran far behind the state ticket, polling some 60,000 fewer votes than defeated gubernatorial candidate Nelson. Since it appears that Republicans contributed more of La Follette's 84,160 votes than did Democrats, Coolidge's 75,733 majority may be considered somewhat less than the margin he would have received had the contest been limited to a two-man race.[50]

In the closest state contest, Republican Sam A. Baker won the governorship by only 5,872 votes, while other Republican candidates for state offices enjoyed margins of 40,000 to 50,000. Viewed in this light, it appears that Nelson's handling of the affidavits charging him with membership in the Klan made him a stronger candidate than he otherwise would have been. On the other hand, it could be pointed out that Nelson, with Pendergast support, split the Kansas City vote with Baker; carried outstate by nearly 40,000 votes; but lost St. Louis by about the same margin.[51] From these facts, one could reason that Nelson's refusal to denounce the Klan in unequivocal terms cost him the support of anti-Klan Democrats and independent voters in both Kansas City and St. Louis and thereby lost the election.

Another factor that may have spelled the difference between victory and defeat for Nelson was the failure of Shannon Democrats in Kansas City and Jackson County to deliver a large vote for the Pendergast-backed candidates. The customary "fifty-fifty" arrangement between the Rabbit boss and the Goat leader that had previously kept Jackson County Democrats united on general election day had been in the process of breaking down since the spring mayoralty contest. When Pendergast-supported candidates beat Shannon men in the August primary, the Rabbit boss, realizing that Democratic victories in state and county contests would mean the undisputed ascendancy of his rival in Kansas City and Jackson County, gave the word to his supporters to "knife" the ticket.[52]

The new strength Negro voters of Kansas City and St. Louis brought to the Republican ticket also figured significantly in the defeat of Nelson and other Democratic candidates. In wards where Republicans traditionally outpolled Democrats, additional votes from the colored newcomers boosted the G.O.P.'s margins substantially over those achieved in the elections of 1920 and 1922. In other wards where Democrats had polled a majority of the votes in the two preceding elections, the Negro vote helped erase or diminish the traditional Democratic margin. The conviction of old and new Negro citizens alike that a vote for Nelson would be a vote for the Klan was reflected in the gains Republicans posted in the Negro-populated wards.[53]

The impact of Negro voters revealed itself also in the

congressional contests in those districts with a large colored population. The new Negro electorate in the southeast counties that constituted the Fourteenth Congressional District clearly contributed to the defeat of incumbent Democrat J. F. Fulbright. In 1922 Fulbright had carried the district by 3,323 votes, winning in 6 of the 7 major cotton-producing counties. The influx of over ten thousand permanent Negro tenant farmers and transient cotton pickers into the area in 1923 and 1924, however, reduced the margin of Democratic victories in 4 of the counties. In Pemiscot County the strength added to the Republican ticket by Negro newcomers helped turn a 1,000-vote Democratic majority in 1922 into an 800-vote Republican majority in 1924.[54]

In St. Louis, the increased Negro registration in the Eleventh District proved almost too much for Representative Harry B. Hawes to overcome in his bid for a third term in the House. Since 1922 three thousand colored voters had been added to the Eleventh District's rolls so that, as Hawes expressed it, "my opponent had 11,000 negroes to go with." [55] No Democrat had spoken more frequently in denunciation of the Klan than Hawes, but when Negroes in the district pressed him for a commitment to support a federal antilynching bill, he demurred, on the ground that the legislation compromised states' rights. The *St. Louis Argus*, a Negro newspaper, urged colored voters to support Hawes's Republican opponent, who not only had denounced the Klan, but favored a federal antilynching bill as well.[56] Waging his campaign almost exclusively on a civil and religious liberty platform, Hawes won re-election by a margin of fewer than 2,000 votes. Two years earlier, he had achieved an easy 24,839 to 17,188 victory over Republican Bernard Bogy. Hawes was one of nine Democratic congressional candidates to win election in 1924; Republicans increased their delegation in the House from four to seven.[57]

In spite of the high hopes of harmonizers, 1924 was yet another year of dissension for the Missouri Democracy. Divergent views on cultural and social issues, which produced hostility between the rural and urban wings of the party, kept Democrats in turmoil and disunity. Both factions demonstrated their power with almost equal effect: Rural Democrats played a crucial role in rejecting the favorite-son candidacy of Senator Reed, dominated and at times controlled the national convention delegation, and saw their favorite gain the gubernatorial nomination; urban Democrats impaired the effectiveness of the pro-McAdoo forces and, more important, either bolted or stayed away from the polls in the November election. Consequently, a divided party suffered defeat.

The problem facing the Democratic party in Missouri involved more than a reunification of its warring wings. The continuing influx into Missouri of persons traditionally recruited to the Republican party, particularly Southern Negroes, threatened to relegate the once dominant Democratic party to permanent impotence. The party's return to power demanded the construction of a broader, united coalition. The task began in 1925.

CHAPTER 6

HAWES AND HARMONY

WHEN FRANKLIN D. ROOSEVELT'S now familiar circular letter of December, 1924, reached Missouri's delegates to the recently adjourned Democratic National Convention, it evoked responses that reflected the divided nature of the party in state and nation. Urban Democrats urged the adoption of a program to combat the illiberalism of prohibitionists and Klan sympathizers; rural Democrats railed against the economic conservatism of the party's eastern wing. Other suggestions from Missourians and from Democrats around the country, embracing every position within the party, helped convince Roosevelt that the Democratic party should formulate a set of fundamentals upon which all could agree.[1]

An all-inclusive stand, yet one distinctly different from that of the Republicans, Roosevelt discovered, constituted a return to the principles of Thomas Jefferson. Roosevelt, his biographer Frank Freidel points out, even tried to function as another Jefferson. While corresponding with distinguished members of the party as well as with lesser Democrats and gaining ideas from everywhere, the New Yorker also employed a variety of means of disseminating the Democratic point of view. The most persistent theme pushed by Roosevelt was the idea that the national Democracy should commit itself to a progressive program. He failed, however, in his efforts to bring conservatives and progressives together in conference for the purpose of establishing progressive issues for the 1926 election. Conservative Democrats, Roosevelt found, were quite willing to accept Thomas Jefferson's creed, but they were unwilling to translate his principles into a progressive program that was realistic enough to meet the needs of twentieth-century society.[2]

If Roosevelt was the "new Jefferson" on the national scene, his counterpart in Missouri was Congressman Harry B. Hawes. No one in the state worked more persistently and diligently during 1925 and 1926 to harmonize warring Democratic factions than the St. Louis congressman, and no Missourian was more eminently qualified for promoting harmony under the Jeffersonian banner than Hawes. In 1901, the centenary of the third President's inauguration, Hawes had led a contingent of Missourians to Monticello, thus dramatizing a revival, albeit brief, of Jeffersonianism. Under Hawes's direction, a Jefferson Club flourished for a while after the turn of the century in St. Louis, helping to carry the city for the Democrats and playing an important part in launching the political career of progressive Governor Joseph Folk. But as Folk's political star ascended, Hawes and the Jefferson Club passed from the scene.

In 1916 Hawes returned to politics and won a seat in the state legislature, where he provided leadership for the passage of the State Highway Act of 1917, commonly known as the Hawes Road Law. This legislation, which initiated the state's modern highway program, was supplemented in 1920 by a $60,000,000 highway bond issue. Hawes played the key role in the passage of the bond issue, too, by directing a vigorous state-wide campaign as president of the Missouri Good Roads Federation. These efforts in behalf of good roads earned him popularity with Democrats and Republicans alike. In the split in the Democratic party over the League of Nations, Hawes steered a middle course and refused to align himself with either the Reed or Wilson faction. By retaining the support of most anti-League Irish Democrats in his urban district, Hawes became one of two Democrats elected to Congress from Missouri in 1920. Re-elected in 1922 and again in 1924, Hawes distinguished himself in the House as an aggressive spokesman for cultural liberalism. He was proud of his attacks upon the Klan and boasted that he was the first member of Congress to speak out against the secret organization from the floor of the House.[3]

Unlike Roosevelt, Hawes did not undertake his self-appointed harmonizing work with the principal aim of committing the Missouri Democracy to a progressive program. He wanted the party's nomination for the United States Senate and, once nominated, he wanted a united party behind his candidacy. For these reasons, during his 8,000-mile speaking tour around the state in 1925 he avoided any discussion of specific issues that divided the party. Instead, he emphasized such Jeffersonian themes as states' rights and individual liberties. In this manner Hawes promoted a new revival of Jeffersonianism, and, more importantly, party harmony and his candidacy for the Senate in 1926.[4]

Other Democrats joined Hawes in his campaign for party harmony. Bennett Clark sounded the keynote for unity in Kansas City at the 1925 Jefferson Day banquet — the first such observance held anywhere in Missouri for several years. "We must cease to fight about things which don't count," Clark advised, "and return again to the principles of Thomas Jefferson. I am willing to let bygones be bygones; I know that I have been mixed up in these factional fights as much as anybody."[5]

Not all Kansas City Democrats, however, were willing at first to join in the quest for harmony. Joe Shannon, still sulking from his defeat in primary contests with Pendergast Democrats in 1924, his ranks thinned out by the defection of the Cas Welch faction to his rival's organization, refused to line up with Pendergast in the movement for a new city charter. In February, 1925, when Kansas Citians voted 37,363 to 8,871 to place the city under a mayor-council-manager government, only Shannon's Ninth Ward returned a majority against the change.[6] Consequently, Shannon Democrats were ignored in the Democratic convention that nominated a slate of candidates for the November city election. Not until Pendergast offered Shannon a third of city and county patronage did the Rabbit leader agree to back the candidates of the Goat boss. As it turned out, Shannon's support materially helped the Pendergast-dominated Democratic organization to elect five of the nine councilmen. Hence, when the new City Council took office for a five-year term in April, 1926, Democratic control of Kansas City, through the instrumentality of a united Pendergast-Shannon organization, was secure.[7]

In the spring municipal election of 1925 in St. Louis, an effort toward harmony by that city's Democrats brought their mayoralty candidate William Igoe within 3,000 votes of upsetting Republican Victor Miller. Igoe's good showing resulted in part from his popularity as a former congressman from St. Louis. His victory in several German wards may have been due to his vote against the declaration of war in 1917, as some political observers believed, but his lack of sympathy with prohibition probably played an even more important part in attracting the German vote. His opponent Miller, a former city police commissioner, had alienated the wets of the city with his strict enforcement of prohibition laws. The 120,000 votes for Igoe, the largest number ever received by the Democrats in a St. Louis municipal election, were due principally, however, to the united endeavors of all factions to poll the full Democratic vote and at the same time effectively exploit weaknesses in the Republican camp.[8]

Democrat Igoe got an unexpected and significant boost from the St. Louis Negro voters, owing chiefly to the unpopularity of the G.O.P.'s mayoralty candidate. The *St. Louis Argus* had supported Miller's opponent in the Republican primary, on the ground that the former police com-

missioner had taken a soft stand on the Ku Klux Klan. Since
the Klan at no time had more than a very limited membership in St. Louis, a more accurate statement of the Negroes'
grievance against Miller was an apparent lack of sympathy
for the aspirations of the race. The *Argus* recalled that
Governor Hyde — not Miller, whom the Governor had ap-
pointed to head the St. Louis Police Board — deserved credit
for the appointment of the city's first colored policeman in
1921. After Miller won the nomination the *Argus* endorsed
Democrat Igoe. Similarly, prominent Negro Republicans
Homer G. Phillips and George L. Vaughn came out for
the Democrats' candidate, and both spoke in Igoe's behalf
in the colored wards of the city.

Miller, however, through other Negro leaders such as
Jordan Chambers, rallied most of the city's colored voters
behind his candidacy to carry all of the Negro wards. Nevertheless, Democrats had made inroads into the Negro Republican ranks. The *St. Louis Argus*, which claimed that nearly
100 per cent of the city's Negroes had voted Republican in
1924, estimated that from six thousand to eight thousand Negroes, or approximately 30 per cent of the number of colored
persons voting, had cast ballots for Igoe.[9] Democrats, in
losing the mayoralty election, also lost the patronage and
policy decisions that could have been used to induce further
defection from the colored Republican ranks. Still, they stood
ready to gain the support of Negroes as they were alienated
by the Miller Administration.

Negroes' discontent with the new Republican state administration, a reality almost from the outset, also indicated
a favorable future for Missouri Democrats. Convinced that
colored citizens had provided Governor Baker with his margin of victory in 1924, the Negro press of Kansas City and
St. Louis quickly turned on the Republican governor after
few political appointments came to their race.[10] When the
Governor delayed the reappointment of Lincoln University's

president, a chorus of Negro protest was raised against the Administration until two Republican members of the school's Board of Curators voted with the Democratic State Superintendent of Schools for the retention of former Governor Hyde's appointee.[11] Baker further alienated Negro leaders by failing to consult with them on the interim appointment of St. Louis Republican George H. Williams to the seat in the United States Senate vacated upon the death of Selden Spencer in May, 1925. The Baker Administration should know, the *St. Louis Argus* heatedly commented, "that the colored people of this state are not bound politically to any star chamber candidate selected behind closed doors by a few bosses who feel that they have our votes in their pockets." The *Kansas City Call* made its attitude clear when it called for the appointment of Baker's political enemy, Walter C. Dickey of Kansas City.[12]

With the approach of the 1926 election, Democrats found their party in better shape than at any time in years. In Kansas City, a majority of Democratic councilmen were slated to take office in April, 1926. St. Louis Democrats, though defeated in the municipal election of 1925, demonstrated that they could unite, organize, and attract support from groups that were traditionally aligned with the Republican party. The state organization, united and revitalized by the efforts for harmony made by Harry B. Hawes and others, ended the year free of debt for the first time since the disastrous 1920 campaign; in addition, the state committee had obtained financial pledges amounting to $35,000 from active organizations in every congressional district for the 1926 campaign.[13]

Furthermore, it appeared that Harry B. Hawes had not only quieted factionalism, but also had established himself as the party's favorite for the senatorial nomination. The state's leading dry Democrat, Wilson supporter Charles M. Hay, found "no disposition on the part of our friends to make a fight,"[14] so he thereupon announced in November, 1925, his "definite and final" decision to remain out of the race for the Senate. Although he emphasized harmony in this announcement, Hay asserted his belief that the party would meet defeat unless it accepted the Eighteenth Amendment and quit warring over religious and racial questions. Hay confided privately to friends that, should Hawes get the nomination — and he fully expected that the St. Louisan would — "we shall have to determine our course in the light of the stand he takes on certain fundamental things."[15]

Specifically, Hay and other dry Wilson Democrats wanted to know how closely Hawes would follow the lead of Jim Reed and his own past inclinations on major questions, such as the World Court, prohibition, and farm relief legislation. Senator Reed had established himself as the implacable foe of the United States' participation in the World Court, and drys of the state felt that the Senator deserved their label, "champion of the wets in the Senate." Reed also opposed the McNary-Haugen farm bill and denounced it as an "unconstitutional" scheme that, if tried, would "produce something akin to a revolution in thirty days."[16] At the end of 1925, Hawes's current stand on prohibition and farm relief remained unknown. In the past, though, he had expressed a willingness to work for the modification of the Volstead Act, and when the McNary-Haugen bill came before the House for the first time in 1924, he voted against it.[17] It was possible, of course, that as a senatorial candidate Hawes would alter his position to the satisfaction of drys and of the economically pinched farmers of the state. Wilson Democrats were pleased with his support of the Burton Resolution in March, 1925. That resolution, which proposed the laying of groundwork for the United States' entrance into the World Court, also received the support of the other eight Democratic congressmen from Missouri.[18]

When the Senate took up the debate on the World Court

in January, 1926, Republican Senator George H. Williams voted with Reed against the entry of the United States into the international body.[19] Since Williams had already indicated he would be a candidate for election in his own right in 1926 and appeared to Hawes as the Republican most likely to be his opponent in the general election, the St. Louis Democrat faced a dilemma. In spite of assurances to Charles Hay that he would take a pro-World Court stand in the campaign and despite Tom Pendergast's promise of support regardless of his stand on the issue, Hawes had no desire to give anti-World Court Democrats a reason to vote for Williams.[20] On the other hand, if both candidates were against the United States' membership in the World Court, that issue would be eliminated as a factor in the campaign.

Thus, in his formal announcement of candidacy in late April, Hawes declared that, although he favored the principle of international justice, he was "unprepared to advocate the entrance of the United States now into the World Court." His position, Hawes explained, resulted from an unwillingness "to involve the United States in problems upon which Europeans themselves cannot agree."[21] Although his statement left some room for maneuvering as the situation might dictate in the Democratic primary, in effect Hawes's stand amounted to opposition to the United States' entry into the World Court.

Hawes's about-face at once angered and surprised Wilson Democrats and so agitated Charles Hay that he briefly entertained the idea of running in the general election campaign on an independent ticket as a pro-World Court candidate. An even more urgent spur to Hay, however, was his conviction that Hawes would soon come out for a liberalization of the Volstead Act. Since Williams was known to have wet views, the nomination of both men would leave drys without a candidate; yet, Hay reasoned, a dry independent candidate could conceivably win the election. Firing off letters to the president of the state Women's Christian Temperance Union, Nelle Burger, the superintendent of the Missouri Anti-Saloon League, and dry Wilson Democrats, Hay quietly began laying the groundwork for opposition to Hawes's candidacy. Then, almost as suddenly as he had conceived the idea of his independent candidacy, Hay abandoned it. A wiser course of action, he believed, would be to persuade one of the two dry candidates who were opposing Hawes for the senatorial nomination to withdraw.[22]

In the race for the Democratic senatorial nomination besides Hawes were Judge Ewing Cockrell of Warrensburg; Willis H. Meredith of Poplar Bluff, a lawyer; and Robert I. Young of St. Joseph, a farmer. As in 1922, no one gave serious thought to Young's candidacy, and very few believed either Cockrell or Meredith had a chance of gaining the nomination, since neither had the organization or resources to take the nomination away from the popular Hawes. If anything, both men in the race assured Hawes's nomination, since their identical stands as advocates of the World Court, farm relief legislation, and prohibition without modification would result only in a division of the rural vote. Each man, confident of success, refused to withdraw.[23]

From early May to mid-July, dry Democrats, officers of the Women's Christian Temperance Union, and officials of the Anti-Saloon League worked frantically but unsuccessfully for the withdrawal of either Cockrell or Meredith. The first plan of the drys involved a private poll of Anti-Saloon League members in an effort to determine which candidate had more strength among prohibitionists. After Cockrell received word that more drys favored Meredith, he quickly denounced the poll, on the ground that the League's membership was partial to Meredith, a director of their organization.[24]

Finally, with the primary little more than two weeks away, the W.C.T.U.'s president, Mrs. Burger, proposed a formula that was satisfactory to the two dry Democrats. Meredith, Mrs. Burger announced, would run only for the short term in the Senate, which began the day after the November election when Williams' term as interim appointee ended and continued to the opening of the full Senate term on March 4, 1927; the candidate for the full term would be Judge Cockrell. This arrangement would permit dry Democrats to vote for both men in a united effort to beat Hawes. The maneuver elated prohibitionists, but since it was proposed so late in the campaign and so much discord had been engendered among Cockrell's and Meredith's supporters, it offered little chance of success.[25] More significantly, the episode revealed the large and active involvement of the dry organizations in Democratic politics.

The turn of events undoubtedly pleased Hawes, since his dry opponents spent much of the primary campaign in denouncing each other, which left them little time to attack him. Hawes wisely watered down his intention, which he had announced earlier, to work for the modification of the Volstead Act "so as to permit the manufacture and sale of beer not intoxicating in fact." Instead, he dwelt on old Jeffersonian themes and on his newly formulated conviction that the farmers needed relief legislation. In addition, he continued to stress party harmony, even advising Democrats to form harmony rather than Hawes clubs.[26]

The prohibition issue and the activity of wets and drys produced even more acrimony in the Republican campaign than in the contest among Democrats. Although the Anti-Saloon League and the W.C.T.U. classed Senator Williams as a wet because of his lack of sympathy for the Eighteenth Amendment, Blodgett Priest, a lawyer in St. Louis who was Williams' major wet challenger in the primary, charged that, because of his support of the Volstead Act, Williams was a dry. A staunch supporter of both the prohibition amendment and federal enforcement was Kansas Citian David

Proctor. Friends of Senator Williams were skeptical of Priest's candidacy, in the belief that dry supporters of Proctor had engineered the entrance of a second wet candidate in order to split the wet vote. When former Governor Hyde made this accusation in the pages of the *Kansas City Star*, Walter C. Dickey, a supporter of Proctor, brought a three-million-dollar libel suit against Hyde and the *Star*.[27]

Similarly, the issue of farm relief produced more dissension among Republicans than among Democrats in the senatorial race, particularly between the supporters of Senator Williams and Proctor. Williams, like Congressman Hawes, had voted for the McNary-Haugen farm relief measure in Congress during the spring session of 1926, thereby gaining the backing of the *Missouri Farmer* and the *Missouri Ruralist*. Proctor, whose hopes rested primarily on a large vote in dry, rural Missouri, engaged the *Missouri Farmer*'s editor William Hirth in a bitter exchange after Hirth publicized the former state senator's past record as an opponent of farm cooperatives. Despite Proctor's assurances that he would work for the farmer in the Senate, Hirth concluded that the Kansas City dry was "not entitled to the vote of a single farmer in Missouri."[28]

The primary vote reflected the greater interest developed in the Republican campaign as more Missourians voted for G.O.P. than for Democratic candidates. Senator Williams easily won the Republican senatorial nomination, carrying both major cities and outstate as well and polling nearly 100,000 more votes than his closest contender, David Proctor. On the short-term balloting in the Democratic contest, Hawes outpolled Meredith 166,478 to 94,388; for the long term Hawes's vote totaled 162,921 to Cockrell's 105,936. Hawes greatly outdistanced his opponents in St. Louis and Kansas City, but his outstate vote topped second-best Cockrell's total by only a few thousand votes.[29] Evidently, Hawes's emphasis upon harmony, his late but strong endorsement of farm relief legislation, and his ability as a campaigner weighed more heavily in his favor with outstate Democrats than his wet, anti-World Court position.

The nomination of wets by both parties in the senatorial contest disappointed the drys and seemed to offer them no alternative except that of supporting the less objectionable candidate. Mrs. Burger, however, immediately announced that the temperance society would support neither candidate. Instead, the head of the W.C.T.U. stated that the organization's 15,000 members would devote their energies to the defeat of the referendum that was to be brought before the electorate and that would propose the repeal of the state's bone-dry prohibition laws.[30]

Proposition Number 4, the popular name of the referendum for repeal, was assured a place on the general election ballot through the petitioning of the Missouri branch of the National Association Against the Eighteenth Amendment. The rationale behind the proposition was that most Missourians resented the intrusion of federal prohibition enforcement officers in the police affairs of the state. Therefore, the argument ran, a majority of citizens would consent to the repeal of the state's prohibition law and the statutes pertaining to its enforcement, thus placing the onus of prohibition and its enforcement fully upon the federal government. The outcome, wets believed, would be a ground swell of support throughout the nation for the repeal of the Eighteenth Amendment. The wet organization also contended that the vote on Proposition Number 4 would indicate that a majority of Missourians opposed prohibition.[31]

The Association Against the Eighteenth Amendment surely could not have anticipated the extensive nonpartisan opposition by both wets and drys to their repeal proposition. The Anti-Saloon League and the W.C.T.U., instrumental in forming the "Citizens Organization Opposed to Proposition Number 4," brought together in that organization well-known Missourians of both major political parties, including three former Democratic governors, two former Republican governors, and the Republican incumbent, Governor Baker. Senatorial candidates Hawes and Williams came out strongly for the retention of the state's prohibition laws, and both the Democratic and the Republican platforms contained planks calling for the defeat of the wet-sponsored proposition. Senator Reed also announced his opposition to the wets' move and advised Mrs. Burger that, while he opposed the outlawing of alcoholic beverages, he favored laws regulating the manufacture and sale of liquor.[32]

The wets, in effect, acknowledged defeat even before the balloting when William H. Stayton, head of the National Association Against the Eighteenth Amendment, advised wet voters in Missouri to withhold their support from the repeal movement.[33] The fact that both parties had nominated wet candidates for the Senate, Stayton reasoned, plainly indicated that Missourians were opposed to prohibition; therefore, a vote to ascertain the state's sentiment on prohibition was unnecessary. Clearly, the wet organization desired to disassociate itself from a losing cause. Moreover, by taking this stand Stayton denied the drys the opportunity to boast after the election that the referendum represented a clear-cut mandate for the continuation of prohibition.

The referendum took none of the pressure off the senatorial candidates; in fact, the prohibition issue dominated the fall campaign as it had the primary contests. Immediately after the primary balloting, Williams issued a statement that Hawes had "blundered in calling for the modification of the Volstead Act" since he could not be "in harmony with the rest of the ticket." Obviously, he meant that Hawes's stand contrasted sharply with that of the rural congressional candidates in his party, who opposed any change in the federal dry laws.[34]

Williams' efforts to create dissension in the Democratic

camp over the prohibition issue, however, were convincingly and quickly dispelled as Judge Cockrell and Willis Meredith, defeated dry aspirants to the Senate, wired pledges of support to Hawes.[35] After the campaign got under way in September, Cockrell and Meredith, joined by Charles M. Hay, took to the stump in dry outstate territory in Hawes's behalf. "When the choice is between a wet Democrat and a wet Republican," Hay asked his dry audiences, "what excuse has a dry Democrat for refusing to support the party nominee?"[36] Senator Reed, speaking primarily to wet urban audiences, contrasted Hawes's pledge to work for the liberalization of the Volstead Act with Williams' commitment to support the federal laws that enforced prohibition. When Breckinridge Long joined the Hawes campaign late in October, Republicans faced a united opposition for the first time since the Democrats' split in 1919 and 1920.[37]

This unity caused former Governor Hyde to complain that Hawes and his supporters were simply trying to harmonize away their inconsistencies:

> if you ask Mr. Hawes whether he is wet or dry, he will answer "harmony." If you ask him whether he is for the World Court, he will intone the gospel of harmony. If you should inquire of his record . . . he will still say harmony, harmony, harmony.[38]

Actually, Hawes clearly spelled out his position on the major issues during the campaign. This frankness was especially true of his stand on farm relief legislation, as William Hirth observed in the *Missouri Farmer*. Hirth reminded farmers that both Wlliams and Hawes had voted for the McNary-Haugen bill in 1926 and that Hawes had also fought on the floor for it. Williams, Hirth reported, had voted for the farm relief measure with great reluctance, since he believed it to be "uneconomic and unsound."[39]

The real straddler of issues was Senator Williams who, in addition to his half-hearted support of farm relief legislation, refused to take a clear-cut stand on prohibition. Williams reiterated his conviction that the Eighteenth Amendment was a mistake, yet he promised to uphold the laws to enforce it and maintained silence on whether he would support any movement to liberalize the Volstead Act or to repeal the prohibition amendment. Late in the campaign, when it became clear that Williams did not intend to commit himself to a change in the federal prohibition law, a group of leading Republicans of St. Louis — bankers, businessmen, and industrialists — announced their support for Harry B. Hawes. According to the spokesman of the group, Carl F. G. Meyer, president of the Chamber of Commerce, "we feel compelled to do this because of the frank and unequivocal stand publicly expressed by Mr. Hawes in his favor of an early modification of the Volstead law." Meyer explained that the group considered its action "in the interest of true temperance and for the advancement of public morals and respect for law and order in this country."[40] Any economic motive these Republicans of St. Louis might have had was unexpressed.

Hawes's wet position and Senator Reed's fiery oratory also enabled the Democrats to attract larger audiences than the G.O.P. candidate in the German wards of St. Louis. German-American support for Hawes was boosted further by a blunder by former Governor Hyde. During the war, Hyde related, Hawes had been sent to Germany for the purpose of escorting Mrs. Adolphus Busch home to St. Louis and received $100,000 from the brewing family for his services. While Hawes had in fact received a large fee for aiding Mrs. Busch, Hyde evidently exaggerated the amount to give prohibitionists the impression that Hawes would be a well-paid servant of the Busch brewing interests if elected to the Senate. Although the Busch family had previously supported the Republican party, after this incident the son and grandsons of the aged Mrs. Busch appeared on the platform with Hawes and Reed in several meetings in the German wards and reportedly gave substantial financial contributions to the Hawes campaign.[41]

The efforts of Democrats to capture a large share of the colored vote in St. Louis and elsewhere, though more subdued than the appeals made to the wet Germans, was much more revolutionary, especially when contrasted with the party's attitude toward the Negro voter in 1924. The most readily observed change took place in the party platform. In 1924, when Missouri Republicans called for such measures as better educational opportunities for Negro youth, the Democratic platform was silent on considerations for the colored citizen's welfare.[42] In 1926, however, the Democratic planks not only included a program for Negroes, but, unlike the G.O.P. plank, stipulated that all public institutions for colored persons should be directed and staffed by their own people. With the state administration under Republican control for another two years, Democrats were powerless to deliver any part of their promises; nevertheless, their plank placed the party on record as a friend of the Negro. Furthermore, the Democratic platform endorsed the claim of Negro politicians and editors that Republican political supremacy in Missouri rested upon the support of the colored citizens. Therefore, the Democratic plank concluded, "we urge [Negro] citizens to study impartially political issues and give careful consideration of the effect which the present political exploitation of their race by the Republican party has had upon their welfare."[43]

Democrats of St. Louis and Kansas City no doubt were instrumental in drafting the strong Negro welfare plank; some of the wording followed closely the remarks made by Hawes in his Jefferson Day speech in 1926.[44] Democrats from the cotton-producing counties, though, probably offered no objection to the party's bid for the Negro vote. While deep-seated prejudice against the Negro still existed among the white Democrats of southeast Missouri in 1926, newspapers of the area no longer carried vicious racist attacks against the colored voter on their editorial page. Evidently, the derogatory editorials of 1923 and 1924 reflected the initial fears of whites in reaction to the rapid influx of Negroes into the area. At first no one knew to what extent the racial composition of the Bootheel would change, but by 1926 white editors, evidently convinced that the social equilibrium was in no danger of being upset, shifted from their earlier position from which they had urged that the Negro be excluded from politics to a new one in which they expressed interest in the colored man's vote for Democratic candidates. Further, Democratic politicians who had felt the sting of black power at the polls in 1924 had good reason for opposing the policy that would let the Negro vote go to white Republicans by default.[45]

Equal to, if not more significant than, the shift in the attitude of white Democrats toward the Negro voter was the continuing current of change in traditional Negro attitudes toward both major parties. In St. Louis' Twelfth Congressional District, where many of the city's Negroes resided, colored citizens demonstrated unprecedented political activity in 1926. Crowding the field in the primary race for congressman on the Republican ballot were Negroes Charles Higgins, George L. Vaughn, and Homer G. Phillips. The three candidates together polled a little more than half of the total accorded the winner, veteran congressman and perennial sponsor of a federal antilynching bill, Leonidas C. Dyer.[46] For the first time in the history of St. Louis, a Negro, George B. Vashon, entered the Democratic congressional primary in the Twelfth District. Vashon, whose Democratic affiliation dated back to 1892, was easily defeated by Jewish businessman David Israel; still, the Negro Democrat received a respectable 32.5 per cent of the Democratic vote.[47]

In Kansas City, long-time Democrat William J. Thompkins predicted that several of his race there would desert the Republican ticket, since "more and more Negroes are coming to understand that the Democratic party is the organization that stands for the welfare of the mass of the people."[48] The only colored newspaper then serving the city, C. A. Franklin's *Kansas City Call*, announced editorially shortly before the election that it should be regarded as a Negro rather than as a Republican newspaper. In the same issue the *Call* denounced Senator Williams, calling him "no good, the same as Jim Reed." Hawes was not specifically endorsed by the Negro newspaper, but the Democratic candidate for re-election as state superintendent of schools, Charles E. Lee, ardent supporter of improvements in educational opportunity for Negroes, received unqualified backing.[49]

The election returns reflected the strengths and weaknesses revealed in the primary and fall campaigns. Harry B. Hawes, architect of Democratic harmony, led the party to victory with an impressive vote of 506,015 to 470,654 over Senator Williams. Hawes's position on the issues — culturally liberal on the matter of prohibition, economically liberal on the farm problem — helped him to bridge the rural-urban gap that had hitherto divided the party at the polls. Not only did Hawes carry rural Missouri by approximately 40,000 votes and Kansas City by 15,000, he also came within 2,000 votes of matching Williams' total in St. Louis. Contributing to the Democrat's good showing in the traditionally Republican city were the large vote obtained in the wet German wards and the gains made in the Negro neighborhoods. The *St. Louis Argus*, a supporter of Williams in the campaign, nevertheless commented favorably upon the "head scratching" of Negro voters in the city's several colored wards.[50]

Another impressive feature of the November vote was the 15,000- to 20,000-vote majorities turned out for all major Democratic candidates in Kansas City and Jackson County.

In addition to demonstrating the power of the new and united Pendergast-Shannon organization, the Democratic margins also reflected the recruitment efforts of Irish leader Cas Welch and of colored organizers among the city's Negro residents.[51] According to the *Kansas City Call*, 42 per cent of the city's colored vote went to Democratic candidates, almost doubling the percentage received by Democrats in 1924.[52]

Although most Negroes in the southeast cotton-producing counties cast Republican ballots in 1926,[53] the total Republican effort was not enough to prevent the comeback of former Congressman J. F. Fulbright. Both candidates were pledged to support farm relief legislation, but the G.O.P. nominee had to overcome the record of the district's retiring congressman, Republican Ralph E. Bailey, who had voted against the McNary-Haugen bill. When cotton prices fell sharply as the new crop moved to market in the fall, farmers apparently decided to vote for Democrat Fulbright.[54]

The past record and future promise of support for farm relief legislation also figured importantly in the outcome of other congressional contests in the country districts. Every one of the rural candidates in both parties who had supported the McNary-Haugen bill in 1924 and 1926 and who renewed their pledge in support in the fall campaign won re-election. In all, Democrats won ten of the twelve rural congressional districts and split with Republicans in the four urban districts.[55]

As expected, Missourians voted overwhelmingly against the referendum to repeal the state's dry laws. At best, the 569,931 to 294,388 vote gave a rough approximation of sentiment for and against prohibition. The city of St. Louis and St. Louis, St. Charles, Ste. Genevieve, and Perry counties, all heavily populated by citizens of German ancestry or birth, returned majorities for repeal. Kansas City and the remainder of the state gave margins ranging from a few votes to several thousand against Proposition Number 4.[56]

Over all, the Democratic resurgence in 1926, capped by the election of Harry B. Hawes to the Senate, resulted from the support received from four major discontented elements of the electorate: Urban wets dissatisfied with prohibition; Negroes alienated by municipal and state Republican administrations; farmers who blamed the Coolidge Administration for the lack of a farm relief program; and, finally, Democrats tired of their inability to unite and win.

Harmony, the key to Hawes's victory, was in essence an agreement among Democrats to disagree without bolting the ticket. Reed Democrats could not approve Hawes's espousal of the principles underlying the McNary-Haugen bill any more than dry Democrats could support the St. Louisan's plan to work for a liberalization of the Volstead Act. Both, however, could rationalize their action to critics: Reed Democrats could argue that Williams, like Hawes, had voted for and would continue to support the McNary-Haugen bill; dry Democrats could point out that Williams was, for all practical purposes, as wet as Hawes.

A most important element in the harmony movement, not only for its contribution to success in 1926 but for its implications for 1928 as well, was the political aspirations of the party's two major factional leaders, Senator Reed and Charles M. Hay. Both gave support to Hawes for political reasons of their own: Reed desired the party's endorsement as favorite son candidate for the Presidency in 1928; Hay wanted the party's nomination for United States senator, either in 1928 or 1932. Despite Republican claims to the contrary, no agreement for mutual support in 1928 existed between the wet Senator and the dry senatorial aspirant. The support each man extended to Hawes was simply the politically correct thing to do, since it not only would place the new senator in their debt, but also would reaffirm to the opposing faction each man's loyalty to the party.[57]

It remained to be seen whether harmony would allow Reed and Hay to fulfill their aspirations. Otherwise, the effort for harmony in 1926 would be remembered simply as a brief interlude in the dissension in the Missouri Democracy during the 1920's.

CHAPTER 7

THE 1928 ELECTION

THROUGHOUT 1928 the coming and going of presidential candidates made Missouri one of the crossroads of the national campaign. Republican delegates from every state assembled in national convention at Kansas City in June, and as the campaign ended, nominee Herbert Hoover selected St. Louis as the place from which to issue a last appeal to midwestern voters. Al Smith also visited St. Louis, en route to a major speaking appearance at Sedalia, where an estimated 75,000 Missourians, the largest number ever to attend a political rally in the state, turned out to see and hear the Democratic nominee. It was the favorite son candidacy of Senator Reed, however, that made the Missouri Democracy a focal point for national interest in 1927 and 1928.

Four years earlier, Reed had entered the race for the Democratic presidential nomination, only to suffer a harsh rebuff from the Wilson Democrats of Missouri, who dominated the state convention. By denying the independent Senator a favorite son endorsement that year, Wilson men had ended his candidacy almost as soon as it had begun. In the intervening years, however, old animosities cooled, and Reed and Wilson factions teamed up to elect Democrat Harry B. Hawes to the United States Senate. Reed even shared the same platform in the Hawes harmony campaign with his major antagonist, Charles M. Hay. Then, in September, 1926, Reed revealed that he would not seek re-election, an announcement interpreted by Missourians to mean that he would be a candidate for the Democratic presidential nomination in 1928.[1]

During the next two years Reed's activities in the Senate helped convince many Democrats around the nation that the Senator from Missouri was presidential timber. As chairman of the committee investigating campaign expenditures, he helped expose two of the major Senate scandals of the twenties. Employing his talent as a prosecutor, Reed gathered evidence and marshaled public opinion against Senators-elect William S. Vare of Pennsylvania and Frank L. Smith of Illinois. Each had spent excessive and illegal sums of money to gain nomination and election in 1926, and as a result of the Reed committee's probe, both were denied their seats in the Senate.[2] Antiprohibitionists around the country also applauded Reed's leadership of the counterattack in Congress upon the powerful Anti-Saloon League.[3] From the Senate floor and committee hearing rooms, Reed's frequent criticism of the Coolidge Administration kept his name on the front pages of the country's newspapers. Many Americans shared the opinion of political columnists Frank R. Kent and Charles G. Ross that the Senator from Missouri was the outstanding figure of the Sixty-ninth Congress.[4]

While Reed's favorite son candidacy depended upon the preservation of the harmony that was achieved in Hawes's campaign for the Senate in 1926 between the rural and urban wings of the party, his best chance of gaining the nomination seemed to depend upon another McAdoo-Smith convention deadlock as in 1924. By 1927, however, much of the liberal and labor support as well as the backing from the old Bryan wing of the party had deserted McAdoo. That fall, in soul-searching letters to George Fort Milton of Tennessee, the nationally known historian and editor of the *Chattanooga News*, McAdoo analyzed the leadership situation confronting the dry agrarian wing of the party. Although many Democrats still regarded him as their leader, McAdoo acknowledged that the party was too factionalized for him to lay claim to a large body of followers:

Virginia recognizes the leadership of Glass; Arkansas recognizes Joe Robinson; Missouri apparently recognizes Jim Reed; Maryland recognizes Ritchie; New York recognizes Smith, and there are a number of favorite sons cropping up throughout the country who will doubtless go into the next convention with the backing of these respective states.[5]

The drys, he complained, "concentrate on nobody."[6] Moreover, he asked, who would supply the organizing skills and money to finance his candidacy for the nomination?[7] On September 15, McAdoo publicly announced that he would not be a candidate for the Presidency in 1928.[8]

This dramatic announcement both changed and clarified the situation in Democratic presidential politics. On the one hand, it boosted even higher the political stock of Alfred E. Smith, whose national popularity had climbed to new heights after his election to a fourth term as governor of New York in 1926.[9] On the other hand, by eliminating the prospect of another convention deadlock between the principals of the 1924 convention, McAdoo's withdrawal forced the hands of favorite son candidates like Reed who had anticipated a relatively quiet campaign until convention time.[10]

Reed responded to this new situation with ambitious plans that included national headquarters in Washington, an extensive speaking tour of twenty-seven states in the winter and spring of 1928, and contests for delegates in several presidential primaries. These activities, Reed hoped, would gain him more than a third of the convention votes, thus blocking Smith's nomination and ultimately boosting his candidacy from second to first place. In mid-October, 1927, Reed Democrats in control of the State Democratic Committee arranged a rally at Sedalia to kick off the Senator's national campaign.[11]

Although formally still an unannounced candidate, Reed realized that the press would consider his address to the rally tantamount to a statement of his campaign platform.

He therefore carefully skirted all divisive issues and instead enunciated the political philosophy upon which he was to wage his contest for the nomination:

> Fads, fancies and experimental theories should be disregarded. Principles are eternal and may not be departed from without confusion and disaster. . . . All attempts to inject into our plan of government paternalistic, socialist, or regulatory schemes, are dangerous and may be fatal.[12]

The only important exceptions Reed would allow in an otherwise limited federal program involved internal improvements, such as flood control, development of inland waterways, and irrigation of arid land. These programs had more appeal in the recently flood-ravaged South and the arid West than in any other section of the country; there was nothing in his agricultural program to win progressives and midwestern farmers burdened with farm surpluses and low market prices. A second theme, which allowed Reed to capitalize upon his own role in exposing corruption and graft in national political life, concerned the restoration of frugality and honesty to government. Finally, Reed stressed the need for curbing the centralization of government in order to ensure states' rights and individual civil liberties.[13]

On February 20, a day after voting in the county conventions assured him of Missouri's 36 votes at the Democratic National Convention, Reed began a drive to round up additional delegates in southern and western states. At Dallas, the first stop on the tour, Reed asserted as the major theme of the campaign his belief in Jeffersonian democracy. He waited until he arrived in New Mexico, home of discredited former Secretary of Interior Albert Fall, to cite restoration of honesty to government as a second major issue. Concerning prohibition, the one issue that might swing the dry South and West away from Smith, Reed at first maintained a discreet silence. Finally, at Los Angeles he asserted that prohibition should not be an issue in the campaign. Reed received preferential treatment in the Hearst press and large crowds turned out to hear him wherever he spoke, but the balloting in presidential primaries failed to give the Missouri Democrat the delegate votes of a single state. In the important California primary, Al Smith piled up more votes than Reed and Montana's Senator Thomas J. Walsh combined.[14]

When the Democratic National Convention opened in Houston the last week in June, much of Al Smith's opposition had faded away. Senator Walsh had thrown his support to Smith shortly after the California primary, and on June 19 Governor Albert Ritchie of Maryland released his state's 16 votes to the New York governor. According to Smith's managers, their candidates would receive 700 votes on the first ballot, only 33⅓ votes short of nomination.[15] Once the convention got under way, Reed refused to lead a "stop Smith" movement, and none materialized. Instead, he continued to hope that the antiprohibition Protestant South would turn to him as the more acceptable candidate and thus force the Smith camp, unable to secure a two-thirds vote, to turn also to Reed. Copies of his letter, written in 1926 to Nelle Burger, president of the W.C.T.U. in Missouri, stating his support of the state's dry laws, circulated by the hundreds in convention hall and hotels, and Reed even conferred with Daniel Roper, self-appointed co-ordinator of dry opposition to Al Smith. The boldest move of all was Reed's public declaration that the Eighteenth Amendment must stand "until the moral forces of the nation find a better solution for the liquor traffic."[16]

But the forces behind Smith's candidacy were too well organized to be scattered by this last-minute appeal to dry Democrats. On the first roll call Smith's 724 votes fell only 9 short of nomination; then Ohio switched to Smith and started the rush that put the New Yorker over with 849 votes. The chairman of the Missouri delegation, Tom Pendergast, acting under Reed's instructions, moved during the hectic vote-switching that Smith's nomination be made unanimous. Convention Chairman Joseph T. Robinson, however, ruled Pendergast's motion out of order, since the balloting had not been completed; thus, on the official record Smith ended with a majority rather than with a unanimous vote. Reed, hailed throughout the preconvention period as the "strongest second contender," actually finished a half vote behind Georgia's Walter George. In addition to the 36 votes from Missouri, Reed received 8 from Oklahoma, 4 from Kansas, 2 from Illinois, and 1 each from Pennsylvania and Arkansas.[17] Reed wired congratulations to Smith and addressed the convention in the traditional show of unanimity. Any Democrat, he asserted, could beat Herbert Hoover, nominated by the Republicans a few weeks earlier at their convention in Kansas City. But to Lee Meriwether, his campaign manager, Reed confided his belief that Smith's religion would cost him the electoral votes of every southern state and of most in the West.[18]

When the disappointed Senator returned to Missouri in late July, he found to his further dismay that sentiment for his choice for the party's senatorial nomination, James Collet, a lawyer from Salisbury, was much weaker than that prevailing for his old enemy, Charles M. Hay. Ironically, Hay had intended to wait until 1932 to seek the senatorial nomination and had not entered the race until Reed Democrats slighted him by not inviting him to the rally held in Sedalia in 1927. A ground swell of rural support not only induced Hay to change his mind, but also convinced the city bosses that Hay's nomination was necessary to preserve party harmony. Thus, when Collet entered the senatorial contest in mid-April, Reed's friends withheld organized support. A spokesman for the Pendergast organization announced that Kansas City Democrats were giving exclusive attention to Francis M. Wilson's candidacy for the gubernatorial nomination.[19]

Reed, evidently unable to bear the thought that Charles Hay might occupy his seat in the Senate, was determined to change the complexion of the senatorial race. On the eve of his departure on July 11 for a conference with Al Smith in New York, he launched a vitriolic attack on Hay. Reversing his earlier position that prohibition was not a campaign issue, Reed now asserted that it was "one of the very important propositions before the country." Since Governor Smith had declared that the Volstead Act must be changed, Reed reasoned that the nomination of prohibitionist Hay would "divide Democrats" and would "drag the ticket down to defeat." Recalling his past differences with Hay, Reed accused him of being a bolter, an agent of the Anti-Saloon League, and a friend of the Ku Klux Klan. He concluded his intemperate and unfair attack by comparing Hay to Tom Heflin, the Catholic-baiting United States senator from Alabama.[20]

Hay, in rejoinder, wisely dismissed Reed's attack upon him as "a personal controversy, the only possible effect of which could be to embarrass the national ticket and whatever state ticket the Democrats may nominate."[21] In St. Louis, Senator Harry B. Hawes repeated his pledge, made in February at the State Democratic Convention, to take no part whatsoever in the primary contests. More important, Tom Pendergast, intent on nominating antiprohibitionist Francis M. Wilson governor and fearing reprisals from dry supporters of Hay, affirmed his intention of staying out of the Reed-Hay controversy. A week before the primary Joe Shannon refuted long-standing reports that he favored Hay over Collet.[22] Other than Shannon's belated endorsement, Reed's attack on Hay did not substantially alter the alignment of important party leaders.

Meanwhile, Reed and Collet teamed up for several Kansas

City and St. Louis speeches in which they hammered away at Hay's prohibitionist position while stressing Collet's agreement with Smith's proposal to modify the Volstead Act. Hay, Reed asserted, should be running on the same ticket with Herbert Hoover.[23] If this line of attack caused rural drys to work harder for Hay's nomination, it also caused Hay to associate his campaign more closely with Smith in order not to drop too many wet votes in the cities. At Fayette he paid a glowing tribute to Smith that, for better or worse, linked him to the wet presidential nominee.[24]

In the August primary Hay's strength among rural Democrats enabled him to carry 104 of the 114 counties and to defeat Collet 171,088 to 141,453. Kansas Citians gave Collet 37,058 votes to 9,902 for Hay, and St. Louis went for "Senator Reed's candidate" 25,985 to 8,233. Republicans nominated as their senatorial candidate a dry — United States District Attorney Roscoe C. Patterson of Springfield. Patterson defeated a wet St. Louis businessman, Nathan Frank, by a little more than 10,000 votes. In the gubernatorial contests, wet Democrat Francis M. Wilson's 255,303 total overwhelmed the 69,990 votes receved by the author of Missouri's dry law, State Senator Alfred M. McCawley. Republican nominee Henry S. Caulfield easily outdistanced his closest dry rival by nearly 60,000 votes.[25] Both parties apparently considered ticket balancing important and nominated dry senatorial and wet gubernatorial candidates.

Arguments in favor of harmony and of balancing the ticket to the contrary, Hay realized the validity of Senator Reed's claim that a dry senatorial candidate would find it difficult to campaign for a wet presidential candidate. Outlining this difficulty in a letter to Franklin D. Roosevelt immediately after his nomination, Hay reported that no more than fifty persons in an audience of two thousand at Fayette had applauded his tribute to Governor Smith. On the other hand, Hay wrote, his declaration that he did not agree with Smith on the liquor question was greeted "with a perfect storm of applause." Hay urged that Roosevelt advise Smith to de-emphasize his views on modification of the Volstead Act and to stress, instead, law enforcement and other constructive achievements upon which all Democrats could agree.[26]

In the fall campaign, Hay put into practice the campaign strategy he had suggested for Smith. Although he minimized Smith's proposal to modify the Volstead Act, he also com-mended him for "frankness and straightforwardness in deal-ing with the question" and for his pledge to enforce honestly the prohibition laws. "If the present administration had ap-proached and discharged the enforcement task in that spirit," Hay argued, "there would be no liquor issue in Ameri-can politics." He enthusiastically endorsed Smith as the coun-try's "big, broad progressive Democrat" and praised his stand on such issues as development of water power, regulation of public utilities, and farm relief legislation.[27]

Smith, however, in a major campaign appearance in Mis-souri, failed to capitalize upon his intial support for farm relief legislation — the one issue in the campaign that offered him a good chance of overcoming the prejudices of rural Protestant drys. Missouri farmers and farm groups such as the Missouri Farmers' Association and the Missouri Farm Bureau Federation were greatly disappointed in the failure of Republicans to adopt a farm plank along the lines of the twice-vetoed McNary-Haugen bill. The fact that the farm bill embodied unsound features did not greatly lessen its popularity with Missouri farmers. Indeed, the Democrats' endorsement of that bill's underlying principles held out the prospect of wining support for Smith from the state's farm-ers.[28] Smith's opportunity to gain the farm vote could hardly have been better from the standpoint of audience and set-ting. Farmers predominated in the crowd of seventy-five thousand persons gathered at the state fair grounds in Se-dalia to see and hear the Democratic presidential candidate.

Four hours before his speech, standing room in the coliseum was occupied. The remainder of the overflow crowd, reportedly the largest number ever assembled for a political speech in Missouri, occupied nearby buildings equipped with amplifiers. But Smith spoke not a word about solutions to farm problems; instead, the wet Democrat gave a dry recital of facts and figures contrasting Democratic and Republican governmental costs.[29] Although the Democratic presidential nominee had attracted a tremendous crowd to Sedalia, he probably won little additional support; moreover, he looked nothing like the portrait of a progressive that Hay had painted in numerous campaign speeches.

Confronted with this lack of support from Smith himself, Hay's continuing attempts to replace prohibition with progressive issues made little headway. Patterson, aided by temperance organizations, refused to let Smith's antiprohibition sentiment and Tammany affiliation drop from the campaign. The W.C.T.U., like Patterson, rejected the image Hay projected of Smith as a progressive, social-minded candidate. As a spokesman for the temperance association commented: "Much is made of what he [Smith] does in humanitarian measures for women, yet in New York when thousands of women petitioned him for law on prohibition enforcement he did not listen to their demands."[30] It made no difference to either the Anti-Saloon League or the W.C.T.U. that Hay was more interested in social welfare legislation than Patterson and, unlike his Republican opponent, had a long record of service to the dry cause. Each organization endorsed both senatorial aspirants without distinction of their contributions in behalf of prohibition. Moreover, by concentrating all their efforts on the defeat of Al Smith, the dry organizations abandoned any positive effort in behalf of the state's leading progressive and prohibitionist.[31]

In St. Louis Al Smith's wetness was, on the whole, an unqualified blessing. Most of the city's Catholics and Jews, almost equaling in number the Protestants, refused to equate morality with total abstinence, and many St. Louis Protestants evidently shared this view. In fact, over the years St. Louisans consistently rolled up majorities against prohibition referenda.[32] As an indication of the resentment with the prohibition experiment that was growing there, all three congressmen from the St. Louis area introduced bills in the 1927 and 1928 sessions of Congress to permit the manufacture and sale of beer and light wines.[33] Shortly after Democrats nominated their wet presidential candidate, August A. Busch, the president of St. Louis' Anheuser-Busch brewery, gave Smith an unqualified endorsement. His electon, the brewery head predicted, would mean an end to the Anti-Saloon League's "domination of government" and would allow the establishment of a "real temperance system."[34] The names of several members of the Anheuser and Busch families were prominent in the list of St. Louis citizens who purchased a full page in the *St. Louis Star* to urge independents to vote for Smith. Another advertisement, frankly declaring prohibition an economic and social failure and appealing to voters solely on the ground that Smith would end the "noble experiment," was purchased by influential St. Louisans who were members of the Association Against the Eighteenth Amendment.[35]

More important support for Smith came from the city's less influential but more numerous citizens of German ancestry or birth. Endorsements by the old prestigious Steuben Society and by the recently formed "German-American Smith-for-President League" were indicative of the powerful organized activity in the German community for the wet Democratic presidential candidate. Anti-British prejudice against Hoover, based on his long business association with British firms, formed one element of pro-Smith sentiment among the city's Germans, and a second factor that attracted German Catholics to Smith was his religion. Clearly the most important factor bringing support to Smith's candidacy, however, was the beer-drinker's disgust with the prohibition experiment. With August A. Busch, many Germans believed that a vote for Smith would bring an end to prohibition and would permit the return of beer.[36]

Democrats in St. Louis counted on another element of the electorate to swell the vote for Smith: Party leaders had hope of swinging to their side for the first time a majority of the city's 35,124 registered Negro voters.[37] Several factors operating in the 1928 campaign prompted this sentiment. The white press commented that Smith's commitment to end prohibition made him attractive to Negro voters who were employed as porters and bellmen because many had felt the economic pinch of prohibition.[38] It is more likely, however, that bootlegging offered as many or more opportunities for the Negro as it did for whites. More significant are the editorials of the Negro press and the frequently quoted slogan, "A vote for Al Smith is a vote against the Klan." The editorials argued that Negroes could strike a blow for tolerance by supporting the Democratic nominee even if it meant abandonment of the party of Lincoln.[39] Further, the formation of numerous colored Al Smith clubs and the rhetoric of Negro politicians indicate that Negroes in St. Louis and elsewhere were attracted to the Irish Catholic's candidacy for many of the same reasons Samuel Lubell has attributed to the nation's new immigrants. Negroes and new immigrants, both "underdog" groups, looked upon Smith's candidacy as a revolt against the discriminations and prejudices of a society and culture dominated by old American stock.[40]

The continuing revolution in the attitudes of both white Democrats and colored Republicans also promised to bring new Negro support to Smith and to the rest of the Democratic ticket. "The negroes of St. Louis should be encouraged," a young white lawyer advised gubernatorial candidate Francis M. Wilson, "even if it means turning our back on some of our old traditions."[41] Wilson demonstrated his agreement with this view by actively appealing to colored voters for support and by warmly acknowledging the assistance given the Democratic ticket by Negro citizens.[42] A more dramatic departure from tradition, however, came when St. Louis Democrats backed the congressional candidacy of a young colored lawyer, Joseph L. McLemore.

McLemore's successful bid for nomination by Democrats of the Twelfth Congressional District represented the culmination of an effort begun in 1927 when the thirty-one-year-old Negro lawyer, frustrated by the slow progress of the race under Republicans and inspired by the Democratic creed, assumed leadership in establishing an alliance between his people and white Democrats of St. Louis. Arguing that both Democrats and Negroes were the dispossessed in politics, McLemore asked the white Democratic leadership to support a multipoint patronage program for colored citizens in exchange for the votes of Negroes at the polls. In addition to requests for positions for Negroes at the ward level, McLemore boldly advanced his own candidacy for the Democratic nomination in the Twelfth Congressional District.[43] The City Democratic Committee, swayed by McLemore's reasonable arguments, ratified his program and supported it in good faith during the 1928 campaign. As a consequence McLemore received the Democratic congressional nomination, winning over his white opponent, 2,790 to 1,497, to achieve a first for St. Louis; indeed, journalists claimed that the Negro's nomination for a seat in the House on the Democratic ticket was unprecedented in any southern or border state, if not in the nation.[44] Although his Republican opponent, incumbent Congressman L. C. Dyer, charged that the Negro candidate was a tool of the Democratic party, the *St. Louis Argus*, which for months had been advising Negroes to vote for "men and measures," proudly announced that it would support Democrat McLemore.[45]

Hoover's managers, their confidence buoyed up by polls indicating that Hoover would win by a landslide, nevertheless worried over reports that Smith's wetness would enable him to carry St. Louis and that his stand on farm relief legislation would swing Missouri and the Republican Midwest into the Democratic camp. Therefore it was decided that Hoover should deliver a major farm address in St. Louis on November 2 as the Republican nominee traveled home to California to vote on November 7. Hoover, speaking to a nationwide audience by radio as well as to an overflow crowd at the St. Louis Coliseum, elaborated his plan for the establishment of a federal farm board to deal with the distressed state of American agriculture.[46] Publicly, St. Louis Republicans boasted that Hoover's visit would keep St. Louis and Missouri in the Republican column, but privately, G.O.P. ward leaders conceded the city to Smith. Unofficially, St. Louis Republican campaign headquarters told precinct workers to "save Hoover, but not at the expense of the state and city ticket." According to the *St. Louis Star*, Republican headquarters was also responsible for the 250,000 sample ballots circulated around the city to show voters how to mark their ballot for Smith and for the rest of the Republican ticket.[47]

Although Democrats of Kansas City and Jackson County were now better organized than at any previous time in the twenties, a reverse of the situation in St. Louis threatened. Instead of wet Republican defection to Smith, sizable dry Democratic desertion to Hoover loomed as a real possibility. Kansas City, known as America's largest dry city, had earned that distinction by returning majorities in favor of prohibition when voting on that issue in referenda.[48] An early sign that the area would not support a wet presidential candidate in 1928 came shortly after the Houston convention. William Southern, Jr., editor of the *Independence Examiner* and a lifelong Democrat of Jackson County, told a

Kansas City gathering of W.C.T.U. members that Smith's intention of working for the nullification of the Eighteenth Amendment would lead to lawlessness and to a breakdown of constitutional government; thus he urged the election of Herbert Hoover.[49]

There were other reasons why Missouri's second largest city did not warm to Smith. As a predominantly Protestant, old-stock town, Kansas City did not identify itself with either Smith's Catholicism or the "urban uprising" associated with his candidacy. The *Kansas City Times* even rejected the contention of some political observers that Smith represented American urban feeling and background. Smith, the *Times* argued, embodied the "New York-Baltimore uprising," two centers that, "due to immigration and various other causes, have become more cosmopolitan in tone, more European in thought." Most American urban life, the Republican newspaper concluded, "draws from the country and the small town."[50]

The *Times*'s analysis stopped short of any outright mention of Smith's religion as an impediment to his becoming the nation's Chief Executive. In fact, flagrant attacks upon Smith's Catholicism did not find their way into the press. Furthermore, when Smith dealt with the religious issue at Oklahoma City, detractors such as Editor Southern criticized him for injecting religion into the campaign. The W.C.T.U., which joined the Missouri Anti-Saloon League's superintendent in asking Protestant ministers in Missouri to preach sermons in Hoover's behalf, denied that Smith's faith was at issue. The foes of prohibition, the W.C.T.U.'s president Mrs. Burger claimed, were simply making this charge "as a barrage or smoke screen to deceive the voters and to becloud the situation."[51]

Unprecedented defections from Democratic ranks on election day helped Republicans boost Hoover to a 834,080 to 662,526 victory over Smith. Over two thirds of the 66 counties that had normally voted for Democratic presidential candidates since 1900 cast ballots for Hoover. Ten counties that had never before gone Republican voted for the G.O.P.'s presidential nominee, but most of Little Dixie, the mid-state area originally settled by old-stock southerners and their Negro slaves, returned near-normal pluralities for Al Smith. Other normally Democratic counties, lacking a slave-holding tradition and having a population composed almost entirely of old-stock whites, moved into the Republican column. Apparently, loyalty to the Democratic party commanded more influence over the old-stock Protestant voters of Little Dixie than any other factor. Only 21 Democratic counties remained loyal to Smith.[52] Over all, Republicans carried 91 of the state's 114 counties for Hoover, their best record at any time in the history of the state.[53]

The performance of other Republican candidates in rural Missouri was almost as good as Hoover's. Although Hay ran ahead of Smith by 63,364 votes, he fell behind Patterson's total by 52,360 votes. Francis M. Wilson exceeded Smith's outstate total by 67,119 votes, while losing there to Caulfield by a total of 48,789. Republicans also won 10 of the state's 16 congressional districts, recapturing the Kansas City-Jackson County district and 7 rural congressional seats. In the state legislature, G.O.P. representatives outnumbered Democrats 103 to 47, while the Democrats retained control of the senate with 19 of 34 seats.[54]

On the other hand, while most of normally Democratic rural Missouri moved into the Republican camp, St. Louis, which had not given a Democratic presidential candidate a majority since 1888, went for Smith 176,429 to 161,701.[55] Irish Democrats constituted the core of Smith's support; in fact, their loyalty to the ticket enabled both Smith and Hay to carry all of the normally Democratic wards of the city. Smith, however, ran ahead of Hay in every Democratic ward by margins ranging from 80 to 816 votes per ward. The city's

relatively few new immigrant voters — like their counterparts in eastern urban industrial centers — as well as gradually increasing numbers of Negroes, were attracted to the
Democratic presidential candidate and provided him with
his margin over Hay in the Democratic wards. A more
noticeable swing to Smith, though, took place in the four
German wards of South St. Louis, where traditionally Republican voters deserted Hoover.[56]

The motives that caused voters to give the Democratic
candidate a majority in the Republican city were as numerous and mixed as the precampaign activity in his behalf. Yet
it appears that during the prohibition era St. Louisans generally, when confronted with a choice between a dry and
a wet candidate, voted for the latter. The results of other
elections in the prohibition decade reinforce this conclusion.
In 1922, when Senator Reed ran up a 43,802-vote plurality
over his dry Republican opponent, and again in 1926, when
Harry B. Hawes, more liberal on prohibition than the incumbent, Republican Senator George H. Williams, equaled
Williams' St. Louis total, it was the wet issue that had swung
the German south side to the antiprohibitionists. Finally, in
the four German wards that accorded Smith a majority over
Hoover, Patterson, as dry as Hay, received even more votes
than Smith.[57] Had Hoover been as wet as Smith, the German
voters in St. Louis probably would have remained loyal to
the Republican candidate.

Kansas Citians voted for the 1928 presidential candidates
as they had voted on prohibition referenda. Hoover outpolled every other candidate on the national and state ticket
there, defeating Smith 106,616 to 84,866. Hay lost the city
by a much smaller margin than Smith, his 94,929 total almost
equaling Patterson's 99,872 vote, but Francis M. Wilson,
whom Pendergast hoped would gain the governor's chair,
outpolled Caulfield 100,904 to 92,103.[58]

Democrats who wrote to Franklin D. Roosevelt after the

election cited a number of factors to explain Smith's defeat in Missouri. According to these analysts, voters had rejected the Democratic candidate chiefly because of his religion. Secondary factors, the Missourians believed, were Smith's stand on prohibition and his identification as a Tammany Democrat. These handicaps, coupled with economic prosperity, Roosevelt's informers concluded, were too much for Smith to overcome.[59] Unlike later historians, none regarded "Republican" economic prosperity the prime and insurmountable obstacle to Democratic success.[60]

The chief dissenter from the view that ranked religious prejudice as the leading cause of Smith's defeat was the Protestant prohibitionist Charles M. Hay. In Hay's mind, Smith's wetness constituted the major factor that turned voters away from the Democratic standard. Reasoning from his own experience, Hay pointed out to friends that Kansas City and St. Louis voters had given him only a few thousand votes less than Patterson received. The thousands of rural Democrats who voted the Republican ballot for the first time in their lives, Hay believed, were ultra drys. In rejecting Smith, Hay explained, these dry Democrats also rejected his own senatorial candidacy. "Sister Burger and the Women's Christian Temperance Union," Hay later complained to a friend, "grossly betrayed me and the cause as well."[61]

Attempts to establish the relative importance of the various issues in the election, as William E. Leuchtenburg has written, may be fruitless, however, for "the campaign reflected a deep antagonism between rural and urban America which went beyond any single issue."[62] The postelection editorial of the *Kansas City Star* illustrates this conclusion:

> Smith represented the big city, its cosmopolitanism, its impatience with . . . "the moral yearnings of the rural communities," its absorption in itself, its failure to think nationally. Hoover was the embodiment of the qualities and the standards of the older rural and small city America. In the election . . .

the newer, urban life clashed with the older tradition, and the older American swept to victory.[63]

Despite the stunning Republican victories in state and nation, some developments in the 1928 election encouraged the Democrats of Missouri. In St. Louis the German-American Smith-for-President League announced on November 9 that it would remain active until after the city elections in the spring. The principal objective of the organization, spokesmen stated, would be the election of Democrat John S. Simon to the office of mayor. Democrats had already inserted a wedge into St. Louis municipal government by electing Franklin Miller circuit attorney over the Republican incumbent. In addition, Democrats in St. Louis had gained a great deal of good will among the city's Negroes through the candidacy of Joseph L. McLemore, even though it ended in defeat.[64] Upon this foundation the Democracy was building for the transition of St. Louis from a Republican to a Democratic city.

Another important development, obscured by the Republican success in Kansas City, was the steadily increasing number of Negroes there who were voting the Democratic ticket. According to editor William J. Thompkins, 47 per cent of the city's colored voters had cast Democratic ballots, almost doubling the percentage in 1924.[65] Thompkins, through his editorials in the *Kansas City American* and through his work as director of the Smith-for-President Colored League, had been partly responsible for the increased defection of Negroes from the G.O.P.; the attractiveness of Al Smith to the Kansas City colored community, however, made Thompkins' task easier. Finally, the patronage and favors tendered colored citizens by Democratic leaders assisted the recruitment of Negro voters to the party. With city and county patronage in the hands of the Pendergast organization, Republicans could expect further Negro desertion from the ranks of the G.O.P. in Kansas City and Jackson County.[66]

Although most Negro voters outstate remained loyal to the Republican party in 1928, the campaign revealed new attitudes on the part of traditionally Negro Republicans and old-stock white Democrats. In Sedalia, for example, the Reverend Richard R. Marshall, pastor of the Free Will Baptist Church, urged his congregation to bolt the Republican party. Marshall's activity was not without its dangers: A group of whites abducted the colored pastor and gave him a severe beating for his political proselyting of Negro Republicans. White Democratic politicians of Sedalia and Pettis County, however, encouraged the Negroes' desertion of the G.O.P. by public solicitation of support for their candidacies.[67]

The Republicans of Missouri could not remain complacent in the face of the Democrats' inroads into the Negro vote in the state. Indeed, with the Negro electorate approaching 100,000, continuation of the G.O.P.'s political supremacy in Missouri demanded that the party adopt policies and programs capable of keeping the colored citizens within the Republican camp. The initiation of this attempt by Governor Henry S. Caulfield in 1929 and the counterproposals of Democratic state legislators were to produce a major controversy during the Caulfield Administration.

CHAPTER 8

THE WOOING OF THE NEGRO

DESPITE THE DEMOCRATS' INROADS into Negro Republican ranks throughout the twenties, nowhere in the principal Negro communities of Missouri did a majority of colored citizens vote Democratic in 1928. By 1932, however, nearly half of Missouri's Negroes were casting Democratic ballots, and in some localities, particularly Kansas City, well over a majority had deserted the Republican party. This transition of Missouri Negroes from "Lincoln Republicanism" to "Jeffersonian Democracy" engaged the two major parties in spirited contests for the Negro's allegiance at all levels of government and constituted the principal political development of the years between Al Smith's defeat in 1928 and Franklin Roosevelt's triumph in 1932.

On the surface it appeared that colored politicians had made impressive gains within the Republican party throughout the decade. In 1920 the voters of the Sixth Legislative District of St. Louis sent Attorney Walthall M. Moore to the Missouri House of Representatives, marking the first time a Negro had been elected to that body. Two years later, Crittenden E. Clark, another St. Louis attorney, became the first Negro justice of the peace in the history of the state. In 1924, Moore, coming back from defeat in 1922, was elected to a second term in the House, and in 1926 both he and John A. Davis were elected to the state legislature from districts in St. Louis. The number of Negro legislators increased to three when L. Amasa Knox, the first colored representative elected from Kansas City, joined the two representatives from St. Louis in the House. Yet, these Negro Republicans did not owe their election to white G.O.P. voters; each had gained nomination and election in predominantly colored districts.[1]

The Negro lawmakers also discovered that representation in the state legislature was one thing and influence with their Republican colleagues in the General Assembly another. When the colored representatives tried to enlist the support of fellow Republicans for legislation designed to improve the Negro citizen's welfare, they achieved only limited success. Major disappointments were the failure of bills aimed at providing all colored children a common school education, increased appropriations for Lincoln University, an antilynching law, and improved facilities at eleemosynary and penal institutions. The Negroes' resentment quite naturally mounted with each successive failure.[2]

Following Sam A. Baker's narrow victory over Democrat Arthur W. Nelson in the gubernatorial contest of 1924, Negro leaders intensified their demands for adequate recognition by Republicans of the Negro's support at the polls. Governor Baker, however, gave only a few political appointments to Negroes, and the Republican-controlled General Assembly passed little legislation to benefit the state's colored citizens. An editorial in the St. Louis Argus, written in 1926 when that Negro newspaper was still Republican in politics, summed up the attitude of many Missouri Negroes toward the Republican party: "The fellow who has been dealing out to us in the past, has not given us our just dues and we know it. Therefore, we want a new deal, especially in politics."[3]

Democrats, out of power in the state except in Kansas City, had little opportunity to present their own "new deal" for Negro Missourians. Moreover, in the early twenties most Democrats rejected the Negro's call for equal opportunities. The party platform of 1924, completely silent on the colored citizen's welfare, reflected the Democrats' indifference to or rejection of Negro support. The adoption of a strong Negro welfare plank by Democrats in 1926, however, gave evidence of a new concern and a rising interest in colored voters. Democrats drafted an equally strong Negro welfare plank again in 1928; the same year, Joseph L. McLemore became the first Negro in Missouri, if not in the nation, to win nomination for Congress on the Democratic ticket. During the Baker Administration, then, Democrats demonstrated in a number of ways their sensitivity to the aspirations of the race.[4]

Republicans, by virtue of their meager record of welfare legislation for Negroes during the Hyde and Baker administrations, seemed indifferent to the desires and needs of colored citizens. No one sensed this more strongly than Governor Henry S. Caulfield, and when he took office in January, 1929, the new Republican governor was determined to improve upon the record of his predecessors. Caulfield, in conferences with race leaders before he assumed office, learned that Negroes were most interested in educational legislation. Therefore, in his inaugural message to the Republican-dominated Fifty-fifth General Assembly, he carefully set forth the needs in this area.[5]

The state, Caulfield frankly asserted, had failed to provide its Negro citizens with equality in education. While the University of Missouri had splendid buildings and equipment and adequate operating income, Lincoln University, the state's institution of higher education for colored citizens, was a university in name only. Moreover, Caulfield observed, state law made no provision for the establishment of schools for Negro children in any school district where there were less than fifteen colored children. As a result, for at least 4,000 colored children the state provided no school facilities at all. The state had a duty, Caulfield asserted, to correct deficiencies that were "unjust and unconstitutional" and "humiliating and unkind."[6]

If credit for initiating an improved Negro educational program was the Republican governor's, credit for sponsoring much of the enabling legislation belonged to Democratic lawmakers. In particular, Senator Michael J. Kinney of St. Louis showed a great deal of interest in the legislation. His concern for the Negro's welfare arose from mixed motives of social justice and political expediency: Negroes comprised 40 per cent of Kinney's St. Louis constituency.[7] In the legislative session of 1929 Kinney authored and provided leadership on a bill that reduced the number of children required for the establishment of a rural school district from fifteen to eight. Later, when the House appropriations bill for Lincoln University came to the senate, Kinney and a Democratic colleague tacked on an amendment that provided high school scholarships for Negro youths and a small sum to pay tuition at out-of-state colleges for Negro students to pursue courses that were not available at Lincoln. Republican support, of course, was necessary for the passage of all of these bills, and when the Negro press commented upon the legislation, the three colored Republicans in the House received congratulations. It was Senator Kinney, however, not Governor Caulfield, who was singled out by the *St. Louis Argus* for special recognition.[8] Evidently, the *Argus* assumed that the Governor would sign the bills into law as a matter of course.

The same Negro newspapers that heaped encomiums upon Democrats in the Fifty-fifth General Assembly viewed with growing disfavor the anti-Negro policies pursued by the Hoover Administration. When President Hoover threw the weight of federal appointive power behind "lily-white" G.O.P. organizations in the South in March, 1929, Negro editors in Missouri added their voices to the nationwide protest. More criticism followed, in the spring of 1930, when

Negro Gold Star Mothers were segregated on the pilgrimage to the graves of their sons who had fallen in France in the First World War. The incident that provoked the strongest criticism of Hoover, however, resulted from the President's nomination to the Supreme Court of a jurist regarded by most Negroes as an enemy of their race.[9]

Hoover's nomination of Judge John J. Parker of North Carolina incurred nationwide opposition from Negroes because of a statement the jurist allegedly made in 1920. At that time Parker reportedly said that the Negro lacked both the "desire to enter politics" and the ability to "share the burdens and responsibilities of government." Missouri's Republican State Chairman Bert G. Voorhees, aware of the strong anti-Parker sentiment among Negroes in the state, warned Senator Roscoe C. Patterson that Parker's confirmation would mean "that the Republican party might just as well say good-bye to Missouri, for the next two or three elections at least. It will be the first great affront given by a Republican senate to the Negro race since the days of Abraham Lincoln."[10]

Patterson, however, ignored the advice of Voorhees and other Missouri Republicans and voted with Administration forces for Judge Parker's confirmation; Senator Harry B. Hawes sided with the majority against Parker.[11] The Senate vote received careful attention in the Negro press. Negroes should remember, urged the *Kansas City American*, that Hawes and other Democratic senators were responsible for Parker's defeat, while Patterson and his Republican colleagues had provided most of Parker's support. "Will you so soon forget Senator Patterson as he thinks that you will?" asked the *St. Louis Argus*.[12]

About the same time that President Hoover alienated Negroes everywhere with his nomination of Parker, Missouri's Secretary of State Charles U. Becker infuriated Negroes of the state by discharging Representative Walthall M. Moore, employed in a state office under Becker's control since the end of the 1929 legislative session. Moore's dismissal had taken place immediately after the St. Louis Negro announced that he would enter the Republican primary for the Twelfth District congressional seat held by L. C. Dyer. Becker informed reporters that he had released Moore with great reluctance; he had done so only because one could not campaign and perform office duties at the same time.[13] But Becker candidly told St. Louis Argus editor J. E. Mitchell that "Dyer's friends would not stand for Moore running against the congressman and working in Becker's office." In fact, Becker said, Dyer's supporters had accused him of backing Moore's candidacy, apparently in order to gain Negro support for the race Becker planned to make for the governorship in 1932. Therefore, Becker explained, obviously thinking that Mitchell would hold their conversation in confidence, Moore had to be discharged in order to placate Dyer's supporters.[14]

This was too much for the editor of the Argus. In revealing his conversation with Becker on the front page of his newspaper, the Negro newspaperman blasted both Becker and Dyer. If the Secretary of State should win the Republican nomination for governor in 1932, Mitchell predicted, Negroes would vote for his Democratic opponent in resentment of Becker's treatment of Moore. The Negro editor angrily denounced Dyer as a hypocrite, "who, after posing as a friend of the Negro and receiving their support for sixteen years, had turned against them when a member of the race aspired to political office." Negroes should not overlook the significance of the episode, Mitchell warned:

> This thing is deeper than it appears on the surface. It strikes at every Negro who holds an appointive office in the state under our "good Republicans." The Democrats, two years ago, nominated and supported a Negro for Congress and thought nothing of it. Yet, it's a crime for a Negro to aspire for that

office on the Republican ticket. WE SHOULD THINK OF
THESE THINGS.[15]

With the *Argus'* attack on Becker and Dyer providing the
opening fireworks, the Dyer-Moore contest went on to become the hottest race in the otherwise dull congressional
primary of 1930. Most of the noise came from the Moore
camp, however, as Dyer refused to make a single speech.
Moore's sole concern with the race question, Dyer charged,
was not a valid campaign issue.[16] The colored candidate did,
in fact, argue for his nomination mainly on the ground that
Negroes, who constituted nearly half of Dyer's constituency
and were the largest bloc of Republican voters in that St.
Louis-situated congressional district, deserved to be represented in Congress by a member of their race. When he
opened his campaign, Moore condemned Senator Patterson
for voting for Judge Parker's confirmation to the Supreme
Court, thus underscoring his point that a white Republican
could not be entrusted with the responsibility of advancing
the Negro race.[17]

A factor probably more important than the race question
in determining the outcome of the Twelfth District's congressional primary was the use of Republican patronage in
Dyer's behalf. Democrats, having lost the municipal election
of 1929, had no favors at their disposal to exploit the split
in Republican ranks between Negro insurgents and party
regulars.[18] Dyer's supporters, on the other hand, custodians
of city, state, and national patronage, were able to keep
important Negro leaders such as Jordan Chambers and Judge
Crittenden E. Clark either independent or committed to
Dyer.[19] Another Negro leader, Attorney Silas E. Garner, was
probably fortified against the catcalls he received from his
people when he spoke in Dyer's behalf, by the knowledge
that he would soon receive an appointment to the State Attorney General's staff.[20] In short, the regular Republican organization wielded the tool of patronage to cut Moore's

support from under him, thus helping Dyer to gain an easy 8,658 to 4,572 victory. Since Dyer was unopposed in the general election, Moore's disgruntled supporters had no opportunity to vote for a Democratic candidate.[21]

An effective combination of patronage and policies enabled Kansas City Democrats, dominant in Missouri's second largest city since the municipal election of 1925, to recruit Negroes in ever-increasing numbers. In the city election of March, 1930, 70 per cent of the Negro voters, as compared to 47 per cent in 1928, voted Democratic despite the objections of the *Kansas City Call* and the *Kansas City Star*.[22] Both newspapers had warned Kansas Citians before the election that a Democratic victory would mean domination of the city by Pendergast, Shannon, and Welch for another five years. The *Kansas City American*, voicing the sentiments of most of the Negroes in the city, dismissed the objections raised against the Democratic bosses by the two Republican newspapers:

> What has Kansas City got against Pendergast, Shannon, and Welch? Anyone can gain an audience with either of them on any matter day or night. Each of them employ Negro labor and there is not a Negro church in Kansas City at some time in their struggles that have not had a helpful check from one or all of them. . . . Judging from the contributions they have made the Negroes of Kansas City should entertain a very high regard for Tom, Joe and Cas.[23]

A Negro contributor to the *American's* letter-to-the-editor page had a shorter explanation for the Negroes' switch away from the G.O.P.: Negroes had voted Democratic because they were "tired of feeding on Abraham Lincoln stuff."[24]

Democrats, of course, in addition to their welfare program, also had a patron saint to take Lincoln's place. Eighty years before Lincoln freed the slaves, Joseph Shannon informed colored audiences, Thomas Jefferson had advocated the equality of man and the abolition of slavery. Propounding the theme "Jefferson the original abolitionist," Shannon's numerous speeches in 1929 and 1930 probably contributed, at least in a small way, to the shift of colored voters to the Democratic camp. In addition, the Rabbit boss's appearances before Negro groups helped lay the basis for his candidacy for congressman from the Fifth District.[25]

Shannon's candidacy, backed by every important element of the Jackson County Democracy, exemplified the effective harmonizing of contending factions that had been accomplished by Boss Tom Pendergast. Only six years earlier, when Shannon and Pendergast were at loggerheads, Shannon bolted the Pendergast ticket and helped bring about Harry S Truman's only political defeat.[26] Nevertheless, in 1930, Truman, a candidate for re-election as presiding judge of Jackson County, suggested that Shannon make the race for Congress. Cas Welch, who had broken with Shannon and had gone over to the Pendergast organization in 1924, also overlooked Shannon's perfidious past and asked his followers to back Shannon.[27] Pendergast, satisfied with his role as the dominant boss of the Kansas City-Jackson County Democracy, ratified the endorsements of Truman and Welch by extending his personal support to Shannon.[28]

The only serious Republican challenge in the general election to Democratic control in Kansas City involved the seemingly unimportant office of justice of the peace, held for years by Irish Democrat Casimer J. Welch. Welch's power in the Negro wards resulted mainly from his ability to dispense justice along with favors to his colored constituency. If Welch could be unseated, Kansas City Republicans reasoned, perhaps Negroes could be wooed away from the Democrats. Selected to make the race against Welch was John Wesson, a Negro who received the full support of the *Kansas City Call*. The *Kansas City American*, discounting the *Call's* charge that Welch was an enemy of their race, pointed out that two thirds of the appointments given to Kansas City

Negroes resulted from Welch's influence. Wesson's campaign, waged solely on the argument that Negroes should fill the political offices in the colored wards, had no more prospect of succeeding than did Walthall M. Moore's primary contest against Congressman Dyer in St. Louis.[29]

On election day all Democratic candidates in the Kansas City area scored impressive victories, and every Democrat on the ticket carried Welch's bailiwick — the Second and Fourth wards — by 4-to-1 victories. The efficacy of patronage over race loyalty as a factor in carrying elections was borne out most convincingly in Cas Welch's 5,865 to 1,593 victory over John Wesson. On Thanksgiving Day Welch returned the favors shown him at the polls by treating approximately four thousand Negroes to free turkey dinners.[30]

In other state-wide and congressional contests, the general election of 1930, like the primary contests, was the dullest in years. Much of the apathy could be attributed to the fact that only two offices, Superintendent of Schools and Judge of the Supreme Court, were subject to a state-wide vote. Moreover, since opposing congressional candidates in all but two districts had similar views on prohibition, that issue did not arouse the voters.[31] Only in the Fourth and Fifth districts did the two Democratic candidates adopt wet stands in contrast to the dry positions advocated by their Republican opponents. In the Fifth District race between Joseph Shannon and Edgar C. Ellis, however, neither man made an issue of their respective wet and dry positions.[32] The only real contest over prohibition shaped up in the Fourth District of northeast Missouri, where R. E. Culver and David Hopkins made clear their respective wet and dry sentiments to the Anti-Saloon League and the W.C.T.U. Hopkins' victory over his wet Democratic opponent as well as the nomination and election of other rural drys seemed to many an indication that outstate sentiment still favored prohibition.[33]

The big change from 1928 that helped Democrats win

twelve of the sixteen congressional seats was, of course, the economic depression that had engulfed the country since the stock market crash in October, 1929. According to the market indexes compiled in 1930 by the Federal Reserve banks of St. Louis and Kansas City, business activity in several sectors of the economy in Missouri and surrounding states had fallen off precipitously from 1929 levels. Production in the shoe industry, important in St. Louis and in several towns of eastern and central Missouri, was down about a third; flour mills centered in the Kansas City area operated at about 70–75 per cent capacity; consumption of electrical power for manufacturing purposes had declined nearly 20 per cent; the value of construction contracts awarded was almost half that in 1929; department store sales had declined 10.4 per cent, and the sale of automobiles was down 37 per cent.[34] A survey in St. Louis of persons employed in manufacturing showed that the number of employed persons in 1930 was 21.8 per cent less than at the same time in 1929, and a similar survey in Kansas City revealed a 13.2 per cent reduction in the factory work force from the previous year. Those employed were also taking home smaller pay checks in 1930 than in 1929.[35] Farm prices in 1930 had declined sixteen index points from the 1929 level, and a drought of major proportions in the summer of 1930 made the farmer's plight even worse. The hot, dry weather reduced the corn crop nearly 50,000,000 bushels from the normal yield predicted by agronomists, and of the 76,987,000 bushels harvested, only 55 per cent was of merchantable quality.[36] Farmers and small-town merchants dependent upon the farmers' business could not blame Hoover for the weather, but many fixed the cause for their economic distress upon Hoover's and previous Republican administrations. Thus, rural Missouri returned to its normal Democratic ways in 1930.

The Democratic resurgence in 1930 extended to the state legislature, where Democrats regained control of the Senate and for the first time in seven years secured a majority in the House. Both parties had expended considerable effort to gain control of the General Assembly, since that body was to draw new congressional boundaries. The fight between Democratic and Republican lawmakers over congressional redistricting, most political observers believed, would emerge as a major political battle in the sessions of the Fifty-sixth General Assembly.[37]

Five days after the General Assembly convened, however, an incident took place that plunged the legislators into a totally unexpected partisan battle over legislation involving the welfare of the Negro. The outcome of this contest, as in other recent partisan maneuvers of politicians for the allegiance of the colored voter, furthered the transition of the Negro electorate from the Republican to the Democratic party.

The incident that touched off the legislative encounter occurred at Maryville on January 13. In that small northwest county-seat town a mob of nearly two thousand persons forced county law officers to surrender custody of a Negro charged with the assault-murder of a local white schoolteacher. After chaining the accused man to the roof of the schoolhouse where the crime had been committed, members of the crowd soaked the building with gasoline and applied a torch. The barbarity of the mob's crime brought cries of protest from within and without the state. The fact that sixty National Guardsmen sent to Maryville the day before the lynching had not been alerted and utilized by Nodaway County's sheriff added to the enormity of the outrage. The sheriff had feared a clash between soldiers and the mob and on this basis defended his action as the wisest course. But of the six lynchings in the state since 1921, the *St. Louis Post-Dispatch* acidly commented, "in none of them has the law turned its back with such emphasis as it did . . . at Maryville."[38]

State legislators in both parties, keenly aware of the public indignation over the lynching at Maryville, were not slow to react. Democrat Gil Bourk of Kansas City's Negro-populated Fourth House District was the first to introduce an antilynching bill in the House on January 23. Two weeks later, four Republican representatives from St. Louis, not to be outdone by the Democrats, brought in a second anti-lynching measure.[39] Obviously, both Democrats and Republicans realized the political benefits that would accrue to the party responsible for the passage of the state's first anti-lynching law. An editorial in the *St. Louis Argus*, however, indicated that the greater opportunity for political gain belonged to Missouri's Democrats:

> Politically speaking, the Democrats have the opportunity of their lives to equalize the Negro vote in this state. With the sponsoring of an anti-lynching bill by the Democrats and the power in their hands to pass other legislation favorable to the Negro, it is now a bet as to which party will control the Negro vote in '32.[40]

Republicans, unable to secure the enactment of their anti-lynching bill, grumbled when the Democratic measure passed in the House. A leading opponent of the successful Bourk bill, Republican George F. Heegee of St. Louis County, bluntly denounced it as a "political measure on the part of the majority members of the House to get the Negro vote. I think that it is a joke."[41]

A few days after the passage of the House measure, Senator Michael Kinney pushed through a milder antilynching bill in the Senate.[42] Kinney's bill may have been drafted simply because members of the Senate found the House's legislation too drastic for their liking. However, the Senator from St. Louis may have wanted the credit for authoring an antilynching bill.

In any event, it was the Kinney antilynching bill that passed both houses, thus marking the first time such a measure had gained the approval of the General Assembly. Although Republicans supplied 39 of the 98 affirmative votes in the House, and 8 of the 19 votes in the Senate, the *St. Louis Argus* gave full credit to the Democrats. "There is no doubt in our mind," the Negro newspaper asserted, "but that had the Republican party . . . been in the majority in both the house and senate during the present sesson of the legislature, no anti-lynch law of any kind would have passed both houses." Consequently, the *Argus* concluded, "we are quite sure that the Negroes of the state will see the Democratic party in a different light to what they have in the past."[43]

When the Democrats' antilynching bill came to Governor Caulfield's desk, however, he surprised Negroes by vetoing the measure. The Governor made it clear that he wanted an antilynching law, but one that would provide for the punishment of all law officers who were derelict in their duty of providing protection for their prisoners. The Kinney bill, Caulfield pointed out, applied only to "state or municipal officers" and exempted county sheriffs and their deputies. Thus, Caulfield explained, the bill omitted from its provisions "the very officer . . . upon whose shoulders falls almost exclusively the high duty of protecting the prisoner from mob violence." The enactment of such an inadequate measure, he concluded, would "lull Missourians into a false sense of security."[44]

The *Kansas City Call* was the only Negro newspaper that defended Caulfield's veto, although the *Kansas City American* lamented that the original Bourk bill, replaced by the Kinney measure, had contained all the features deemed essential by the Governor.[45] The *American* also urged the passage of a new bill, but the Governor's veto had come after the end of the legislative session. The *St. Louis Argus*, never a strong supporter of Governor Caulfield, regarded the Governor's explanation for vetoing the Kinney bill as "bunk, pure and simple." There is no evidence to support the *Argus'* further claim that politics played the major part in the Governor's veto.[46] However, Caulfield may have recalled that in 1929, when the legislature passed his educational program for Negroes, the *Argus* gave credit to Senator Kinney and none to the Governor. Certainly, partisan politics had been one of the motivating forces behind the Democrat-sponsored antilynching bill.

Moreover, judging from the editorial response in the Negro press and from the resolution adopted by the National Association for the Advancement of Colored People in St. Louis,[47] Republicans lost to Democrats because of Caulfield's veto. Many Negroes simply added the Governor's rejection of the antilynching bill to the long list of political actions and decisions by Republicans that, the race felt, prevented their achieving first-class citizenship: President Hoover's nomination of Judge Parker to the Supreme Court, Senator Patterson's vote for Parker's confirmation, Charles U. Becker's firing of Walthall M. Moore, and the Dyer-Moore congressional primary fight of 1930. Collectively, these incidents helped loosen the cement of political loyalty that for years had bound Missouri's Negroes to the Republican party.

With the approach of the election year of 1932, the political transition of a majority of the state's colored voters to the party of Jefferson, however, was incomplete. Of the four major Negro population areas of the state — St. Louis, Kansas City, Little Dixie, and the Cotton Delta counties — only in Kansas City had a majority of Negroes shifted to the Democratic party. Nevertheless, colored Democrats were numerous enough in every area of the state in 1931 to warrant the Democrats' claim that Negroes were an integral part of the Missouri Democracy. Thus strengthened, Democrats looked confidently to 1932 as the year of their restoration to power in Jefferson City and in Washington.

CHAPTER 9

RESTORATION TO STATE
AND NATIONAL OFFICE

THE DETERIORATING CONDITIONS IN 1931 that plunged Missouri
and the rest of the nation deeper into economic depression
also brought political despair to the ranks of the Republicans of Missouri. Confronted with a host of dissatisfied
farmers outstate and of unemployed workers in the cities,
few Republicans were eager to run for office in 1932. Con-
versely, the collapse of "Republican prosperity" raised the
Democrats' hopes for victory, and political aspirants flooded
the field in every primary contest. Moreover, the Democratic
presidential nomination, unlike the nominations of 1924 and
1928, carried promise in 1932, for the person nominated by
the Democrats seemed certain to become President of the
United States. Before the restoration of Democrats to office,
though, came the struggle for control of the party in state
and nation.[1]

The conservative-liberal conflict in the national Democracy
between the probusiness element, headed by National Democratic Committee Chairman John J. Raskob, and the forces
opposed to business rule, led by Franklin D. Roosevelt, influenced and in turn was influenced by Democratic politics
in Missouri. The repeal of the Eighteenth Amendment, the
issue that the conservative Raskob hoped would turn Democrats away from a fight on business rule, became the chief
weapon of Bennett Clark against his opponent for the senatorial nomination, prohibitionist and progressive Charles M.
Hay. In presidential politics former Senator James A. Reed,

in his third and last bid for his party's presidential nomination, became an active force in the conservative coalition that was intent on "stopping Roosevelt."[2] Other Missourians, covertly and overtly, worked for the nomination of the progressive Governor of New York. The key figure in the behind-the-scenes machinations for Roosevelt, Tom Pendergast, already a power in the Democratic party, emerged as an even more potent force in state politics; the principal Democratic antagonists of the twenties, Reed and Hay, ended their careers as major political leaders in Missouri. The failure of the conservative Reed and prohibitionist Hay to realize their chief political ambitions signified the changes in the political climate of the depression thirties.

As Democrats were firmly convinced that the economic collapse would bring victory to the party in 1932, so rank-and-file sentiment held that Franklin D. Roosevelt was the man best qualified to preside over recovery. This sentiment manifested itself at a luncheon arranged for junketing Jim Farley, in Kansas City while on tour in the summer of 1931 for the purpose of sounding out support for Roosevelt. Although Jim Reed at first intended to boycott the luncheon for Farley, he attended and heard himself lionized by the diplomatic New Yorker. Reed responded by indicating to Farley his friendliness toward Governor Roosevelt.[3] In September, however, when a Roosevelt admirer publicized plans to start a Roosevelt-for-President organization, Reed made it known that he would "consider it a compliment" if the Missouri delegation voted for him for the presidential nomination. Farley quickly advised the former Senator and other concerned Democrats that the Governor would not sanction any organization for himself in Missouri, in view of the sentiment for Reed there. Roosevelt, wise to Reed's plans, wrote a flattering letter to Reed to express his hope that they could work together for party harmony and solidarity.[4]

"Reed can't be out to win the Democratic nomination for

President," observed *Outlook*. "He must be out to keep some
one else from winning it."[5] In spite of his seventy years,
however, Reed's ambitions for the presidential nomination
were genuine. His private correspondence, public pronouncements, and the course he followed at the Democratic National
Convention make clear that the old Jeffersonian entertained
the hope that his party would call upon him to turn the federal government from its Hamiltonian ways. More realisti-
cally, however, Reed regarded his candidacy as a means of
exerting influence in the selection of a candidate with views
similar to his own.[6]

While conservative Democrats sounded Jeffersonian themes
at the Jackson Day dinner of 1932 in the nation's capital,
Reed sounded the keynote for the annual gathering of the
Democrats of Missouri at Springfield. As though rebuking
in advance Franklin Roosevelt's later call for "bold, persistent experimentation," Reed demanded that Democrats "reject every experimental scheme." The fundamental remedy
for the nation's economic crisis, he insisted, was a return to
Jeffersonian principles. At the close of the meeting at Springfield Reed confided to friends his evaluation of the leading
contenders for the nomination. "His criticism of you," Edward F. Goltra wrote Roosevelt, "was far more severe and
vitriolic than of any of the others, being bitter and abusive;
charging that under no circumstances would you do as the
candidate."[7] Subsequently, Reed used his waning influence
in an unsuccessful attempt to prevent Roosevelt's nomination.

Meanwhile, old anti-Reed Democrats and Roosevelt supporters quietly initiated action to nullify Reed's efforts. With
the tacit consent of Roosevelt's lieutenants Louis M. Howe
and James A. Farley, Ewing Y. Mitchell of Springfield, a
leader in the campaign against Reed's senatorial campaign
in 1922, launched a correspondence campaign for Roosevelt in November, 1931. Mitchell asked delegates to the State

Democratic Convention to support Roosevelt after giving Reed a complimentary vote on the first ballot.[8]

Charles M. Hay, once again a candidate for the senatorial nomination, publicly assumed a noncommital attitude toward the Roosevelt movement, but unreservedly cast his lot against the conservative brand of Democracy being promoted by National Committee Chairman John J. Raskob. In a Jefferson Day speech in 1931, Hay specifically denounced the efforts of Raskob to make prohibition the leading issue of the campaign. Raskob, Hay charged, was a

> mouthpiece of Mammon and a high priest of privilege and concentrated wealth. Farmers, laborers, small businessmen, victims of the tariffs, of combines and extortions, call on him for relief from intolerable economic ills; he suggests in answer that they first determine the percentage of alcohol to go in their drink. They cry for bread, he demands that they ask for a can with foam on it. They demand jobs, he suggests jags.[9]

Hay, anxious that the Democratic party avoid a collision on the prohibition issue so as not to endanger his contemplated candidacy for the senatorial nomination, was equally opposed to the nomination of a reactionary for the Presidency.[10]

Retiring Senator Harry B. Hawes, out of favor with the Pendergast organization and with the ward politicians in St. Louis, had nothing to lose by a forthright rejection of Reed's favorite son candidacy and by open advocacy of Franklin D. Roosevelt's. On the eve of the election of delegates to the national convention by the State Democratic Convention, Hawes advised against any action that might "prevent delegates from exercising their own judgment in preventing a long and destructive deadlock at Chicago." It was a fateful year, Hawes warned, "and no personal aspiration should interfere with party harmony and success." With obvious reference to Reed, Hawes continued: "No man is bigger than his party; no real Democrat will sacrifice its best interests for his own personal advancement this year."[11]

The night before the opening of the national convention, Hawes executed another bold move in Roosevelt's behalf. Without the approval of Texas' favorite son candidate John Nance Garner, Hawes wired Democratic leaders at the convention and around the country that the Texan had agreed to a Roosevelt-Garner ticket. If, as Frank Freidel has concluded, it was Garner himself who played the really decisive role in guaranteeing the nomination of Roosevelt, Hawes's unauthorized action undoubtedly promoted pro-Roosevelt sentiment and may have strengthened Garner's strong conviction that a deadlock should not be permitted to develop at the convention.[12]

But it was Tom Pendergast, the most powerful figure in the Missouri Democracy by 1932, who held the key to the state convention's action in matters of presidential politics. Much of Pendergast's power in Misouri politics hinged upon the ability of his machine to deliver the Kansas City vote to candidates subject to a state-wide vote. However, since Republican Governor Henry S. Caulfield had vetoed the partisan congressional redistricting bill passed by Democratic legislators in 1931, candidates for nomination to the thirteen seats in the House were also subject to a state-wide vote. Theoretically, each congressional candidate who desired the 50,000 to 100,000 votes of the Pendergast organization would pledge support to every other candidate endorsed by Pendergast. Thus, on paper at least, the Kansas City leader had the ability to determine both the state and national Democratic tickets in Missouri. However, as a perceptive reporter for the *St. Louis Globe-Democrat* pointed out, Pendergast could not dictate the nomination of a candidate unless the person made a striking appeal to the rural voters. In reality, then, Pendergast did not possess dictatorial powers, but held the balance of power.[13]

So it was with the instruction of delegates to the national convention: Most Democrats, including Pendergast, realized that party sentiment in the state clearly favored the nomination of Roosevelt. Many Missourians were willing to go along with a complimentary first-ballot vote for Reed, but few wanted to give the delegation to the former Senator to use either in his own behalf or in behalf of candidates other than Roosevelt.[14] Nevertheless, by drawing upon outstate and St. Louis Democrats who were willing to go down the line for Reed and by threatening to withhold election support from leaders who were unwilling to throw blocs of votes under their control to a pro-Reed slate, Pendergast could have forced through a delegation with instructions for Reed. By foregoing a fight to tie the delegation to Reed as in 1928, when the state convention bound delegates to Reed until the Senator released them in writing, Pendergast in effect aligned himself with the Roosevelt forces. The convention instructions that delegates "use all honorable means to nominate Senator Reed for President" would permit Pendergast to decide when delegates loyal to him should go over to Roosevelt. More important, it also meant that pro-Roosevelt delegates unfriendly to Reed could determine individually when "all honorable means" had been exhausted.[15]

When a Smith supporter inquired of Reed the meaning of the convention's instructions, Reed admitted that the situation was less under control than he had desired; nevertheless, he added, "the very worst that can possibly happen would be that two or three might seek to break away." But if Pendergast had ever told Reed of his intention of voting the bloc of voters under his control for Roosevelt after a few complimentary ballots for the former senator (as he reportedly told a Roosevelt scout before the state convention)[16] Reed made no mention of the matter to Smith's backer. Pendergast, Reed wrote,

> has been my friend for thirty years. I do not think it, but I know absolutely that he will stick with me in this fight until I tell him to go elsewhere. And I am very sure he will go to the

person I ask him to. I am very sure he regards Roosevelt just
about as you do; that he is going to this convention to play the
game so as to secure my nomination if possible. And if that
becomes impossible, then to cast his influence and vote for
some candidate who belongs to our branch of the Democracy. . . . I think the sentiment out here among my friends
will be more favorable to Garner than any other candidate,
although a whole lot of them would like to vote for Smith.[17]

Two weeks before the Democratic National Convention Reed
reassured his friend that "you need give yourself no worry
about Pendergast sticking to me as long as I want him."[18]

The balloting during the national convention at Chicago
revealed Reed's poor assessment of the disposition of several
Missouri delegates toward his candidacy, but Pendergast's
activities in his behalf misled the Senator for nearly a year:
When several St. Louis and outstate delegates announced
their intention of deserting Reed on the first ballot, Pendergast came close to exchanging blows with one of the defect-
ing leaders, Louis J. Gualdoni. Later, when reporters asked
Pendergast about the possibility of the entire Missouri delegation going over to Roosevelt on the first ballot, Pendergast replied:

> We are all under instructions to use every honorable means to
> bring about the nomination of Senator Reed. That binds every
> delegate to support Reed until efforts to nominate him are
> exhausted. Reed has been my friend twenty-five years and
> more. He has never failed me when I needed him and I will not
> fail him now. You can say for me that I will vote for Reed for
> 100 ballots if necessary.[19]

On the opening roll call of the states for the Democratic
presidential nomination, however, after the fifty-four Missouri delegates cast the state's 36 votes for Reed and before
the vote was announced, seventeen delegates from St. Louis
and outstate, following the leadership of Gualdoni, changed
their 12 votes to Roosevelt. On the second ballot another

6 votes switched to Roosevelt, and on the third round of balloting Roosevelt picked up 2½ more Missouri votes. Although relatively few in number, the Missouri votes for Roosevelt contributed in a major way to the New Yorker's increased strength after each ballot, and the fatal decline that the anti-Roosevelt forces had hoped for did not materialize. With Roosevelt's nomination virtually assured after California shifted to his camp on the next ballot, Reed informed Pendergast that those delegates who had remained loyal to him could be released. Thus, on the fourth and final roll call, Pendergast joined the rest of the Missouri delegation in casting the state's 36 votes for the Governor of New York.[20]

Although newspapers at the time extolled the Kansas City boss's loyalty to Reed and Reed himself seemed satisfied with Pendergast's performance at Chicago,[21] Bennett Clark later provided Reed with the correct version of Pendergast's perfidious role at the convention. In a letter to Reed in March, 1933, written shortly after he took office as United States senator, Clark related that James Farley had asked him if it were all right for Pendergast to control the appointments at Kansas City as a reward for his support of Roosevelt at the convention in Chicago. Clark informed the new Postmaster General that Missouri's senatorial patronage belonged solely to him. Moreover, Clark added, Pendergast had not supported Roosevelt at the convention, since he had publicly offered to fist-fight Louis J. Gualdoni in Reed's behalf. Farley candidly replied: "Oh, Pendergast was all right. Was with us all the time. Reed had him hog-tied but I saw him every day and he was with us from the start." When Clark protested further, Farley frankly admitted that the President had promised Pendergast the Kansas City patronage *before the convention.*[22] Thus, while the early and important defection of Missourians to Roosevelt came from delegates who were not members of the Pendergast organization, the loose instructions adopted without a fight from Pendergast forces at the state convention made those defections possible. Reed's slim hope of gaining the nomination for himself or of using the Missouri delegation in behalf of a candidate more conservative than Roosevelt was doomed from the start.

Reed's choice to succeed Harry B. Hawes in the United States Senate was destined for success. Bennett Champ Clark, son of the famous Speaker of the House, had often sided with Reed in major battles within the party in the twenties. Although newspapermen regarded Clark as a progressive, he actually had a political philosophy very similar to that of the conservative Reed. True, Clark at first publicly disagreed with Democratic National Committee Chairman Raskob's attempts to make prohibition the major issue of the 1932 campaign, but later he made repeal of the Eighteenth Amendment and the legalization of beer key planks in his campaign platform. And although Clark favored the enactment of a federal relief bill, Arthur M. Schlesinger, Jr., has written that this was one liberal program most conservative Democrats approved. Unlike many conservatives, Clark rejected the sales tax as a means of raising revenue; otherwise, his position on the tariff and his belief in limited government conformed to the traditional party program.[23] Over all, he was a worthy heir to the political tradition of former Senator Reed.

A second entry in the Senate race was Charles M. Howell, a corporation lawyer in Kansas City. Howell, once a member of Reed's law firm, also had a political outlook similar to Reed's. Backed by Tom Pendergast and thus assured of the Kansas City vote, Howell evidently did not wish to offend the drys of rural Missouri with an outright declaration for repeal of prohibition. Therefore, when he announced his candidacy in October, 1931, Howell stated that he would take the same position on the liquor question as that adopted by the Democratic National Convention. The rest of Howell's platform — planks advocating the abolition of "useless boards and bureaus," decentralization of government, and lowering of the tariff — appeared to be patterned after Reed's presidential program.[24] Because of past professional and personal ties with Reed, Howell seemed assured of the former senator's neutrality between himself and Bennett Champ Clark, and Reed did in fact issue a statement of neutrality after Howell announced his candidacy. Privately, however, Reed indicated his preference for Clark, and at the end of the campaign his public speeches clearly displayed a preference for the St. Louisan.[25]

Reed left no doubt in anyone's mind concerning his attitude toward the third senatorial aspirant, perennial candidate Charles M. Hay. If old antagonisms from the party's scrap over the League of Nations and from their disagreement on prohibition were not enough to ensure Reed's opposition, the progressive platform of the St. Louis Democrat guaranteed it. Hay had taken an advanced position on economic and social issues throughout the twenties. His Jefferson Day address of 1931 made clear his fundamental disagreement with the conservative element of the party, and his alignment with the programs of progressives such as Governor Roosevelt and United States Senators Robert F. Wagner of New York and George Norris of Nebraska indicated unmistakably his liberalism. In calling for public works projects, government protection of labor organizations, accident, old-age, and unemployment insurance, farm relief, government ownership of water power sources, and government control and supervision of public utilities and holding companies, Hay's platform foreshadowed many of the important programs subsequently enacted during the New Deal.[26]

Before the Democratic National Convention and the party's adoption of a plank calling for the repeal of the Eighteenth Amendment and the modification of the Volstead Act, political observers placed Hay ahead of his two rivals in the senatorial primary race. According to the analyses of political writers, Howell and Clark would divide the wet vote, and

Hay would sweep to victory on a dry ticket. Hay shared this optimistic outlook, although he feared the adoption of a wet plank by the national convention would injure his candidacy. As wet sentiment within the party and in the state increased, Hay modified his rigid position of no change on the Eighteenth Amendment and the Volstead Act to one whereby the dry laws would be resubmitted to the people, along with a substitute plan for liquor control. Finally, after the convention adopted its outright repeal plank, Hay also moved into the repeal camp, although he continued to maintain his personal belief in the soundness of prohibition. He also continued to argue that economic recovery, not repeal of prohibition, constituted the central issue of the campaign.[27]

Clark, however, astutely gauged the declining strength of sentiment for prohibition outstate and, sensing the advantage that accrued to him as the "original" wet candidate, pressed that advantage even harder after the adoption of the repeal plank at Chicago. Concentrating his fire on his dry opponent in order to accentuate his own wet position, Clark assailed Hay for insisting that prohibition was not an economic issue:

> If Hay says putting 500,000 people to work in the manufacture of beer, spending millions in the rehabilitation of breweries and allied industries and raising a billion dollars a year in taxes, which now goes to bootleggers and racketeers, is not an economic issue, then I fail to understand his process of reasoning.[28]

Clark's economic argument against prohibition received support from spokesmen of the conservative-led and -financed Association Against the Eighteenth Amendment and from representatives of the brewing industry. August A. Busch, president of the Anheuser-Busch breweries in St. Louis, estimated that if beer were legalized his company would require material and equipment costing $7,000,000 and 2,500 additional employees. Other brewery officials in the St. Louis area issued statements indicating the additional money they would expend and the workers they would employ if manufacture of real beer were legalized.[29]

Hay, chiding both Howell and Clark for "wrangling over the question which got wet first and which is the wettest now," attempted to turn the campaign back to strictly economic issues. To emphasize his concern for the farmer's plight, Hay related to rural audiences his activity at the Chicago convention in behalf of a plank calling for long-term, low-interest farm loans. Realizing Hay's popularity with farmers of the state, William Hirth of the Missouri Farmers' Association, an old friend of the Clark family, avoiding alienating those members of the MFA who regarded Hay as a sincere supporter of farm interests; Hirth endorsed both men.[30] Believing that Howell rather than Clark constituted his chief opponent, Hay contrasted his own progressive platform with the fundamentally conservative stand taken by the lawyer-lobbyist of insurance and utilities companies: "A dry can conscientiously support Franklin Roosevelt . . . as the hope of the party for economic relief; but there is no place in the present program for . . . a man who for years has been identified with interests and practices inimical to true democracy."[31]

Despite the best efforts of Hay, the senatorial primary contest ended with prohibition as the central issue and Bennett Clark the party's nominee. By capturing nearly all of St. Louis' vote and by leading the field with 47 per cent of the rural returns, Clark finished well ahead of his opponents with 268,667 votes; Howell's 101,259 votes from Kansas City and Jackson County boosted him to second place, with a 173,266-vote total. Hay, compiling most of his total outstate, ran a disappointing third, with 151,188 votes.[32] Clark, a colonel in command of a Missouri regiment during the First World War and first national commander of the American Legion, won heavy backing from veterans; he attracted further support as the son of the illustrious Speaker and as the protégé of former Senator Reed; and he convinced many Democrats that he could represent them best in the federal government's efforts to end the depression. Both Hay and Tom Pendergast agreed, however, that Clark's effective use of the prohibition issue had gained him the nomination.[33]

Although newspapers hostile to the Pendergast organization had charged that Howell would be dominated by the Kansas City boss if elected to the Senate, neither Clark nor Hay raised this charge against their common rival. It was left for Russell Dearmont, a lawyer of Cape Girardeau and rival of Francis M. Wilson of Platte City for the gubernatorial nomination, to level the charge that Wilson, endorsed by Tom Pendergast, would be controlled by the Pendergast organization if elected governor.[34] The *St. Louis Post-Dispatch* and the *St. Louis Star and Times* lined up with Dearmont; however, the *Kansas City Star*, certainly no friend of the Pendergast organization, unreservedly recommended Wilson to Democrats as a man of both ability and integrity.[35]

Most Democrats agreed with the *Star's* evaluation. Wilson won a decisive 374,289 to 224,377 victory over Dearmont, carrying 84 of the state's 114 counties and falling only 5,000 votes behind Dearmont's total in St. Louis. Kansas City and Jackson County gave Wilson a lopsided eleven-to-one edge over Dearmont, but even without the 110,273 votes he received from the Pendergast organization, Wilson could have emerged the victor with 39,639 votes to spare.[36]

The results of the at-large congressional contests, similar to Howell's unsuccessful senate race and Wilson's successful bid for the gubernatorial nomination, reflected the uneven influence of the Pendergast organization in elections. Twenty-two of the fifty-six candidates ended up on the Pendergast slate, but in the voting the machine gave strong backing to only sixteen aspirants. Four of the twelve incumbents, William Barton, James F. Fulbright, Robert D. Johnson, and

William Nelson, received a large outstate vote but failed of nomination because of a small vote in Kansas City. On the other hand, John D. Taylor of Keytesville, a close friend of Pendergast, received the full machine vote, but lost when rural voters failed to give him sufficient backing. Two other incumbents, Milton A. Romjue and Clyde Williams, fell far short of total machine support, but won nomination when rural voters amassed large totals for them. Thus, while Pendergast's support was crucial for nomination in some cases, in others it was either ineffective or inconsequential.[37]

Commitment to repeal of prohibition was not one of the requirements for Pendergast's backing in the congressional primary, as evidenced by the renomination of long-time drys Cannon, Dickinson, Lozier, Romjue, and Williams. However, all of the dry congressional candidates promptly moved into the wet camp after the primary election.[38] The poor showing of Charles Hay in the senatorial primary and a realization that St. Louis voters would not vote for prohibitionists probably accounted for the shift. If this move did not place the formerly dry Democrats on an equal footing with wet Republican Congressmen L. C. Dyer and Henry Neidringhaus in the campaign, the state and national Democratic plank did so by calling for outright repeal of prohibition and legalization of beer. In fact, wet Republicans were at a disadvantage in that their state plank on prohibition, like the national party's stand, equivocated instead of taking a clearcut position on repeal.[39]

Bennett Clark lost few opportunities to make the voters and his Republican opponent in the senatorial contest, Henry W. Kiel, aware of the differences between the Democratic and Republican planks on the liquor question. "Kiel is not so wet as he claims to be," Clark told St. Louisans. "Mr. Kiel must stand on his party's national and state platforms"; neither plank, Clark reminded his listeners, called for legislation to legalize beer.[40] When Kiel hotly replied that he had been calling for the return of beer since the primary, Clark accused his opponent of disloyalty to Hoover and the Republican party. Republican leaders did in fact circulate nearly a million sample ballots in St. Louis showing "Roosevelt Republicans" how to "ditch" Hoover and support the rest of the ticket.[41]

Democrats met these maneuvers of the Republicans to save St. Louis for their senatorial and congressional candidates by lining up support from German-American societies and by intensive campaigning in the brewery wards. Former Senator Reed, sharing the speaker's platform with officials of the Anheuser-Busch brewery company, tore to shreds the Republican position on the liquor question in several talks around the city. Franklin Roosevelt climaxed these efforts to win the wet St. Louis vote by reiterating his declaration for repeal and legalization of beer, made in his acceptance speech, in a visit to the city on October 22.[42]

As repeal of prohibition dominated the senatorial contest in St. Louis, "bossism" dominated the gubernatorial campaign. Shortly after the August primary, the G.O.P.'s candidate for governor, Edward H. Winter, announced that "Pendergast influence over Wilson" would be the main issue of the fall campaign. Then, quite suddenly on October 12, Wilson died, momentarily halting the gubernatorial campaign in both camps. The campaign was resumed a week later, however, after the Democratic State Committee, which was empowered by state law to fill the vacancy, selected Circuit Judge Guy B. Park as Wilson's successor, and Republicans renewed with vigor their charge of "bossism." [43]

Lending validity to the G.O.P.'s claim that Park had been "handpicked by Pendergast" was the relative obscurity of the candidate and the apparent bypassing of more widely known Democrats. The evidence suggests, however, that Judge Park's selection was a compromise acceptable to Bennett Clark and outstate Democratic committeemen as well as to Tom Pendergast.[44] Farm leader William Hirth, probably the Democrat most concerned over the Republicans' charge that Pendergast would control a Democratic governor, came out for Park three days before the state committee named the Platte City jurist as Wilson's successor.[45] Eventually even Russell Dearmont, still at odds with the Pendergast organization, gave Park his personal endorsement.[46]

While Democratic leaders reacted favorably to Judge Park's nomination, Republicans entertained hope that the party's rank and file would turn to the G.O.P.'s candidate, Winter. Clever use of pamphlets and newspaper advertisements by the Republican campaign committee made it appear that Winter's opponent for governor was not Park, but Tom Pendergast. Campaign literature featured a picture of the Kansas City boss nattily attired in formal dress, top hat and all (the picture had been cropped from a photograph of his daughter's wedding party), under captions reading "Beat the Boss!" and "Shall Missouri Be Boss-Controlled?"[47]

Despite these efforts by Republicans to promote defection among the Democrats over the bossism issue, the Missouri Democracy entered the fall campaign more united than at any time since the party split over the League in 1919. The chief unifying factor that brought the once warring wings of the party into harmony was a common conviction that the return of prosperity depended upon the election of Democrats to state and national office. Charles M. Hay, for example, although concerned over the possibility of Pendergast's domination of state government[48] and dissatisfied with the party's commitment to repeal of prohibition, insisted that economic issues were paramount. It was imperative, Hay advised friends, that Democrats gain control of government, because Republicans had become indifferent to the needs of the people.[49] Similarly, economic considerations helped bring to the aid of the ticket Democrats who had been opposed to Roosevelt's nomination. The foremost of the old Jeffersonians,

Jim Reed, had appealed for harmony at the convention in Chicago. Reed even wrote Roosevelt a friendly letter of advice concerning party organization; by mid-September the former Senator was out campaigning for the entire ticket. When the charge of socialism was hurled at Roosevelt, Reed came strongly to his defense. Hoover, Reed asserted, had already established "capitalistic Socialism, inaugurated not for the benefit of the common man or the small merchant, but for the benefit of the great banks and trust companies."[50] Thus, while many Democrats had reservations about some of the candidates and disagreed with parts of the party platform, concern over the Republicans' response to the economic crisis prompted these party members to overcome their differences in order to achieve the common objective of turning Republicans out of office.

The failure of the Hoover and Caulfield administrations to cope adequately with the problems underlying and extending the depression also became a dominant theme in the campaign of the Democratic candidates. Nevertheless, when solutions for the nation's economic ills were advanced, they conformed for the most part to old Jeffersonian principles of limited government. Judge Park's promise to hold state governmental services at a minimum was echoed by other Democratic seekers of state and national office. Bennett Clark cited both the Federal Farm Board and the Reconstruction Finance Corporation as examples of unwarranted activity by the federal government. The return of prosperity, Clark asserted, depended upon lowering the tariff. None of the candidates adopted a position anywhere close to the progressive stand taken by Charles M. Hay in the primary.[51]

Republicans countered the Democrats' attacks upon G.O.P. policies vigorously. "Remember," Henry Kiel told a St. Louis audience, "that over seventy-five per cent of the great industries of St. Louis have been fostered and developed under the protective tariff system." Kiel also defended the

Federal Farm Board and the Reconstruction Finance Corporation as significant undertakings of the Hoover Administration to deal with depression and recovery.[52] Winter
declared that he would make economy and efficiency bywords
of his administration and charged that Missourians could
look forward only to high cost of state government under a patronage-dispensing, Pendergast-dominated governor.
"Prosperity can only come back with Herbert Hoover," pro-
claimed G.O.P. newspaper advertisements, but most Missourians, certain that the Hoover Administration had not
brought them prosperity at all, remained unconvinced.[53]

On November 8, Democrats returned to state and national
offices in the greatest political landslide in the history of Missouri. From the top to the bottom of the ticket, in traditionally
Republican St. Louis and outstate counties, Democrats swept
to unprecedented victories. Roosevelt led the ticket with
1,025,406 votes to Hoover's 564,713, a 460,693-vote margin
that exceeded his advantage in every other state except in
his own New York. Other Democratic candidates, faced with
stronger opponents than Hoover and confronted with troublesome state as well as national issues, achieved less impressive
yet substantial margins.[54]

The influence of the three key campaign issues — beer,
bossism, and economic conditions — manifested themselves
most noticeably in the returns from traditionally Republican
St. Louis. Roosevelt's 102,890 plurality led the ticket, although Bennett Clark carried one more ward than Roosevelt. In the south-side brewery wards Roosevelt received a
better than two-to-one margin over Hoover; Clark, opposed
by the dripping-wet Kiel, ran about 3,000 votes behind Roosevelt in the same wards. St. Louisans accorded the smallest
plurality of all to Governor-elect Park. Projected into the
campaign at a very late stage and receiving the brunt of the
Republicans' opposition because of an alleged subservience
to Tom Pendergast, Park ran ahead of his G.O.P. rival by

44,219 votes but fell approximately 35,000 votes behind the rest of the state ticket in the city.[55]

Tom Pendergast's ability to deliver the Kansas City vote was demonstrated in a most convincing fashion in the wards controlled by his organization. Pendergast Wards 1, 2, 3, 4, 9, and 11 rolled up a 66,103 to 15,266 advantage for Roosevelt over Hoover; nine of the city's remaining ten wards went for Roosevelt 75,614 to 45,710. Only the "silk-stocking" Republican Eighth Ward in the fashionable southwest corner of the city gave a majority to Hoover. Judge Park, given about the same total as that accorded Roosevelt in the Pendergast wards, came within 4,000 votes of matching the performance of other Democrats on the state ticket.[56]

Although Park ran about 25,000 votes behind the rest of the Democratic slate outstate, he still shared in the Democratic ground swell and finished with a 968,551 to 629,438 advantage over Winter. Clark's 1,017,046 to Kiel's 575,174 was a more typical vote, however, as Democrats captured all of the state administrative offices and every one of the thirteen congressional seats. In the state legislature Democrats elected 140 of the 150 members of the house and carried all of the senatorial elections to gain a 27-to-7 advantage in the upper chamber. The votes for this spectacular showing came uniformly from all sections of Missouri. In fact, 107 of the state's 114 counties went Democratic in presidential voting, including 14 counties that previously had an unbroken record of loyalty to the Republican party.[57]

A more significant and enduring feature of the election of 1932 than the shift of traditionally Republican counties to the Democratic party was the continuing defection of Negroes from the Republican party. According to an estimate published in the St. Louis Argus, twenty thousand of the city's Negroes, or 50.5 per cent of the number participating in the election, voted Democratic.[58] The St. Louis Post-Dispatch, however, noted that the only wards in St. Louis to return majorities for Hoover were Negro Wards 5, 6, 19, and 23. These wards gave Hoover 54.5 per cent of the vote to 45.5 per cent for Roosevelt. In Wards 4, 16, 17, and 20, where Negroes constituted from 20 to 32 per cent of the voting population, Roosevelt received from 59.6 to 64.1 per cent of the vote, or about 10 per cent less than he achieved in several other wards. Apparently, the colored voters in St. Louis remained loyal to the G.O.P., but only by a small majority.[59] In Kansas City, however, a large majority of Negroes cast Democratic ballots. Voters in the Negro Second and Fourth wards outdid their performance of 1930 when 59.7 per cent voted Democratic by giving Roosevelt 77.5 per cent of the 1932 vote.[60] Figures for the scattered outstate Negro vote are difficult to ascertain, but a sampling of published election returns and the correspondence of politicians reveals that Negro Democrats outnumbered Negro Republicans at the polls in Hannibal and St. Joseph and in Pemiscot County.[61] Judging from these sources, it appears that for the first time a majority of Missouri Negroes voted for the Democratic party in 1932.

"The people wanted bread, clothing, and the necessities of life, and the Negro was no exception," commented the *St. Louis Argus*. The voters, the Negro newspaper added, had judged Hoover either incapable or indifferent.[62] Even without the economic distress of 1932, however, many Missouri Negroes would have deserted the G.O.P. that year. Since the mid-twenties, articulate spokesmen for the race had been calling for a "new deal," to little avail. As more and more colored citizens saw their aspirations frustrated by apathetic Republicans, they began to shift their allegiance to the Democratic party. Astute Democrats, aware of the importance of the colored vote in the reconstruction of a majority coalition, aided this transition by liberal policies within the party and patronage. The depression, as Arthur M.

Schlesinger, Jr., has suggested, merely accelerated a political process that was already in progress.[63]

The depression and dissatisfaction with the Republican response to the economic crisis, however, were unquestionably the chief factors responsible for the restoration of Democrats to power. These considerations, on the one hand, brought about wide-scale defections among traditionally Republican voters and, on the other, united Democrats for the common objective of ousting Republicans from office.

Thus, the election of 1932 brought an end to many of the disastrous party battles of the twenties. New conflicts loomed over the horizon, but the Democratic coalition of the thirties would be broad enough to afford the loss of disaffected Democrats.

CONCLUSION AND EPILOGUE

DIVERSE CULTURAL, ECONOMIC, AND SOCIAL ISSUES that produced antagonisms between rural and urban Democrats in the decade following the First World War divided the Missouri Democracy and relegated the party to minority status throughout most of the twenties. The breakup of the party's once dominant coalition of rural, old-stock citizens and the Irish of the cities began in 1919 when a fierce internecine battle erupted over the League of Nations. Disagreement over the question of the United States' participation in the World Court in 1925 and 1926 revived the quarrel between rural Wilson Democrats and the anti-League Irish Democrats, but by the mid-twenties conflict over domestic issues such as farm relief legislation, Ku Kluxism, and prohibition had become more important sources of controversy among Democrats.

The national prominence of Senator James A. Reed gave added significance to the party's battles in Missouri. Reed, the leading Democratic opponent of the League of Nations, provided forceful, unwavering opposition to the new world order. This in itself was enough to bring down upon the Democratic irreconcilable the wrath of President Wilson, but because the President and his supporters conducted the fight for the League along responsible party lines, Reed's opposition was regarded by the Wilson men as party treason. Consequently, the President became a participant in the efforts of Wilson Democrats in Missouri to read the independent Senator out of the party, and the Wilson-Reed feud, central to the disruption of the Missouri Democracy, had its disturbing effect upon national Democratic politics. Despite strong opposition from pro-League Democrats and Wilson himself, the Senator from Missouri won renomination and re-election in 1922, but the presidential nomination to which Reed aspired evaded his grasp. Nevertheless, in 1924, 1928, and again in 1932, Reed played an influential role in the party's selection of a presidential nominee.

Prohibition proved to be an issue with many ramifications in the politics of the dry decade, but its major effects were twofold. Its first effect was as a persistently disruptive factor in both parties, since it reversed the traditional partisan response of many Democrats and Republicans. It became almost axiomatic that when a wet candidate faced a dry opponent, the wet would receive the votes of antiprohibitionists in both parties. Senator Reed's success in 1922 resulted largely from the support given him by wet Republicans, and assistance from the same voters helped elect Democrat Harry B. Hawes to a seat in the Senate in 1926. Two years later, the defection of wet German Republicans enabled Al Smith to carry St. Louis and marked the first time a Democratic presidential candidate had obtained a majority there since 1888. Outstate dry Democrats, however, flocked to Hoover, more than offsetting Smith's victory in St. Louis and allowing Hoover to carry the state.

The second major effect of prohibition was evidenced in the senatorial contest of 1932, when the prohibition issue produced the defeat of a dry progressive, Charles M. Hay, and promoted the election of a wet conservative, Bennett Clark. Although Hay's conversion from individualistic, morally oriented reform to mass economic reform was almost complete by 1932, his support of the dry cause over the years obscured his advocacy of advanced liberal programs. Thus, the conservative Clark, an avowed wet, rode the crest of sentiment for repeal of prohibition to victory over Hay.

Later, he triumphed over his wet Republican opponent, Henry W. Kiel.

Despite their senatorial defeats at the hands of Democrats, Republicans were able to place Missouri in the G.O.P. column in presidential and gubernatorial voting throughout the twenties by submerging most of their differences and by capturing the votes of disaffected Democrats. In addition, the influx of southern Negroes into the state during the decade added new voters to the Republican rolls. Negro support for Republican candidates proved crucial in several contests, especially in the gubernatorial election of 1924, when Republican Sam A. Baker gained a narrow victory over Democrat Arthur W. Nelson.

The significance of Negro support for the G.O.P., however, seemed lost on the ascendant Republicans — but not on the Democrats. Capitalizing upon the Negroes' discontent with the policies of the Republican state and national administrations, Democrats campaigned on several fronts in the 1920's to woo the Negro from the G.O.P. The Pendergast organization in Kansas City, with a record of recruitment dating back to the 1880's, attracted Negroes to the Democratic standard in even greater numbers after it gained control of Kansas City's municipal government in 1926. St. Louis Democrats made less spectacular inroads into the Negro Republican ranks, but they broke precedent in 1928 by backing the congressional candidacy of Joseph L. McLemore, thus marking the first time that Democrats anywhere had nominated a Negro for Congress. Many Negroes, impressed by the cultural liberalism of Al Smith, broke with the Republican party in 1928, also. Finally, Democrats in the state legislature were responsible for the introduction and passage of legislation that was important to colored citizens. These efforts of Democrats played a significant part in bringing about a shift of a majority of Missouri's Negro voters to the Democratic party in 1932. The tasks of the state and national

Democratic administrations during the thirties were to expand and enlarge the liberal policies for Negroes that had been initiated and implemented by Missouri's Democrats in the late twenties.

The collapse of "Republican prosperity" in 1929 and the ensuing depression foreshadowed the end of twelve years of unbroken Republican rule in state and nation in 1932. In the fierce fight for party control that preceded the general election, a majority of Missourians rejected the conservative policies of presidential aspirant James A. Reed for the liberalism of Franklin D. Roosevelt. Despite fundamental differences between old and new Jeffersonians over the proper role of the federal and state governments and despite the reluctance of some party members to support the Pendergast-backed candidate for governor, Democrats united for the fall campaign. On election day the party's broadened coalition of farmers, laborers, old-stock Irish and Yankees, Negroes and newer ethnic groups, wets and drys restored Democrats to power. The long era of Republican ascendancy was over.

The primary catalyst in the formation of the coalition that returned Democrats to office in 1933 was the widespread discontent of the voters with the Republican efforts to end the depression. Distressed citizens expected an expanded program of action, and the new state and federal administrations responded. Although Governor Guy B. Park and his Democratic successor Lloyd C. Stark failed to sponsor a comprehensive state-wide new deal for Missouri, a program of direct relief, old-age assistance, and increased state aid for public institutions and education was implemented, financed by old taxes and a new general sales tax that was inaugurated in 1934.[1] Moreover, Missouri welcomed nearly one billion dollars in federal monies that were pumped into the state by the Roosevelt Administration from 1933 to 1937 to promote relief, recovery, and reform.[2]

The patronage that accompanied the federal funds became

a powerful tool in the hands of Democratic politicians, particularly Kansas City Boss Tom Pendergast. According to Lyle W. Dorsett, Boss Tom received control of all federal work relief in the state;[3] Pendergast's politics at the convention had paid off. Further, through his influence with Governor Park, Pendergast gained a large share of state patronage. Combined federal and state patronage, then, aided the Kansas City machine to exercise power on a state-wide basis after 1932.[4]

One of the chief beneficiaries of the powerful Pendergast organization was Harry S Truman. Although Truman's assets as an efficient administrator in Jackson County won him state-wide recognition and support before his senatorial campaign of 1934, the backing of the machine that year enabled Truman to achieve a victory over two other candidates in the Democratic primary. In the general election, Truman's endorsement of Roosevelt's New Deal helped him to achieve an easy victory over the reactionary Republican incumbent, Roscoe C. Patterson.[5]

Old Wilson Democrats, unsuccessful in their efforts to gain elective office during the twenties, also came into their own with the inauguration of the state and national Democratic administrations. Breckinridge Long won appointment as Ambassador to Italy, Ewing Y. Mitchell became Assistant Secretary of Commerce, and Charles M. Hay, after serving as Counselor of St. Louis during the early thirties, accepted at different times a number of legal and administrative assignments from the Roosevelt Administration.[6]

Pendergast politics and New Deal programs, however, did not sweep everything in their path. Senator Bennett Clark, angry with the Roosevelt Administration's channeling of patronage through Pendergast and unhappy with the President's expansion of government, became an early member of the conservative coalition in Congress.[7] Former Senator James A. Reed expressed his disagreement with the New Deal by providing leadership in the conservative Liberty League and by forming the anti-Roosevelt National Jeffersonians. During the presidential campaign of 1936 Reed campaigned for Landon in Maine and against Roosevelt everywhere. Both rural and urban conservative Democrats, a definite minority of the party, followed Reed away from Roosevelt into the Republican camp.[8]

By 1936 the Democratic state political pot, too, came to a boil again when an avowed anti-Pendergast Democrat, William Hirth, lost a closely contested gubernatorial nomination to the machine-supported candidate, Lloyd C. Stark. Shortly after Stark took office, however, he initiated action to curb the power of the Pendergast organization. Eventually, Tom himself, promoter of a fraudulent insurance scheme and evader of the federal income tax, received a prison sentence in 1939, thus terminating his influence as a Democratic leader.[9]

The demise of the boss's influence had its expected impact upon Missouri politics. In the state's Democracy, power shifted away from Kansas City to St. Louis, a Democratic city since the municipal election of 1933. In the senatorial contest of 1940, only Harry S Truman's unblemished record as an ardent New Dealer prevented his defeat. In the gubernatorial race, St. Louisan Lawrence McDaniel found the incubus of his association with Pendergast too much to overcome; Forrest C. Donnell won the governorship in an extremely close race and became the state's only Republican chief executive in the three decades since 1932. Later in the forties, when Donnell and James P. Kem won election to the United States Senate, Missouri was represented by two Republican senators in Washington for the first time since the 1870's. In other senatorial contests since 1932, Missourians elected Democrats Thomas C. Hennings, Jr., Stuart Symington, and Edward V. Long. Another Democrat, Frank P. Briggs, received appointment to the seat in the Senate that was vacated by Harry S Truman when Truman was elected Vice-President in 1944. Except for the mid-forties, when Republicans outnumbered Democrats in both Congress and the state legislature, Democrats dominated the state's congressional delegation and both houses in the Missouri General Assembly.[10]

With the single exception of 1952, when Dwight D. Eisenhower broke the Democrats' hold on the state's presidential electoral votes, a majority of Missourians supported Democratic candidates from Roosevelt to Lyndon B. Johnson. The elevation of Vice-President Harry S Truman to the Presidency upon the death of Franklin D. Roosevelt in 1945 gave Missouri, for the first time in its history, a native son in the White House. Most of President Truman's fellow citizens approved of his leadership; in the presidential election of 1948 only Texas' nearly half-million-vote plurality for Truman exceeded the more than quarter-million-vote margin given him in Missouri.[11]

For the most part, farmers and urban workers remained loyal to the national Democratic ticket, but the most faithful member of the Democratic coalition was the Negro voter. When some farmers and city dwellers shifted back to the Republican party in the forties and fifties, Negroes continued to support the party of the New Deal and the Fair Deal.[12] Not only did the percentage of Negro voters who cast Democratic ballots increase steadily after the initial defection from the G.O.P. in the 1920's, but the Negro population itself, fed by unceasing migration of Negroes from the Deep South to St. Louis, Kansas City, and other Missouri cities, grew by leaps and bounds. In the decade of the forties, for example, Missouri's white population increased 3 per cent; the increase in the Negro population was 21 per cent. In the mid-sixties Negroes constituted more than 30 per cent of St. Louis' population, and one in five Kansas Citians was colored. Continuing liberal policies for the Negro's welfare was the cement that bonded the Negro to the Democracy and helped keep the cities in the Democratic camp.[13]

While the coalition that brought Democrats to power in Missouri and in the nation in 1933 has suffered both election setbacks and continuing defections and dissension, it has been sufficiently broad enough to maintain a durable majority that is capable of dominating political life in the United States.

NOTES

INTRODUCTION

1. Arthur S. Link, "What Happened to Progressivism in the 1920's?" *American Historical Review*, 64 (July, 1959), 834.

2. Professor Link provides a representative sampling of the recently published literature of the twenties in his essay, 834–35; for an excellent bibliographical essay on the literature of the twenties, see Burl Noggle, "The Twenties: A New Historiographical Frontier," *Journal of American History*, 53 (September, 1966), 299–314.

3. Frank Freidel, *Franklin D. Roosevelt:* Vol. II, *The Ordeal,* and Vol. III, *The Triumph.* Although Freidel's volumes remain the best comprehensive account of Democratic politics during the twenties, other scholars have made recent additions to the literature. Among the articles (the following list is not intended to be complete) are: Lee N. Allen, "The McAdoo Campaign for the Presidential Nomination in 1924," *Journal of Southern History,* 29 (May, 1963), 211–28, and "The Underwood Presidential Movement of 1924," *Alabama Review,* 15 (April, 1958), 83–93; David B. Burner, "The Breakup of the Wilson Coalition of 1916," *Mid-America,* 45 (January, 1963), 18–35, "The Democratic Party in the Election of 1924," *Mid-America,* 46 (April, 1964), 92–113, and "The Brown Derby Campaign," *New York History,* 46 (October, 1965), 356–80; William G. Carleton, "The Politics of the Twenties," *Current History,* 47 (October, 1964), 210–15, 242; Paul A. Carter, "The Campaign of 1928 Re-examined: A Study in Political Folklore," *Wisconsin Magazine of History,* 46 (Summer, 1963), 263–72, and "The Other Catholic Candidate: The 1928 Presidential Bid of Thomas J. Walsh," *Pacific Northwest Quarterly,* 55 (January, 1964), 1–8; Robert E. Hennings, "California Democratic Politics in the Period of Republican Ascendancy," *Pacific Historical Review,* 31 (August, 1962), 267–80; Richard Hofstadter, "Could a Protestant Have Beaten Hoover in 1928?" *The Reporter,* 22 (March 17, 1960), 31–33; Nevin E. Neal, "The Smith-Robinson Arkansas Campaign of 1928," *Arkansas Historical Quarterly,* 19 (Spring, 1960), 3–11; James T. Patterson, "F.D.R. and the Democratic Triumph," *Current History,* 47 (October, 1964), 216–20, 243–44; David H. Stratton, "Splattered with Oil: William G. McAdoo and the 1924 Presidential Nomination," *Southwestern Social Science Quarterly,* 44 (June, 1963), 62–75; Richard L. Watson, Jr., "A Political Leader Bolts — F. M. Simmons in the Presidential Election of 1928," *North Carolina Historical Review,* 37 (October, 1960), 516–43. Recent books are: Wesley M. Bagby, *The Road to Normalcy: The Presidential Campaign and Election of 1920;* Stanley Coben, *A. Mitchell Palmer: Politician;* Clarence H. Cramer, *Newton D. Baker: A*

Biography; Dewey W. Grantham, Jr., *The Democratic South*; J. Joseph Huthmacher, *Massachusetts People and Politics, 1919–1933*; Burl A. Noggle, *Teapot Dome: Oil and Politics in the 1920's*; Elmer L. Puryear, *Democratic Party Dissension in North Carolina, 1928–1936*; Alfred B. Rollins, Jr., *Roosevelt and Howe*; Gene Smith, *When the Cheering Stopped: The Last Years of Woodrow Wilson*.

4. Recently, two historians of the 1920's have called for state and local studies of politics to provide more nearly conclusive information about the role of ethnic factors in the political behavior of the electorate, the impact of prohibition upon politics, and the nature and strength of conservatism and progressivism in the twenties. See John D. Hicks, "Research Opportunities in the 1920's," *The Historian*, 25 (November, 1962), 1–13, and J. Joseph Huthmacher, "Urban Liberalism and the Age of Reform," *Mississippi Valley Historical Review*, 64 (September, 1962), 231–41. I have been greatly influenced by Huthmacher's study, *Massachusetts People and Politics, 1919–1933*, particularly by his analysis of the role of ethnic factors in politics.

5. Lee N. Allen, "The McAdoo Campaign," 216–17.

6. For a critical discussion of the sectional and rural-urban hypotheses of politics, see William Diamond, "Urban and Rural Voting in 1896," *American Historical Review*, 46 (January, 1941), 281–305; Samuel J. Eldersveld, "Influence of Metropolitan Party Pluralities on Presidential Elections Since 1920," *American Political Science Review*, 43 (December, 1949), 1189–1206; Carl N. Degler, "American Political Parties and the Rise of the City: An Interpretation," *Journal of American History*, 51 (June, 1964), 41–59; and V. O. Key, Jr., *Politics, Parties, and Pressure Groups*, 250–79. These and other factors, especially ethnic, are also presented in Samuel Lubell, *The Future of American Politics*.

CHAPTER 1

1. Centennial speech of James A. Reed, *Kansas City Star*, August 9, 1921; see also Walter Williams, *The State of Missouri: An Autobiography*, 6, 9.

2. "An Open Letter to Mr. Alfred E. Smith of New York and Mr. William G. McAdoo of California," Jefferson City *Daily Capital-News*, March 1, 1927.

3. John H. Fenton, *Politics in the Border States*: . . . , 8-11; Floyd C. Shoemaker, *History of Missouri and Missourians*, 278–79, 291–92.

4. Homer Clevenger, "Missouri Becomes a Doubtful State," *Mississippi Valley Historical Review*, 39 (March, 1943), 542–46.

5. Clevenger, "Missouri Becomes a Doubtful State," 551–52.

6. Clevenger, "Missouri Becomes a Doubtful State," 549–55; State of Missouri, *Official Manual of Missouri for the Years 1919–1920*, 412, 417–18. Cited hereafter as *Official Manual* for specific years.

7. United States Department of Commerce, Bureau of the Census, *Negroes in the United States: 1920–1932*, 9–12; *St. Louis Argus*, January 9, 1925.

8. Lyle W. Dorsett, "Alderman Jim Pendergast," *Bulletin of the Missouri Historical Society*, 20 (October, 1964), 9; Franklin D. Mitchell, "Embattled Democracy: Missouri Democratic Politics, 1918–1932," unpublished doctoral dissertation, University of Missouri, Chap. 6; Bureau of the Census, *Negroes in the United States, 1920–1932*, 24.

9. United States Department of Commerce, Bureau of the Census, *Fourteenth Census of the United States, 1920 (State Compendium, Missouri, 1921)*, 30, 31, 51, 53–55; Shoemaker, *History of Missouri and Missourians*, 290–91.

10. Foreign-born voters of northern European origins predominated in both cities. Kansas City's 10,148 foreign-born citizens, by nationality, included 1,906 Germans, 1,348 Russians, 1,186 Irish, 970 Italians, and 845 English (*Kansas City Times*, October 29, 1924). The 29,141 foreign-born citizens of St. Louis, by nationality, included 11,681 Germans, 3,512 Austrians, 3,231 Irish, 3,036 Russians, 1,803 English, 1,136 Italians, and 601 Canadians (*St. Louis Globe-Democrat*, October 23, 1924). "Foreign-born," as used here, refers to naturalized citizens born outside the United States.

11. Bureau of the Census, *Fourtenth Census (State Compendium, Missouri)*, 4–6, 135 ff.; *Negroes in the United States, 1920–1932*, 24; Fenton, *Politics in the Border States*, 160–61, 163–64.

12. William S. Rossiter, *Increase of Population in the United States, 1910–1920*, Census Monographs, I, 66–68.

13. United States Department of Commerce, Bureau of the Census, *Abstract of the Fourteenth Census of the United States: 1920*, 886.

14. Rossiter, *Increase of Population in the United States*.

15. Bureau of the Census, *Abstract of the Fourteenth Census*, 500, 504, 920–22, 1169.

16. Bureau of the Census, *Abstract of the Fourteenth Census*, 569–70.

17. United States Department of Commerce, Bureau of the Census, *Religious Bodies: 1926*, I, *passim*.

18. Arthur M. Hyde to Lloyd E. Worner, Jr., August 11, 1943, Lloyd E. Worner, Jr., Letters (Western Historical Manuscripts Collection, University of Missouri); Robert P. Friedman, "The Candidate Speaks: Arthur M. Hyde," *Missouri Historical Review*, 61 (October, 1966), 51–61; Floyd C. Shoemaker, *Missouri and Missourians: Land of Contrasts and People of Achievement*, III, 84–85.

19. Louis G. Geiger, *Joseph W. Folk of Missouri*, Chap. 3; Ernest Kirschten, *Catfish and Crystal: The Bicentenary Edition of the St. Louis Story*, Chap. 25; Fenton, *Politics in the Border States*, 128–29; William Rufus Jackson, *Missouri Democracy: A History of the Party and its Representative Members — Past and Present*, *passim*. Voters elected Clark to the United States Senate in 1932; Dickmann won the contest for Mayor of St. Louis in 1933.

20. Bureau of the Census, *Abstract of the Fourteenth Census*, 110; Bureau of the Census, *Religious Bodies: 1926*, I, 66. Protestants comprised 60 per cent of the total church membership in Kansas City; a large number of citizens who claimed no church membership were unaffiliated Protestants.

21. William M. Reddig, *Tom's Town: Kansas City and the Pendergast Legend*, 33–34.

22. Dorsett, "Alderman Jim Pendergast," 3–14.

23. "James A. Reed," *National Cyclopaedia of American Biography*, 34, 9–11.

24. Reddig, *Tom's Town*, 50–51, 66–67.

25. Reddig, *Tom's Town*, 98–100; *Missouri Democrat* (Kansas City), April 19, 1929; Dorsett, "Kansas City Politics: A Study of Boss Pendergast's Machine," *Arizona and the West*, 8 (Summer, 1966), 107–18.

26. Reddig, *Tom's Town*, 35–37, 115–22; Charles P. Blackmore, "Joseph

B. Shannon, Political Boss and Twentieth Century 'Jefferson'," unpublished doctoral dissertation, Columbia University, *passim.*

27. My description of Missouri's political areas draws heavily upon the analyses provided in three sources: Fenton, *Politics in the Border States,* Chap. 7; Morran D. Harris, "Political Trends in Missouri, 1900–1954," unpublished Master's thesis, University of Missouri, *passim*; and Robert M. Crisler, "Missouri's 'Little Dixie'," *Missouri Historical Review,* 42 (January, 1948), 130–39.

28. Charles G. Sellers, Jr., "Who Were the Southern Whigs?" *American Historical Review,* 59 (January, 1954), 341.

29. *Biographical Directory of the American Congress, 1774–1961,* 658, 698.

30. Jackson, *Missouri Democracy,* I, 525; *Kansas City Star,* September 2, 1926.

31. Harry S Truman, *Memoirs,* Vol. I, *Year of Decisions,* 220.

32. "Arthur Mastick Hyde," *National Cyclopaedia of Biography,* B, 182–83; Henry Taylor, Jr., and W. A. Bingham, *A General History of Shelby County, Missouri,* 123; Reddig, *Tom's Town,* 100–101, 140–41.

33. Walter B. Williams and Floyd C. Shoemaker, eds., *Missouri, Mother of the West: Missouri Biography,* Vol. I, 8, 9.

34. *Biographical Directory of the American Congress, 1774–1961,* 1433.

35. Fenton, *Politics in the Border States,* 160–61.

36. V. O. Key, Jr., *American State Politics: An Introduction,* 217–18.

CHAPTER 2

1. Arthur S. Link, *Wilson,* Vol. V, *Campaigns for Progressivism and Peace, 1916–1917,* 8, 38–48, 135–36.

2. Arthur S. Link, *Wilson the Diplomatist,* 154–55; see also Richard L. Watson, Jr., "Woodrow Wilson and His Interpreters," *Mississippi Valley Historical Review,* 44 (September, 1957), 207–36.

3. "James A. Reed," *National Cyclopaedia of American Biography,* 34, 9–11; Bert A. Smith, "The Senatorial Career of James A. Reed," unpublished Master's thesis, University of Missouri, Chaps. 1–3; Ralph A. Stone, "Two Illinois Senators Among the Irreconcilables," *Mississippi Valley Historical Review,* 50 (December, 1963), 464.

4. Arthur S. Link, *Wilson,* Vol. II, *The New Freedom,* 145–47; E. David Cronon, "Woodrow Wilson," in *America's Ten Greatest Presidents,* Morton Borden, ed., 209 ff.; James MacGregor Burns, *The Deadlock of Democracy: Four-Party Politics in America,* 119–23, 130–36, 142–47.

5. Link, *Wilson, The New Freedom,* 147.

6. Burns, *The Deadlock of Democracy,* 132–33, 143–47.

7. *Congressional Record,* 65th Cong., 1st Sess., June 14, 1917, 3598. Reed, of course, was espousing the concept of the proper relationship between a legislator and his constituents, pronounced in the eighteenth century by the British statesman Edmund Burke.

8. Charles G. Ross, "Reed of Missouri," *Scribner's,* 83 (February, 1928), 151–52.

9. Smith, "The Senatorial Career of James A. Reed," 28–31; Ruth Towne,

"The Public Career of William Joel Stone," unpublished doctoral dissertation, University of Missouri, 237.

10. Editorials, *St. Louis Republic*, June 18, 25, July 19, 1917. In its editorial of July 19, 1917, the *Republic* (owned by David R. Francis, one-time governor of Missouri, a political foe of Senator Reed, and U. S. Ambassador to Czarist Russia) contended that "in his present attitude, Reed does not represent ten per cent of the people of Missouri, excluding alien enemies and traitors."

11. Excerpt quoted in the *Kansas City Star*, August 24, 1917.

12. George Soule, "Concerning Senator Reed," *The New Republic*, 14 (March 23, 1918), 237.

13. Lee A. Meriwether, *Jim Reed: "Senatorial Immortal,"* 62–65; Smith, "The Senatorial Career of James A. Reed," 48; *Kansas City Star*, March 18, 1919.

14. *St. Louis Star*, January 8, 1919.

15. One indication of sentiment for the League in the spring of 1919 is afforded by the *Literary Digest* poll of daily newspapers in the country. Newspapers in the north central states section, which included Missouri, responded as follows when asked their opinion of American entrance into the League: 85 "yes," 29 "no," and 70 "conditional." "Nation-Wide Press Poll on the League of Nations," *Literary Digest*, 61 (April 5, 1919), 15.

16. Jefferson City *Daily Capital-News*, March 11, 1919. Spencer was elected to the Senate in November, 1918, to serve out the remaining two years of Senator Stone's term. Stone died in April, 1918; Democrat Zenophon P. Wilfley served from Stone's death to Spencer's election. *Biographical Directory of the American Congress, 1774–1961*, 1638, 1816.

17. Jefferson City *Daily Capital-News*, March 14, 1919.

18. *Kansas City Star*, March 18, 1919.

19. Jefferson City *Daily Capital-News*, March 19, 1919.

20. Jefferson City *Daily Capital-News*, March 20, 1919.

21. *St. Louis Star*, March 21, 1919.

22. Jefferson City *Daily Capital-News*, March 22, 1919.

23. *Kansas City Star*, March 20, 1919.

24. *Kansas City Star*, March 21, 1919.

25. *Kansas City Star*, March 21, 1919.

26. Bernard M. Garfinkel, "The Political Career of Charles Martin Hay," unpublished Master's thesis, University of Missouri, Chap. 2; *St. Louis Star*, March 19, 1919.

27. *Kansas City Star*, May 26, 1919.

28. *Kansas City Star*, June 1, 1919; *St. Louis Star*, May 20, 1919.

29. *Kansas City Star*, June 1, 1919.

30. *Kansas City Star*, June 1, 1919.

31. *Kansas City Star*, June 1, 2, 1919.

32. Tumulty to Wilson, March 26, 1919, Joseph P. Tumulty Papers (Library of Congress).

33. Wilson to Edward J. Goltra, April 16, 1919, Woodrow Wilson Papers (Library of Congress).

34. Goltra to Wilson, May 20, 1919, Wilson Papers.

35. Wilson to Goltra, May 20, 1919, Wilson Papers.

36. Goltra to Tumulty, June 4, Wilson to Tumulty, June 4, 5, 7, 10, 14, 1919, Wilson Papers.

37. *Kansas City Star*, August 1, 1919.

38. Wilson to Goltra, August 11, 1919, Wilson Papers.

39. Thomas A. Bailey, *Woodrow Wilson and the Great Betrayal*, 23–28.

40. *St. Louis Globe-Democrat*, August 9, 1919.

41. *St. Louis Star*, August 11, 1919.

42. *Kansas City Star*, August 8, 1919; *St. Louis Globe-Democrat*, August 1, 1919.

43. *St. Louis Globe-Democrat*, August 12, 1919.

44. *St. Louis Globe-Democrat*, August 12, 1919.

45. Goltra to Francis, August 15, 1919, David R. Francis Papers (Missouri Historical Society, St. Louis).

46. *St. Louis Star*, July 24, 1919; Wesley M. Bagby, *The Road to Normalcy: The Presidential Campaign and Election of 1920*, 154–55. See also pre-election analysis: *St. Louis Star*, October 5, 30, 1920, and *St. Louis Globe-Democrat*, October 30, 1920.

47. *St. Louis Star*, August 12, 1919.

48. *St. Louis Star*, August 22, 1919; *St. Louis Globe-Democrat*, August 12, 1919.

49. *St. Louis Star*, August 22, 1919.

50. John M. Blum, *Joe Tumulty and the Wilson Era*, 207–10.

51. Wilson to Goltra, September 3, 1919, Wilson Papers; *St. Louis Star*, September 5, 6, 1919.

52. *St. Louis Star*, September 6, 1919.

53. *St. Louis Star*, September 9, 1919.

54. *St. Louis Star*, September 12, 1919.

55. Bailey, *Wilson and the Great Betrayal*, 114, 132–33, Chaps. 11–12.

56. Long to Edward M. House, August 28, 1919, Edward M. House Papers (Yale University Library).

CHAPTER 3

1. Thomas A. Bailey, *Woodrow Wilson and the Great Betrayal*, 216–17.

2. Long to F. W. Bronaugh, January 16, 1920, Bronaugh-Bushnell Papers (Western Historical Manuscripts Collection, University of Missouri).

3. William Rufus Jackson, *Missouri Democracy: A History of the Party And Its Representative Members — Past and Present*, III, 515–16; James F. Watts, Jr., "The Public Life of Breckinridge Long," unpublished doctoral dissertation, University of Missouri, Chaps. 1–2.

4. Long Diary, March 3, 1919, 62, Breckinridge Long Papers (Library of Congress).

5. Long Diary, March 20, 1919, 79, Long Papers.

6. Although a draft of the Wilson plan has been dated January 26, 1920, by the Library of Congress' custodian of the Wilson papers, John M. Blum has shown that the proposal had its inception in December, 1919. See his *Joe Tumulty and the Wilson Era*, 232–33, 315.

7. Bailey, *Wilson and the Great Betrayal*, 214–15.

8. *St. Louis Star*, January 13, 1920.

9. *St. Louis Star*, January 15, 1920.

10. Bailey, *Wilson and the Great Betrayal*, 215.

11. *St. Louis Star*, January 14, 17, 1920.

12. *St. Louis Post-Dispatch*, February 9, 1920; *St. Louis Star*, January 20, 30, February 21, 1920.

13. *St. Louis Globe-Democrat*, February 27, 1920.

14. *St. Louis Star*, January 29, 30, March 22, 1920.

15. At the State Convention Reed received the support of the entire Kansas City delegation and all or part of the delegation from Carroll, Platte, Randolph, Knox, and St. Louis counties. The City of St. Louis' twenty-eight wards gave Reed unanimous support except for Wards 13, 17, 25, 26, and 28. *St. Louis Star*, April 22, 1920; *Kansas City Star*, April 23, 1920.

16. *Independence Examiner*, April 22, 23, 1920; *Kansas City Post*, April 22, 1920; *St. Louis Star*, April 22, 23, 1920.

17. *Kansas City Times*, May 11, 1920.

18. *Kansas City Star*, June 28, July 3, 4, 5, 6, 1920.

19. *Kansas City Star*, June 29, 1920.

20. *St. Louis Star*, July 9, 15, 1920.

21. State of Missouri, *Official Manual, 1921–1922*, 489–90, 492.

22. James M. Cox, *Journey Through My Years*, 405.

23. Diary, August 8, 1920, 38–39, Long Papers.

24. *St. Louis Star*, October 11, 18, 1920.

25. *Kansas City Post*, October 13, 1920.

26. *Kansas City Post*, October 27, 1920; *Kansas City Star*, October 13, 1920; *St. Louis Star*, October 16, 1920.

27. Reed also supported Spencer's charge that Wilson had promised at Versailles to send American troops to guarantee the boundaries of Rumania, in case of attack. This charge brought public denials from both Presidential Secretary Tumulty and President Wilson. *St. Louis Star*, October 12, 22, 1920; Blum, *Joe Tumulty and the Wilson Era*, 253.

28. *St. Louis Star*, October 25, 1920.

29. *St. Louis Star*, October 23, 1920; *Kansas City Post*, October 24, 1920.

30. *St. Louis Star*, October 14, November 1, 1920.

31. *St. Louis Star*, October 14, 1920.

32. Since Frank Freidel wrote that "there is nothing to indicate that anti-League Irish and Germans deserted the Democratic party in any greater proportion than the population as a whole [in the 1920 election]," *(Franklin D. Roosevelt*, Vol. II, *The Ordeal*, 88), at least two scholars have taken exception. J. Joseph Huthmacher, in *Massachusetts People and Politics, 1919–1933*, argues that this conclusion overlooks the matter of relative degree of voter participation. His analysis of political records of Massachusetts cities reveals that Irish and new immigrant people failed to register and vote, while old-stock Republicans flocked to the registration booths and polls. This indifference, Huthmacher concludes, constituted party desertion (42 ff.). Similar conclusions for Boston, Chicago, and New York City have been reached by David B. Burner ("The Breakup of the Wilson Coalition of 1916," *Mid-America*, 45 (January, 1963), 30 ff.). The lack of data prevents a similar analysis for Kansas City and St. Louis, since either voter registration records or precinct returns, or both, are not available for the 1920's. Austin Hill, Deputy Secretary of State, to author, March 4, 1964; Harry Leitz, Director of Elections, St. Louis, to author, February 26, 1964.

33. *Official Manual, 1921–1922*, 31–35, 77, 80, 297–309; Hawes also made known his views against prohibition, received the support of retiring Eleventh District Congressman William I. Igoe, and spent $9,135 on his campaign, while his Republican opponent spent less than $500. *St. Louis Star*, November 8, December 1, 1920.

34. Wesley M. Bagby, *The Road to Normalcy: The Presidential Campaign and Election of 1920*, 141–58, 161; Duane Meyer, *The Heritage of Missouri: A History*, 586; Lloyd E. Worner, Jr., "Missouri and the National Election of 1920," unpublished Master's thesis, University of Missouri, 182–84.

35. Bailey, *Wilson and the Great Betrayal*, 338–39; Long Diary, 1920, 40, Long Papers; *St. Louis Star*, November 3, 1920.

CHAPTER 4

1. *St. Louis Globe-Democrat*, November 21, 1920.

2. *St. Louis Star*, October 23, 1920; *Kansas City Post*, October 25, 1920.

3. Long Diary, 1922, 11, Breckinridge Long Papers; Lee A. Meriwether, *Jim Reed: "Senatorial Immortal,"* 109. Meriwether quotes Reed as telling J. L. Baity, the Senator's private secretary, in the spring of 1922 that he would not run for re-election, since "I can never win in the face of Wilson's bitter opposition, and I am tired of the struggle, tired of being misunderstood" (106). While Reed indicated to friends that he might retire, his activities in late 1921 and early 1922 suggest that he planned to seek renomination with the strong conviction that he could win a third term in the Senate. See William Rufus Jackson, *Missouri Democracy: A History of the Party and Its Representative Members — Past and Present*, I, 339.

4. See Folder 8, Charles M. Hay Papers (Western Historical Manuscripts Collection, University of Missouri); Long Diary, 1922, 11–12, Long Papers.

5. Long Papers; Breckinridge Long to Edward M. House, November 5, 1920, Edward M. House Papers.

6. Hay to George Stivers, April 19, 1922, Hay Papers; William T. Kemper to David R. Francis, April 14, 1922, Edward F. Goltra Papers (Missouri Historical Society, St. Louis).

7. Hay to A. C. Parsons, March 23, 1922, Hay Papers.

8. The best critical account of Wilson's formulation of the doctrine of responsible party government is Austin Ranney, *The Doctrine of Responsible Party Government: Its Origins and Present State*, Chap. 3.

9. *St. Louis Star*, January 1, 8, 1922; *St. Louis Globe-Democrat*, January 8, 1922.

10. *St. Louis Star*, March 21, 1922; *St. Louis Globe-Democrat*, March 22, 1922.

11. *St. Louis Star*, March 22, 1922.

12. Long to Wilson, February 9, 1922, Long Papers.

13. *St. Louis Globe-Democrat*, May 8, 1922. In a letter to John C. Higdon, a St. Louis patent attorney and twice an unsuccessful seeker of the Democratic senatorial nomination, Wilson urged the aspirant "not to complicate the contest in Missouri" by becoming a candidate for the nomination. "If you believe in my political leadership, Wilson wrote, "I think it will be wise for you to accept . . . [my advice]." Robert I. Young, St. Joseph farmer and political unknown, entered the senatorial race, but the press largely ignored his candidacy so that the contest remained essentially a two-man race. In

the 1922 primary election Young polled 9,979 votes. *St. Louis Star*, May 3, 1922; *Official Manual, 1923–1924*, 306–7.

14. Long to Wilson, March 25, 1922, Long Papers.
15. Wilson to Long, March 28, 1922, Long Papers.
16. Wilson to Long, March 28, 1922, Long Papers.
17. Long asked Wilson for permission to use the letter denouncing Reed at an appropriate time in the primary campaign. (Long to Wilson, April 1, 1922, Long Papers.) Wilson, however, never gave his consent; consequently, the letter was never public during the 1922 campaign.
18. Long to Wilson, April 3, 1922, Long Papers.
19. John Randolph Bolling to Long, April 6, 1922, Long Papers.
20. Wilson to Long, April 5, 1922, Long Papers.
21. For Meriwether's account of the episode, see his biography of Reed, *Jim Reed: "Senatorial Immortal,"* 49–50, 112–14.
22. *St. Louis Globe-Democrat*, April 18, 1922. "I beg that you will do me the courtesy of publishing this letter," Wilson wrote the editor of the *Globe-Democrat*.
23. *St. Louis Globe-Democrat*, April 18, 1922; editorial, *St. Louis Star*, April 18, 1922. For another view of Reed's role in the framing of the Federal Reserve bill, see Arthur S. Link, *Wilson*, Vol. II, *The New Freedom*, 51–52.
24. *St. Louis Globe-Democrat*, April 19, 1922.
25. Long Diary, 1922, 20–23, Long Papers; *St. Louis Star*, April 28, 1922, editorial, May 6, 1922.
26. Meriwether, *Jim Reed*, 114–17; *St. Louis Star*, May 5, 6, 1922.
27. Jefferson City *Democrat-Tribune*, May 6, 1922.
28. *St. Louis Globe-Democrat*, May 8, 1922.
29. *St. Louis Globe-Democrat*, May 10, 21, 1922.
30. *St. Louis Globe-Democrat*, June 4, 1922.
31. See Ranney, *The Doctrine of Responsible Party Government*, Chap. 3.
32. *St. Louis Globe-Democrat*, June 2, 14, 17, July 15, 16, 1922; *Kansas City Times*, July 6, 1922.
33. *St. Louis Star*, July 16, 1922; Jack M. Bain, "A Rhetorical Criticism of the Speeches of James A. Reed," unpublished doctoral dissertation, University of Missouri, 104–6; *St. Louis Globe-Democrat*, July 4, 1922. In St. Louis, Mrs. Nat Brown organized a Reed-for-Senator-Club to offset the effects of the "Rid-Us-Of-Reed" group. The literature of both organizations may be found in Box 1, Goltra Papers. During the general election campaign, newswoman Mrs. W. W. Henderson of LaPlata often traveled with the Reed campaigners and spoke in the Senator's behalf. *St. Louis Star*, October 25, 1922.
34. *St. Louis Globe-Democrat*, July 5, 1922; *Missouri Farmer*, 14, (June 15, 1922), 1, 9, 12.
35. *Missouri Farmer*, 14 (June 15, 1922), 3, 8, 9, 12; (July 1, 1922), 3, 4, 8; (July 15, 1922), 4.
36. Long Diary, 1922, 5, 48–56, Long Papers.
37. Long Diary, 54–56; Long Papers; *St. Louis Globe-Democrat*, June 7, 1922; *St. Louis Star*, July 21, 1922.
38. See Chap. 2.
39. *Official Manual, 1919–1920*, 427. St. Louisans voted against a state dry law 102,736 to 14,510.
40. *St. Louis Star*, January 5, 1920.

41. *St. Louis Star*, March 25, 1922; *St. Louis Globe-Democrat*, May 18, June 17, July 16, 1922.

42. *St. Louis Globe-Democrat*, June 9, 1922.

43. Long Diary, 1922, 46–48, 50–52, Long Papers.

44. *Kansas City Times*, July 19, 1922.

45. *Kansas City Times*, July 27, 1922.

46. Editorial, *St. Louis Star*, July 28, 1922; *St. Louis Globe-Democrat*, July 21, 1922.

47. W. R. Hollister to Ewing Y. Mitchell, June 20, July 28, 1922, Ewing Young Mitchell Papers (Western Manuscripts Collection, University of Missouri). Hollister called Mitchell's attention to *Revised Statutes of Missouri*, Sections 4839, 4840, and 4841, the laws governing primary election procedures.

48. Long Diary, 1922, 38, Long Papers; *Kansas City Times*, July 20, 1922; *St. Louis Star*, July 21, 1922.

49. *Kansas City Times*, July 21, 1922; *St. Louis Globe-Democrat*, July 21, 1922.

50. *Official Manual, 1923–1924*, 306–7; Morran D. Harris, "Political Trends in Missouri, 1900–1954," unpublished Master's thesis, University of Missouri, *passim*.

51. *St. Louis Star*, August 6, 8, 1922.

52. Many leading Republicans agreed with Long's contention. Attorney-General Jesse W. Barrett, in an appeal to Republicans to support their senatorial nominee, said that if the Republican party owed a debt of gratitude to Jim Reed, "that debt has been more than paid by the thousands of Republicans who went into the Democratic primary and saved his senatorial neck." *St. Louis Star*, October 22, 1922.

53. Long Diary, 1922, 48–55, 71–72, 92, Long Papers; Ranney, *The Doctrine of Responsible Party Government*, Chap. 3.

54. Wilson to Long, April 11, 1922, Long Papers. "There is no use of being afraid of Reed," Wilson wrote, "and if he is gone after without gloves he will do the fearing."

55. *Kansas City Times*, July 6, 1922; *St. Louis Globe-Democrat*, July 6, 7, 1922. Reed had maneuvered Long into the exchange of a pledge of support before Long realized that the primary might not be a true test of Democratic sentiment.

56. *St. Louis Star*, August 9, October 7, 1922; extensive literature and the financial records of the "League of Loyal Democrats" may be found in Box 1, Goltra Papers; Hay to George W. Hay, August 23, 1922, Hay Papers.

57. *St. Louis Star*, October 4, 15, 20, November 3, 1922; *Kansas City Star*, November 5, 1922.

58. *St. Louis Star*, October 1, 15, 17, 24, 1922.

59. *St. Louis Star*, October 6, November 1, 1922.

60. John Randolph Bolling to W. R. Hollister, June 29, 1922, Long Papers. Bolling, personal secretary of the former President, wrote Long's campaign manager that Wilson would "treat every speech of Senator Reed about him with contemptuous silence." Shortly after the November election ex-Governor Lon Stephens made public a letter of October 27 from the former President: "I do not think I ought to attempt any advice as to the election," Wilson wrote Stephens. Despite this disclaimer, the rest of Wilson's letter was an implicit

endorsement of the anti-Reed activities of the League of Loyal Democrats. *St. Louis Post-Dispatch*, November 8, 1922.

61. This is suggested in correspondence between Long and Edward M. House, April 26, 1922, House Papers.

62. Long to Wilson, October 19, 1922, House Papers; *St. Louis Star*, October 16, 1922.

63. *Official Manual, 1923–1924*, 264–67, 270–71, 307–9; *St. Louis Star*, November 8, 9, 1922. One Democrat who did not support Reed was Harry S Truman. Jonathan Daniels quotes Truman as saying: "I never liked Reed. I hated his guts after the way he treated Wilson. I supported him the first two times he ran, but the third time I was against him." Jonathan W. Daniels, *The Man of Independence*, 100.

64. *Official Manual, 1923–1924*, 264. Kansas Citians favored a state dry law in a 1918 referendum by the extremely close vote of 19,473 to 19,457. *Official Manual, 1919–1920*, 427; *Kansas City Star*, November 8, 9, 1922.

65. *St. Louis Globe-Democrat*, November 9, 1922.

66. *Official Manual, 1923–1924*, 306–7; Long Diary, 1922, unnumbered page, November 8, 1922, Long Papers.

67. "Why 'Lone Wolf' Reed Came Back," *Literary Digest*, 74 (August, 1922), 15–16.

CHAPTER 5

1. United States Bureau of the Census, *Negro Population: 1790–1915*, 49, 93; United States Bureau of the Census, *Negroes in the United States: 1920–1932*, 24, 26, 32, 761–66. The out-of-state Negroes who migrated to southeast Missouri and St. Louis came principally from Mississippi and Arkansas. The Negroes who migrated to Kansas City came mainly from Arkansas and Texas (36); State of Missouri, *Biennial Report of the Missouri Negro Industrial Commission, 1923–1924, 1925–1926*, 77.

2. John H. Fenton, *Politics in the Border States*, 160–61; United States Bureau of the Census, *Negroes in the United States*, 761–66.

3. Lyle W. Dorsett, "Alderman Jim Pendergast," unpublished Master's thesis, University of Kansas City, 37, 55–56, 61.

4. Paul Bestor to Arthur M. Hyde, November 8, 1922; C. F. Bloker to Arthur M. Hyde, March 1, 1923, Arthur M. Hyde Papers (Western Historical Manuscripts Collection, University of Missouri).

5. Hyde to Harry M. Daugherty, September 28, October 8, 1923, Hyde Papers.

6. See the editorials in the Charleston *Enterprise-Courier*, October 18, November 15, 1923, October 16, 30, 1924, and the Caruthersville *Democrat-Argus*, November 21, 1924.

7. J. H. Whitecotton to Francis Wilson, April 9, 1924, Francis M. Wilson Papers (Western Historical Manuscripts Collection, University of Missouri); Ewing Y. Mitchell to Daniel C. Roper, September 12, 1924, Ewing Young Mitchell Papers; Long to House, November 13, 1923, Breckinridge Long Papers.

8. Franklin to Hyde, October 29, 1923, Hyde Papers.

9. Franklin to Hyde, December 8, 1923, Hyde Papers.

10. Hyde to Franklin, November 3, 1923, January 2, 1924, Hyde Papers.

11. *Kansas City Sun*, February 23, 1924.

12. Breckinridge Long to W. R. Hollister, April 14, 1923, Hollister to Long, April 20, 1923, Long Papers. Although Wilson men dominated the state delegation to the 1924 National Democratic Convention, only 2 votes were cast for the minority report that asked for immediate commitment to the League. *St. Louis Globe-Democrat*, June 29, 1924.

13. Statement of Mitchell, February 28, 1924, Mitchell Papers.

14. John Higham, *Strangers in the Land: Patterns of American Nativism, 1860–1925*, 286–99; Francis M. Wilson to J. H. Whitecotton, April 14, 1924, Wilson Papers; *Kansas City Times*, February 28, 1924; *St. Louis Globe-Democrat*, April 17, 1924. In April, 1924, Klan officials in Missouri claimed a membership of 150,000, but most politicians believed that number was too large. A membership of 100,000 seems closer to fact, judging from Klan activities as described in the press of the state and in the two Klan newspapers circulated in Missouri, the *Klan Kourier* (later the *Missouri Kourier*), published in St. Louis, and the St. Joseph *Missouri Valley Independent*. *Kansas City Times*, April 30, 1924.

15. *St. Louis Globe-Democrat*, December 1, 1923.

16. *St. Louis Globe-Democrat*, December 2, 10, 12, 1923.

17. *St. Louis Globe-Democrat*, December 10, 11, 13, 17, 22, 1923.

18. *St. Louis Globe-Democrat*, December 17, 1923, January 15, 1924; Breckinridge Long to Daniel G. Roper, December 11, 1923, Long Papers; George F. Milton, Jr., to William G. McAdoo, December 20, W. R. Hollister to McAdoo, December 14, Hollister to David Rockwell, December 14, 1923, McAdoo to Thomas L. Chadbourne, January 16, 1924, William G. McAdoo Papers (Library of Congress).

19. *Kansas City Times*, January 28, 29, 1924; *St. Louis Globe-Democrat*, January 29, 1924.

20. Charles M. Hay to C. E. Betts, August 6, 1923, Charles M. Hay Papers.

21. *St. Louis Globe-Democrat*, December 17, 1923.

22. *Kansas City Times*, January 29, 1924; Milton L. Fox to McAdoo, January 29, David Rockwell to McAdoo, January 31, 1924, McAdoo Papers.

23. *Kansas City Times*, February 2, 1924; *St. Louis Globe-Democrat*, February 2, 1924; Burl A. Noggle, *Teapot Dome: Oil and Politics in the 1920's*, 234; Lee N. Allen, "The McAdoo Campaign for the Presidential Nomination in 1924," *Journal of Southern History*, 29 (May, 1963), 220; Breckinridge Long to C. C. Oliver, February 1, 1924, Long Papers; David H. Stratton, "Splattered with Oil: William G. McAdoo and the 1924 Presidential Nomination," *Southwestern Social Science Quarterly*, 44 (June, 1963), 65–66.

24. Stratton, "Splattered with Oil," 65–66.

25. *St. Louis Globe-Democrat*, February 3, 1924; *Kansas City Times*, February 4, 1924.

26. *Kansas City Times*, February 2, 1924.

27. Long to C. C. Oliver, February 2, 1924, Oliver to Long, February 2, 1924, Long Papers. Long not only directed the fight against Reed in Missouri, but he also contributed the major portion of the campaign funds. After the state convention Long wrote McAdoo that he had "put up fourteen thousand dollars . . . all done in your name." Long to McAdoo, April 24, 1924, Long Papers.

28. *Kansas City Times*, February 19, 1924.
29. *Kansas City Times*, February 28, 29, March 1, 3, 1924.
30. Long to McAdoo, February 26, 27, David Rockwell to McAdoo, February 26, 28, George F. Milton, Jr., to McAdoo, February 28, 1924, McAdoo Papers.
31. McAdoo to Long, February 26, 27, 1924, McAdoo Papers.
32. McAdoo to Long, February 27, 28, 1924, McAdoo Papers.
33. George F. Milton, Jr., to Brice Claggett, March 3, 1924, McAdoo Papers.
34. Roper to McAdoo, January 24, 26, 1924, McAdoo Papers. Fordyce denied being a party to political blackmail, but admitted that he had called upon Roper and "expressed the hope that Reed would not be opposed in his home state." His remarks, Fordyce explained, were made in answer to questions raised by Roper. *St. Louis Globe-Democrat*, March 3, 4, 1924.
35. *St. Louis Globe-Democrat*, March 3, 1924.
36. *St. Louis Globe-Democrat*, March 10, 1924.
37. *Kansas City Times*, March 24, 1924.
38. *St. Louis Globe-Democrat*, March 8, 1924. While meeting for a post-election analysis of the causes for Reed's defeat, Bennett Champ Clark, Ed Glenn, Samuel Lazarus, and William Igoe concluded that "primarily and chiefly, this infernal Ku Klux Klan outfit is responsible for the result." Clark to Reed, March 12, 1924, James A. Reed Papers (Reed Residence, Kansas City).
39. *St. Louis Globe-Democrat*, April 15, 16, 17, 1924.
40. *St. Louis Globe-Democrat*, June 25, 29, 1924.
41. *St. Louis Globe-Democrat*, June 24, 27, 30, 1924; *Kansas City Times*, July 2, 3, 7, 1924; *Official Report of the Proceedings of the Democratic National Convention, 1924, passim.*
42. Newton C. Gillham to Davis, June 4, 10, Henry L. Jost to Davis, June 18, Xenophon P. Wilfley to Davis, June 18, 1924, John W. Davis Papers (Yale University Library).
43. The source for this account of the gubernatorial primary and general election campaigns is, mainly, John Judson Large, Jr., "The 'Invisible Empire' and Missouri Politics: The Influence of the Revised Ku Klux Klan in the Election of 1924 as Reported in Missouri Newspapers," unpublished Master's thesis, University of Missouri.
44. Although an official of the organization assured Klansmen on the eve of the general election that Nelson would not take orders from Pendergast, it is quite likely that Pendergast agreed to provide Nelson with support in the primary and general elections only if Nelson would agree to appoint Pendergast Democrats to key Kansas City positions, particularly election and police commissioners, and to give the machine a fair share of state patronage. *St. Louis Globe-Democrat*, November 4, 1924; *Official Manual, 1925–1926*, 440–41.
45. *St. Louis Globe-Democrat*, October 23, 1924.
46. *St. Louis Globe-Democrat*, October 29, November 2, 3, 1924; there is some question whether Senator Reed's anti-Klan pronouncements helped or hindered Nelson's campaign. The pro-Klan St. Joseph *Missouri Valley Independent* quite naturally concluded that Reed's denunciation of the Klan had brought about Nelson's defeat; editorial, November 13, 1924.

47. Reed to Davis, October 16, Davis to Reed, October 18, 1924, Davis Papers.

48. *Kansas City Times*, October 4, 11, 1924.

49. Ewing Y. Mitchell to Daniel G. Roper, October 24, 1924, Mitchell Papers.

50. *St. Louis Globe-Democrat*, November 6, 7, 9, 1924; *Official Manual, 1925–1926*, 194, 243–44. One student of the 1924 election has concluded that in the southern and border states, La Follette drew his small vote almost equally from the two parties. David B. Burner, "The Democratic Party in the Election of 1924," *Mid-America*, 46 (April, 1964), 112. However, in St. Louis City and County, where La Follette received 40.1 per cent of his Missouri vote, newspapers reported that German Republicans had supplied much of La Follette's support. *St. Louis Globe-Democrat*, November 8, 1924, and the *St. Louis Post-Dispatch*, November 9, 1924. A St. Louis Socialist newspaper estimated that a third of La Follette's St. Louis vote had come from Socialists; *St. Louis Labor*, November 8, 1924.

51. *Official Manual, 1925–1926*, 243–44.

52. *Kansas City Times*, February 16, 28, March 9, April 14, June 26, August 8, October 4, November 5, 12, 1924; *St. Louis Globe-Democrat*, November 6, 1924. One of the victims of Shannon's bolt was Harry S Truman, Pendergast's candidate for judge of the Jackson County Court. Truman's defeat is a good example of how cultural and social forces played a more important role than economic factors in the 1924 election. Although Truman's excellent record of supervising the expenditures of his office earned him the endorsement of the Republican *Kansas City Star*, the Klan of Jackson County endorsed the Republican candidate. *Kansas City Times*, November 4, 1924. On the other hand, Truman did not have the endorsement of one Klan-proscribed group: The Kansas City National Association for the Advancement of Colored People informed the readers of the Negro newspaper, the *Kansas City Call*, that Truman's reply to their questionnaire was "unsatisfactory." The questions the N.A.A.C.P. asked Truman are not known. *Kansas City Call*, October 31, 1924.

53. St. Louis Wards 4, 5, 6, 20, and 23 housed many of the Negro new-comers to that city and showed substantial Republican gains over their 1920 presidential and gubernatorial vote. *Official Manual, 1921–1922*, 385; *Official Manual, 1925–1926*, 325; editorial, *St. Louis Argus*, November 7, 1924. The heavily Negro-populated Eighth Ward of Kansas City, under the leadership of Irish Democrat Cas Welch, had turned out 300– and 400–vote Democratic majorities in 1920 and 1922. But in 1924 the Eighth Ward went Republican by about 300 votes. Although Welch told his supporters to support Pendergast candidates in 1924, Shannon may have persuaded some of Welch's Negro followers to bolt, thus accounting for the ward's switch to the Republican column.

54. *Official Manual, 1923–1924*, 269; *Official Manual, 1925–1926*, 407. Fulbright to Ralph L. Lozier, November 12, 1924, Ralph L. Lozier Papers (Western Historical Manuscripts Collection, University of Missouri). After the 1924 election several Democratic newspaper editors complained that white Republicans had forced Negroes to vote the G.O.P. ticket. See editorials in the Charleston *Enterprise-Courier*, November 6, 1924, Caruthers-

ville *Democrat-Argus,* November 21, 1924, and the *Dunklin Democrat,* November 14, 1924.

55. Hawes to Ralph L. Lozier, November 13, 1924, Lozier Papers.

56. Editorial, *St. Louis Argus,* November 9, 1923, October 31, 1924.

57. Hawes to Ralph L. Lozier, November 13, 1924, Lozier Papers; *Official Manual, 1925-1926,* 407; *Official Manual, 1923-1924,* 269.

CHAPTER 6

1. See Box 9, Group XI, Franklin D. Roosevelt Papers (Franklin D. Roosevelt Library, Hyde Park); Frank Freidel, *Franklin D. Roosevelt,* Vol II, *The Ordeal,* 201-3.

2. Freidel, *The Ordeal,* 203-13.

3. William Rufus Jackson, *Missouri Democracy: A History of the Party and Its Representative Members — Past and Present,* Vol. II, 114-17; Louis G. Geiger, *Joseph W. Folk of Missouri,* 14-16, 22-27, 129-30.

4. Hawes to Charles M. Hay, February 19, 1926, Charles M. Hay Papers; *St. Louis Post-Dispatch,* September 14, 15, 1925; for a discussion of the national revival of Jeffersonianism during the 1920's, see Merrill D. Peterson, *The Jefferson Image in the American Mind,* 347-55.

5. *Kansas City Times,* April 14, 1925.

6. *Kansas City Times,* February 17, 25, 1925; Charles P. Blackmore, "Joseph B. Shannon, Political Boss and Twentieth Century 'Jefferson,'" unpublished doctoral dissertation, Columbia University, 336-37.

7. Blackmore, "Joseph B. Shannon," 340-42; *Kansas City Star,* September 11, 14, 1925; *Missouri Democrat* (Kansas City), October 23, November 6, 1925. The *Missouri Democrat* came into existence in October, 1925, as a weekly newspaper purporting to be the state organ for the Missouri Democracy. In reality it served as the voice of the Pendergast organization in local and state Democratic politics.

8. *Kansas City Times,* April 8, 1925; *St. Louis Globe-Democrat,* April 4, 6, 8, 9, 1925.

9. Editorials, *St. Louis Argus,* November 7, 1924, February 20, 27, March 6, 20, 27, April 3, 10, 1925; *St. Louis Globe-Democrat,* April 2, 3, 4, 8, 1925. The statement of the St. Louis Colored Democratic Club expressed the feeling of many Negroes toward the outgoing Republican city administration: "The election of Mr. Igoe will be the most stunning blow to the Ku Klux Klan that can be delivered, and it will undo the Jim Crow deviltry of the only Jim Crow city administration that has ever disgraced St. Louis, and it will not lessen one iota the representation that our colored population have in jobs." *St. Louis Argus,* March 27, 1925.

10. "It will be impossible for the Republican party in Missouri to count on the Negro in the future if his real service in 1924 goes unpaid," warned the *Kansas City Call,* January 23, 1925. A few days later the *St. Louis Argus* reminded the Governor "not to forget us," February 6, 1925.

11. *Kansas City Call,* May 8, June 19, 1925.

12. Editorial, *Kansas City Call,* May 22, 1925; editorial, *St. Louis Argus,* July 17, 1925.

13. *St. Louis Globe-Democrat,* June 29, 30, September 16, 1925; *Missouri Democrat,* December 1, 1925.

14. Hay to C. E. Betts, November 12, 1925, Hay Papers.

15. Hay to Ovid Bell, November 2, 1925, Hay Papers; *St. Louis Globe-Democrat*, November 2, 1925; *St. Louis Post-Dispatch*, November 2, 1925.

16. *St. Louis Star*, January 19, 24, 1926; Andrew Sinclair, *Prohibition: The Era of Excess*, 350; *Congressional Record*, 69th Cong., 1st Sess., June 24, 1926, 11858–60. The McNary-Haugen Bill of 1926 provided for the orderly disposal of surplus crops by an agricultural export corporation. In short, it involved the use of federal power to obtain "parity" prices for farm products. John D. Hicks, *Republican Ascendancy, 1921–1933*, 198–99.

17. *St. Louis Globe-Democrat*, April 6, 1920, October 30, 1922; *Congressional Record*, 68th Cong., 2d Sess., June 3, 1924, 10340–41.

18. *Congressional Record*, 68th Cong., 2d Sess., March 3, 1925, 5413.

19. *Congressional Record*, 69th Cong., 1st Sess., January 25, 1926, 2678–79.

20. *Biographical Directory of the American Congress, 1774–1961*, 1820. Hawes to Charles M. Hay, February 19, 1926, Hay Papers; *Missouri Democrat*, April 16, 1926.

21. *Kansas City Times*, April 28, 1926; *St. Louis Star*, April 28, 1926.

22. See Folders 49A and 50A, Box 2, Hay Papers.

23. Charles M. Hay to Willis H. Meredith, December 16, 1925, July 2, 1926, Meredith to Hay, July 9, 1926, Ewing Cockrell to Hay, July 10, 1926, Hay Papers.

24. *Kansas City Times*, June 24, July 1, 1926; *St. Louis Star*, June 18, 25, July 2, 1926.

25. Burger to Charles M. Hay, July 19, 1926, Hay Papers; *Kansas City Times*, July 17, 1926; *St. Louis Star*, July 17, 19, 1926.

26. *Kansas City Times*, July 26, 1926; *St. Louis Star*, June 16, July 17, 1926.

27. *Kansas City Times*, July 1, 1926; *St. Louis Globe-Democrat*, July 8, 13, 15, 23, August 3, 1926; *St. Louis Star*, June 16, 1926.

28. *Missouri Farmer*, 18 (July 15, 1926), 10–11; (August 1, 1926), 8; *Missouri Ruralist*, 68 (August 1, 1926), 2.

29. *Official Manual, 1926–1927*, 298–99.

30. *St. Louis Star*, August 5, 1926.

31. *St. Louis Star*, May 12, 1926; *Kansas City Times*, May 25, 1926; *St. Louis Globe-Democrat*, May 12, 1926.

32. *St. Louis Star*, August 24, 1926; *St. Louis Globe-Democrat*, September 12, 1926; *Official Manual, 1926–1927*, 326, 365.

33. *St. Louis Star*, August 31, September 2, 1926.

34. *St. Louis Star*, August 5, 1926.

35. *St. Louis Globe-Democrat*, August 5, 6, 1926.

36. *St. Louis Star*, October 5, 12, 1926.

37. *St. Louis Star*, October 27, 28, 29, 1926; *St. Louis Globe-Democrat*, October 31, 1926.

38. *St. Louis Star*, September 16, 1926.

39. *Missouri Farmer*, 18 (October 15, 1926), 12; the *Missouri Ruralist* endorsed Williams in its November 1, 1926, issue; the Missouri Farm Bureau Federation did not endorse either candidate. *Missouri Farm Bureau News*, October 29, 1926.

40. *St. Louis Globe-Democrat*, October 31, 1926; *St. Louis Post-Dispatch*, November 1, 1926.

41. *St. Louis Star*, October 22, 27, 28, 29, 1926.
42. *Official Manual, 1924–1925*, 486, 528–29.
43. *Official Manual, 1926–1927*, 325, 366.
44. *St. Louis Globe-Democrat*, April 14, 1926.
45. See pages 64–65; see also the subtle analysis of the Caruthersville *Democrat-Argus* editorial, November 5, 1926.
46. *St. Louis Argus*, July 16, 30, August 6, 1926; *Official Manual, 1926–1927*, 303; *St. Louis Globe-Democrat*, April 14, 1926; *Biographical Directory of the American Congress, 1774–1961*, 841.
47. *St. Louis Argus*, July 16, 30, August 6, 1926; *Official Manual, 1926–1927*, 303.
48. *Missouri Democrat*, October 29, 1926.
49. *Kansas City Call*, October 29, 1926.
50. *Official Manual, 1926–1927*, 192–93; *St. Louis Post-Dispatch*, November 3, 1926; *St. Louis Star*, November 3, 1926; editorial, *St. Louis Argus*, November 5, 1926.
51. *Missouri Democrat*, November 5, 12, 1926. The Pendergast organization had white and colored workers stationed at the polls to prevent illegal voting by Negro Republicans.
52. *Kansas City Call*, November 5, 1926; Democrats captured 27 per cent of the Kansas City Negro vote in 1924. *Missouri Democrat*, March 14, 1929.
53. Editorial, Caruthersville *Democrat-Argus*, November 5, 1926; *Missouri Democrat*, November 19, 1926.
54. *St. Louis Star*, October 18, November 3, 1926.
55. *Missouri Farmer*, 18 (October 15, 1926), 12; *Official Manual, 1926–1927*, 302–3.
56. *Official Manual, 1926–1927*, 294–95.
57. *St. Louis Globe-Democrat*, September 8, 1926; Hay to T. C. Alford, November 26, 1926, Hay Papers.

CHAPTER 7

1. See pages 69–75, 96, 102–03; *St. Louis Star*, September 6, 7, 1926.
2. Bert A. Smith, "The Senatorial Career of James A. Reed," unpublished Master's thesis, University of Missouri, 116–29; Vare was convinced that he was the victim of Reed's presidential ambitions. See Samuel J. Astorino, "The Contested Senate Election of William Scott Vare," *Pennsylvania History*, 28 (April, 1961), 200.
3. Andrew Sinclair, *Prohibition: The Era of Excess*, 277, 300.
4. Frank R. Kent, "Senator 'Jim' Reed," *Forum*, 78 (July, 1927), 66; Charles G. Ross, "Reed of Missouri," *Scribner's*, 83 (February, 1928), 152.
5. McAdoo to Milton, August 27, 1927, William G. McAdoo Papers.
6. McAdoo to Milton, September 7, 1927, McAdoo Papers.
7. McAdoo to Milton, August 27, 1927, McAdoo Papers.
8. McAdoo to Milton, September 15, 1927, McAdoo Papers.
9. Milton to McAdoo, September 2, 1927, McAdoo Papers.
10. Unsigned article, "Senator 'Jim' Reed as Presidential Timber," *Literary Digest*, 92 (February 5, 1927), 12–13; unsigned article, " 'Jim' Reed's Opening Blast," *Literary Digest*, 93 (October 29, 1927), 10–11.

11. "'Jim' Reed's Opening Blast," 10–11; Lee A. Meriwether, *Jim Reed: "Senatorial Immortal,"* 158–76; *Kansas City Times,* October 13, 14, 1928.

12. *Missouri Democrat,* October 14, 1927.

13. *Missouri Democrat,* October 14, 1927.

14. *St. Louis Star,* February 16, 21, 27, May 2, 1928; Meriwether, *Jim Reed,* 163–64; *Kansas City Times,* May 3, 1928.

15. *St. Louis Star,* May 5, June 19, 1928.

16. *St. Louis Star,* June 20, 23, 26, 1928; *Kansas City Times,* June 25, 27, 1928; George F. Milton to William G. McAdoo, July 9, 1928, McAdoo Papers.

17. *St. Louis Star,* June 29, 1928.

18. Meriwether, *Jim Reed,* 175–76. Meriwether relates that a committee, "obviously official," offered Reed the vice-presidential nomination. Reed snapped in reply, "I appreciate the compliment you are paying me, but I do not care for a back seat in a hearse" (175). It is doubtful if anyone connected with Smith headquarters had anything to do with the committee Meriwether mentions. Franklin D. Roosevelt wanted a dry, Protestant Southerner, preferably Cordell Hull of Tennessee, as Smith's running mate. Frank Freidel, *Franklin D. Roosevelt,* Vol. II, *The Ordeal,* 334; Senator Joseph Robinson of Arkansas, mentioned most often by the press as Smith's choice, became the vice-presidential nominee.

19. *St. Louis Star,* January 16, April 16, 20, July 2, 7, 1928; Hay to Mr. and Mrs. J. W. Estes, October 18, 1927, Charles M. Hay Papers; *St. Louis Globe-Democrat,* October 14, 18, 25, 1927.

20. *St. Louis Globe-Democrat,* July 11, 1928.

21. *St. Louis Star,* July 13, 1928.

22. *St. Louis Star,* July 14, 27, 1928; *Kansas City Journal-Post,* July 15, 1928; *St. Louis Globe-Democrat,* July 17, 27, 1928.

23. *St. Louis Star,* July 31, August 2, 1928; *St. Louis Globe-Democrat,* August 1, 2, 3, 5, 1928.

24. *Kansas City Times,* August 3, 1928.

25. *Official Manual, 1929–1930,* 428–31.

26. Hay to Roosevelt, August 10, 1928, Group XVII, Franklin D. Roosevelt Papers.

27. *St. Louis Post-Dispatch,* August 23, 1928; Bernard M. Garfinkel, "The Political Career of Charles Martin Hay," unpublished Master's thesis, University of Missouri, 133–45.

28. William A. Hirth to N. H. Gentry, October 22, 1928, William Hirth Papers (Western Historical Manuscripts Collection, University of Missouri); *Kansas City Times,* June 12, 13, 1928; *Missouri Farmer,* 20 (November 1, 1928), 3; *Missouri Ruralist,* 70 (October 15, 1928), 4.

29. *Kansas City Times,* October 17, 1928.

30. *St. Louis Star,* September 29, 1928; *Kansas City Star,* October 2, 1928.

31. This situation has a parallel in California. According to Gilman M. Ostrander, "In the 'twenties . . . the Anti-Saloon League, having — on paper at least — achieved the millennium, was no longer officially interested in progress." (*The Prohibition Movement in California, 1848–1933,* 189.) For Hay's interest in social welfare legislation and activity in behalf of prohibition, see Garfinkel, "The Political Career of Charles Martin Hay," Chap. 3.

32. Bureau of the Census, *Religious Bodies: 1926,* I, 66; *Official Manual, 1919–1920,* 427; *Official Manual, 1926–1927,* 294–95.

33. *St. Louis Globe-Democrat,* November 25, 1927; *St. Louis Post-Dispatch,* November 2, 1928.

34. *St. Louis Star,* August 16, 1928; *Missouri Democrat,* August 24, 1928.

35. *St. Louis Star,* October 31, 1928.

36. *Missouri Democrat,* October 26, 1928; *St. Louis Star,* October 26, November 1, 1928.

37. *St. Louis Star,* October 9, 1928.

38. *St. Louis Star,* October 5, 1928; *Kansas City Star,* October 14, 1928.

39. *Kansas City American,* September 20, 27, October 4, 18, November 1, 1928; *Kansas City Call,* October 19, 26, November 2, 1928; *St. Louis Argus,* September 7, 1928.

40. *St. Louis Argus,* September 7, 1928; Samuel Lubell, *The Future of American Politics,* 35–43; *St. Louis Star,* November 3, 1928.

41. John J. Nangle to Wilson, February 29, 1928, Francis M. Wilson Papers.

42. Wilson to W. G. Mosley, August 12, 1928, F. M. Wilson Papers; *Kansas City Call,* October 12, 19, 26, November 2, 1928; *St. Louis Argus,* November 2, 1928.

43. McLemore to author, March 3, 1966; *St. Louis Argus,* February 10, August 10, October 19, 1928.

44. *Missouri Democrat,* September 21, 1928; *St. Louis Argus,* September 7, 1928.

45. Editorial, *St. Louis Argus,* November 2, 1928. The *Argus* endorsed neither Hoover nor Smith.

46. *St. Louis Star,* November 3, 1928.

47. *St. Louis Star,* November 1, 4, 1928.

48. *St. Louis Star,* October 26, 1928; *St. Louis Globe-Democrat,* October 29, 1928.

49. *Kansas City Journal-Post,* July 25, 1928.

50. Bureau of the Census, *Religious Bodies: 1926,* I, 66; editorial, *Kansas City Times,* June 27, 1928; for an able discussion of Smith's failure — even unwillingness — to establish a national identity, see David B. Burner, "The Brown Derby Campaign," *New York History,* 46 (October, 1965), 356–80.

51. Editorial, *Independence Examiner,* October 1, 1928; Missouri Women's Christian Temperance Union, *Annual Report, 1928,* 49.

52. *Official Manual, 1929–1930,* 208–9, 237–38; Morran D. Harris, "Political Trends in Missouri, 1900–1954," unpublished Master's thesis, University of Missouri, 18, 29–30, 100. The ten traditionally Democratic counties that broke precedent by voting for a Republican presidential candidate for the first time in 1928 were Cass, Clay, Clinton, Henry, Iron, Marion, Pike, Pulaski, Saline, and Vernon counties. For a map showing the percentage of slaves in the population in each county in 1860, see Duane Meyer, *The Heritage of Missouri: A History,* 317. This pattern of voter behavior in the traditionally Democratic counties of Missouri conforms partly to that of the Deep South's "black belt" and old settled Southern counties once having a high concentration of Negro residents. The votes of many Negroes of Little Dixie, attracted to the candidacy of Al Smith, undoubtedly helped offset the defection of white voters to the G.O.P. See V. O. Key, Jr., *Southern Politics in State and Nation,* 318–29.

53. Harris, "Political Trends in Missouri," 100.

54. *Official Manual, 1929–1930*, 105–8; *St. Louis Post-Dispatch*, November 7, 1928; *St. Louis Star*, November 7, 1928.

55. In the three-cornered election of 1912, when Roosevelt, Taft, and Wilson contested for the Presidency, Wilson's plurality in St. Louis fell 12,410 votes short of a majority. Harris, "Political Trends in Missouri," 29.

56. *Official Manual, 1929–1930*, 237, 326. In the four German wards, 10, 11, 12, and 13, Smith outpolled Hoover 30,470 to 27,165.

57. *Official Manual, 1929–1930*, 237, 326; Patterson defeated Hay in the four German wards, 30,684 to 26,718.

58. *Official Manual, 1929–1930*, 221, 277.

59. 1932 Campaign Correspondence, 1928–1933: Missouri Abstract, Democratic National Committee Papers (Franklin D. Roosevelt Library, Hyde Park).

60. See Richard Hofstadter, "Could a Protestant Have Beaten Hoover in 1928?" *Reporter*, 22 (March 17, 1960), 31.

61. Hay to Rev. Martin T. Haw, April 18, 1931, Hay Papers. "Mrs. Burger," Hay confided to Haw, "happens to be one of the very few persons against whom I have any bitterness in connection with the last [1928] election." A statistical analysis of the 1928 presidential voting in Missouri also refutes the view of contemporary Democrats that Protestants who voted against Smith because of his religion played the major role in the Catholic candidate's defeat and supports the belief of Hay concerning the importance of prohibition in the election. See Richard A. Watson, "Religion and Politics in Mid-America: Presidential Voting in Missouri, 1928 and 1960," *Midcontinent American Studies Journal*, 5 (Spring, 1964), 33–55.

62. William E. Leuchtenburg, *The Perils of Prosperity, 1914–1932*, 237.

63. *Kansas City Star*, November 8, 1928.

64. *St. Louis Star*, November 9, 1928; editorial, *St. Louis Argus*, November 9, 1928; Joseph L. McLemore to author, March 3, 1966. White Republican L. C. Dyer defeated McLemore 24,701 to 17,609. *Official Manual, 1929–1930*, 410.

65. *Missouri Democrat*, March 14, 1929; *Kansas City American*, February 27, 1930. Democrats garnered 27 per cent of the Kansas City Negro vote in 1924.

66. *Missouri Democrat*, March 14, 1929.

67. *Sedalia Democrat*, November 4, 5, 1928; see also Caruthersville *Democrat-Argus*, August 10, October 19, 1928.

CHAPTER 8

1. *St. Louis Argus*, January 7, 1921, November 24, 1922, November 7, 1924; *Missouri Democrat*, January 7, 1927; November 9, 1928; *Kansas City American*, November 16, 1928.

2. See pages 63–66, 86–88.

3. *Kansas City Call*, May 8, June 19, 1925; *Missouri Democrat*, November 12, 1926; editorial, *St. Louis Argus*, July 9, 1926.

4. See pages 98–100, 115–16; party platforms are published in the *Official Manual of Missouri*.

5. *St. Louis Argus*, January 11, 1929.

6. *St. Louis Argus*, January 18, 1929; *St. Louis Star*, January 14, 1929.

7. Kinney's Thirty-first Senatorial District included several precincts in Negro Wards Four, Five, and Six. *Official Manual, 1931–1932,* 313; *Kansas City American,* February 26, 1931; *St. Louis Argus,* June 7, 1929. See also Robert Irving Brigham, "The Education of the Negro in Missouri," unpublished doctoral dissertation, University of Missouri, Chaps. 6–7, 10.

8. *St. Louis Argus,* June 7, 1929.

9. Elbert Lee Tatum, *The Changed Political Thought of the Negro, 1915–1940,* 118–37; *St. Louis Argus,* March 29, June 6, 1930; *Kansas City American,* March 7, April 10, 17, 1930.

10. Tatum, *Changed Political Thought,* 118–37; Richard L. Watson, Jr., "The Defeat of Judge Parker: A Study in Pressure Groups and Politics," *Mississippi Valley Historical Review,* 50 (September, 1963), 221; *St. Louis Globe-Democrat,* April 17, 1930.

11. *Congressional Record,* 71st Cong., 2d Sess., May 7, 1931, 8487; in a letter to Jesse W. Barrett, Senator Patterson insisted that the political implications of Parker's nomination were only a minor consideration in determining his vote. Patterson to Barrett, May 8, 1930, Jesse W. Barrett Papers (Western Historical Manuscripts, University of Missouri).

12. Editorial, *Kansas City American,* May 15, 1930; editorial, *St. Louis Argus,* May 16, 1930.

13. *St. Louis Globe-Democrat,* April 13, 1930.

14. *St. Louis Argus,* April 11, 1930.

15. *St. Louis Argus,* April 11, 1930.

16. *St. Louis Star,* August 2, 4, 6, 1930; *St. Louis Post-Dispatch,* August 3, 1930.

17. *St. Louis Argus,* May 16, 1930.

18. In the 1929 St. Louis municipal election, incumbent Republican mayor Victor Miller defeated Democrat Lawrence McDaniel 108,696 to 101,582. Miller carried seventeen of the city's twenty-eight wards, including all of the Negro wards and the South Side German wards. *St. Louis Star,* April 3, 6, 1929; for a list of the kind and quantity of patronage Miller's administration gave to the Negroes of St. Louis, see the *St. Louis Argus,* March 29, 1929.

19. Chambers, an unsuccessful candidate for constable, formed an independent organization in the Nineteenth Ward to advance his candidacy, thus avoiding any tie-up with either Dyer or Moore; Clark remained loyal to Dyer and lost his bid for renomination as a justice of the peace. *St. Louis Argus,* May 16, June 27, August 1, 8, 1930; in its editorial of September 19, 1930, the *Argus* excoriated the Negro representatives on the Republican Central City Committee who had neither "race loyalty or guts enough to come out and support a Negro for Congress."

20. *St. Louis Argus,* August 1, September 19, 1930.

21. *St. Louis Argus,* August 8, 1930; *Official Manual, 1931–1932,* 274, 294. Democrat John Cochran was also unopposed for re-election in the Eleventh Congressional District. It is possible that Democrats and Republicans in St. Louis agreed to avoid contests in the two congressional districts.

22. *Kansas City American,* March 20, 27, 1930; *Missouri Democrat,* March 14, 1929; *Kansas City Star,* March 20, 1930.

23. *Kansas City American,* March 27, 1930.

24. *Kansas City American,* March 27, 1930.

25. *Kansas City American,* December 5, 1929, January 30, 1930. Kansas

City Negro Democrats also appropriated Jefferson's birthday to replace Lincoln Day celebrations. Roy Dorsey, a prominent Republican until he deserted to the Democrats in the city election of 1930, presided over the Jefferson Day festivities in 1930. Dorsey's loss to the Republican party, commented the *Kansas City American* in its April 3, 1930 issue, "was the greatest blow [the G.O.P.] has received locally in years." *Missouri Democrat*, April 25, 1930; Charles P. Blackmore, "Joseph B. Shannon, Political Boss and Twentieth Century 'Jefferson'," unpublished doctoral dissertation, Columbia University, 361–64.

26. See page 80, and note 52, Chap. 5.

27. Blackmore, "Joseph B. Shannon," 376, 383, 385.

28. Blackmore, "Joseph B. Shannon," 385; *Kansas City Star*, November 3, 1930.

29. *Kansas City American*, October 30, November 6, 1930. The *American* termed the *Call*'s anti-Welch editorials an "outrage."

30. *Kansas City American*, December 5, 1930; *Kansas City Star*, November 5, 1930.

31. *St. Louis Globe-Democrat*, October 20, 24, 1930; *St. Louis Star*, October 24, November 3, 1930.

32. *Kansas City Star*, October 24, November 6, 1930.

33. According to a St. Joseph newspaper, the wet Democrat evidently underestimated the strength of the W.C.T.U. *St. Joseph News-Press*, November 5, 1930.

34. Federal Reserve Bank of St. Louis, *The Monthly Review of Agricultural, Industrial, Trade and Financial Conditions in the Eighth Federal Reserve District*, December, 1930, *passim*; Federal Reserve Bank of Kansas City, *The Monthly Review of Agricultural, Industrial, Trade and Financial Conditions in the Tenth Federal Reserve District*, December, 1930, *passim*.

35. State of Missouri, *Fiftieth, Fifty-first, and Fifty-second Annual Reports of the Missouri Industrial and Labor Commission: 1929–1931, passim*.

36. Federal Reserve Bank of Kansas City, *Monthly Review*; J. C. Grady, "Missouri Farm Prices Since 1910," *Missouri Agricultural Experiment Station Research Bulletin*, No. 508, University of Missouri, 15.

37. *St. Louis Star*, August 9, 1930; *St. Louis Globe-Democrat*, November 6, 1930; *Official Manual, 1931–1932*, 104.

38. *St. Louis Argus*, January 16, 1931; *St. Louis Globe-Democrat*, January 13, 14, 15, 16, 17, 1931; *St. Louis Post-Dispatch*, January 12, 13, 15, 16, 18, 25, 1931; see also Proctor Neal Carter, "Lynch Law and the Press of Missouri," unpublished Master's thesis, University of Missouri, *passim*.

39. Editorial, *St. Louis Argus*, January 23, 1931; the Republican-sponsored antilynching bill was introduced by Representatives Huber, Goener, Wolff, and Williams. *Journal of the House of the State of Missouri*, Fifty-sixth General Assembly, February 4, 1931, 155.

40. *St. Louis Argus*, editorial, March 13, 1931.

41. *St. Louis Argus*, April 10, editorial, April 17, 1931.

42. *St. Louis Argus*, April 17, May 1, 8, 1931.

43. *St. Louis Argus*, editorial, May 8, 1931; Democrats provided 59 of the 98 affirmative votes in the House and 11 of the 19 affirmative votes in the Senate in the voting on the Kinney antilynching measure. The total House vote was 98 to 4, with 48 not voting; the total Senate vote was 19 to 7, with

8 not voting. *Journal of the House of the State of Missouri*, Fifty-sixth General Assembly, April 14, 1931, 1032.

44. *Kansas City Times*, May 13, 1931.

45. Editorial, *Kansas City American*, June 11, 1931. Editorials in both the *American* and the *St. Louis Argus* took C. A. Franklin of the *Kansas City Call* to task for upholding Caulfield's veto of the antilynching bill. *Kansas City American*, June 4, 1931, and *St. Louis Argus*, May 29, 1931.

46. Editorial, *St. Louis Argus*, May 15, 1931.

47. *St. Louis Argus*, May 29, 1931.

CHAPTER 9

1. *St. Louis Globe-Democrat*, December 14, 1931; William E. Leuchtenburg, *Franklin D. Roosevelt and the New Deal, 1932–1940*, Chap. 1.

2. Arthur M. Schlesinger, Jr., *The Age of Roosevelt*, Vol. I, *The Crisis of the Old Order, 1919–1933*, Chap. 27.

3. *Missouri Democrat*, July 24, 1931; Frank Freidel, *Franklin D. Roosevelt*, Vol. III, *The Triumph*, 209.

4. *Missouri Democrat*, September 25, 1931; *St. Louis Globe-Democrat*, September 12, 17, 23, 1931; Farley to Bennett Champ Clark, September 23, Roosevelt to Reed, October 9, 1931, Democratic National Committee Papers.

5. Unsigned article, "It Won't Be Reed," *Outlook*, 159 (October 7, 1931), 165–66.

6. *St. Joseph News-Press*, January 17, 1930; Reed to Daniel H. Coakley, May 11, 1932, James A. Reed Papers.

7. Schlesinger, *The Crisis of the Old Order*, 282; *Missouri Democrat*, January 15, 1932; Goltra to Roosevelt, February 8, 1932, Edward F. Goltra Papers.

8. Frank P. Walsh, old Kansas City progressive residing in New York City, acted as liaison between Mitchell and Roosevelt's managers. For the correspondence between Mitchell, Walsh, Louis M. Howe, and James A. Farley, see Box 134, Frank P. Walsh Papers (New York Public Library, New York City). Much of this correspondence has been printed in Chapter I of Mitchell's book, *"Kicked In and Kicked Out of the President's Little Cabinet."* A great deal of correspondence between Mitchell and Democrats in Missouri concerning Mitchell's efforts to prevent an instructed delegation for Reed to the National Democratic Convention may be found in the Ewing Young Mitchell Papers (Western Historical Manuscripts Collection, University of Missouri). See also Franklin D. Roosevelt to Ewing Y. Mitchell, April 14, 1932, Democratic National Committee Papers. Roosevelt thanked Mitchell for "most enlightening information which you sent me . . . [clarifying] the Missouri situation. Frankly, I did not want to be put in the position of seeming to challenge the loyalty of your fellow citizens to their own favorite son. I have written, however, to the gentlemen whose names you have sent me to thank them for their personal interest and their desire to influence the primary decision." After assuming the Presidency, Roosevelt named Mitchell Assistant Secretary of Commerce.

9. Bernard M. Garfinkel, "The Political Career of Charles Martin Hay," unpublished Master's thesis, University of Missouri, 148.

10. Garfinkel, "Charles Martin Hay," 150; Hay to William T. Kemper,

April 20, 1931, Hay to Moses Greenwood, April 24, 1931, Charles M. Hay Papers.

11. *St. Louis Globe-Democrat*, March 28, 1932.

12. Joseph B. Shannon, one of the recipients of Hawes's telegram, voted for Reed on the first three ballots at Chicago, but devoted his time at the convention to promoting the Roosevelt-Garner ticket. Charles P. Blackmore, "Joseph B. Shannon, Political Boss and Twentieth Century 'Jefferson,'" unpublished doctoral dissertation, Columbia University, 401–2; a photostatic copy of the Hawes telegram to Shannon of June 27, 1932, is in the Reed Papers. James A. Farley, *Behind the Ballots: The Personal History of a Politician*, 132–33; Freidel, *The Triumph*, 309; Senator Key Pittman shared Hawes's apprehensions over a deadlocked convention and teamed up with Hawes to promote a Roosevelt-Garner ticket. Fred L. Israel, *Nevada's Key Pittman*, 96–98.

13. Robert B. Dishman, "Machine Politics — Kansas City Model," unpublished Master's thesis, University of Missouri, 86; *St. Louis Globe-Democrat*, December 19, 1930.

14. For a survey of Roosevelt sentiment in Missouri, see 1932 Campaign Correspondence, 1928–1933: Missouri Abstract, National Democratic Committee Papers. The results of the Jesse I. Straus poll of Missouri delegates and alternates to the 1928 Democratic National Convention, included in the national committee's correspondence, showed Roosevelt ahead of Reed 19 to 13. Reed's name, incidentally, was left off the Straus poll, so Missourians had to write it in.

15. *St. Louis Globe-Democrat*, March 29, 1932.

16. Freidel, *The Triumph*, 277.

17. Reed to Daniel H. Coakley, May 11, 1932, Reed Papers.

18. Reed to Coakley, June 15, 1932, Reed Papers.

19. *St. Louis Globe-Democrat*, June 27, 1932.

20. *St. Louis Globe-Democrat*, July 2, 1932; *St. Louis Post-Dispatch*, July 1, 1932; *Kansas City Times*, July 1, 1932; Freidel, *The Triumph*, 305–11.

21. *Missouri Democrat*, July 1, 1932; *Kansas City Star*, July 3, 1932. The *Star* also observed that Pendergast had not offended Roosevelt by his course of action; Reed singled out State Democratic Chairman Charles Greenwade as the influential leader who was working against him at Chicago. Reed to John J. Schneider, July 11, 1932, Reed Papers.

22. The italics are Clark's. Clark to Reed, March 22, 1933, Reed Papers; according to Louis J. Gualdoni, he and Charles Lemp of St. Louis had informed Pendergast in December, 1931, a few months before the State Democratic Convention, that they intended to vote for Roosevelt at Chicago. When the Missouri delegation caucused on June 27, 1932, at the convention, Pendergast "blasted me because I announced at the caucus that I would vote for Roosevelt on the first ballot," relates Gualdoni. "Later, during this same convention, Pendergast and I got our heads together on several matters and were on intimate terms." Gualdoni to author, undated (received June 13, 1964, in reply to letter of author, June 9, 1964).

23. *St. Louis Star*, January 7, 1932; Schlesinger, *The Crisis of the Old Order*, 282.

24. *Missouri Democrat*, October 23, 1931, January 8, 1932.

25. *Kansas City Times*, December 10, 1931; Reed to John J. Schneider, July 11, 1932, Reed Papers.

26. Garfinkel, "Charles Martin Hay," 150–51; *St. Louis Post-Dispatch*, December 6, 1931; speech, May 10, 1932, Hay Papers.

27. Garfinkel, "Charles Martin Hay," 153–54, 158; speech, July 30, 1932, Hay Papers.

28. *St. Louis Globe-Democrat*, July 21, 22, 1932.

29. *St. Louis Globe-Democrat*, May 2, 13, 1932; *St. Louis Star*, July 8, 1932.

30. Garfinkel, "Charles Martin Hay," 157–58; *Missouri Farmer*, 24 (July 1, 1932), 8–9.

31. Speech, July 25, 1932, Hay Papers.

32. *Official Manual, 1933–1934*, 400–401.

33. Garfinkel, "Charles Martin Hay," 163; Dishman, "Machine Politics — Kansas City Model," 85; the state-wide voting on the question of Missouri's stand on the repeal of the Eighteenth Amendment reveals the outstate shift against prohibition by early 1933. The totals were 503,642 in favor of repeal, 156,961 opposed. See *Official Manual, 1933–1934*, 594.

34. According to Harry S Truman, Dearmont was disgruntled because he had failed to receive Pendergast's endorsement. Truman himself was promoted by friends for the Democratic gubernatorial nomination, but withdrew from the race when the Pendergast organization endorsed Wilson. *Missouri Democrat*, May 13, 20, June 5, 1931; see also Franklin D. Mitchell, "Who is Judge Truman?: The Truman-for-Governor Movement of 1931," *Midcontinent American Studies Journal*, 7 (Fall, 1966), 3–15.

35. See editorials in the *St. Louis Post-Dispatch* and the *St. Louis Star and Times* for July and August, 1932; *Kansas City Star*, August 1, 1932.

36. *Official Manual, 1933–1934*, 402–3.

37. *Official Manual, 1933–1934*, 412–23; Dishman, "Machine Politics — Kansas City Model," 86; *Kansas City Star*, July 26, 1932; John H. Fenton, *Politics in the Border States*, 136–37.

38. *St. Louis Star and Times*, September 1, 1932.

39. *St. Louis Star and Times*, September 13, 14, 1932.

40. *St. Louis Globe-Democrat*, November 3, 1932.

41. *St. Louis Globe-Democrat*, November 3, 1932; *Kansas City Star*, November 6, 1932.

42. *St. Louis Star and Times*, October 6, 22, November 3, 4, 1932.

43. *St. Louis Star and Times*, August 17, October 12, 18, 1932; *Kansas City Times*, October 18, 1932.

44. Editorial, *St. Louis Globe-Democrat*, October 18, 1932; *Kansas City Star*, October 12, 1932; *St. Louis Post-Dispatch*, October 12, 15, 18, 1932. See also Franklin D. Mitchell, "Embattled Democracy: Missouri Democratic Politics, 1918–1932," unpublished doctoral dissertation, University of Missouri, 276–78.

45. *Kansas City Star*, October 15, 1932.

46. *St. Louis Globe-Democrat*, November 4, 1932.

47. See, for example, the advertisement published in the *Columbia Missourian*, November 5, 1932. The G.O.P. primary featured a comical parallel: As Winter hammered away at the "handpicked candidate of Pendergast," the disgruntled Charles U. Becker, defeated in the primary by Winter, charged

that Republican bosses had "stolen" the gubernatorial nomination from him. Becker even launched a write-in campaign in his own behalf, but Republicans refused to take his charges and candidacy seriously. *Kansas City Journal-Post,* November 6, 1932; *St. Louis Globe-Democrat,* October 18, November 1, 7, 1932.

48. Hay to Mrs. Henry N. Ess, September 2, 1932, Hay Papers; see the *Missouri Farmer,* 24 (November 1, 1932), 8, for William Hirth's defense of Judge Park against the "bossism" charge and an argument for the Democrat's election on the ground that the G.O.P. nominee could not bring efficiency and economy to state government.

49. Hay to Harry H. Woodring, August 17, 1932, Hay to Homer H. Gruenther, August 18, 1932, Hay Papers.

50. *Official Report of the Proceedings of the Democratic National Convention at Chicago, Illinois, June 27 to July 2, inclusive, 1932,* 329–31; Reed to Roosevelt, July 5, 1932, Democratic National Committee Papers; *Missouri Democrat,* September 23, October 19, 1932.

51. *St. Louis Globe-Democrat,* October 29, 30, 1932; *Kansas City Star,* November 6, 1932. One of the best sources for the campaign speeches of the Democratic candidates is the *Missouri Democrat,* September–November, 1932.

52. *St. Louis Globe-Democrat,* October 28, 30, November 1, 1932.

53. *Columbia Missourian,* October 27, November 5, 1932.

54. *Official Manual, 1933–1934,* 214 ff. Socialist presidential candidate Norman Thomas received 16,374 votes from Missourians; Communist candidate William Z. Foster received a scant 568 votes; *St. Joseph News-Press,* November 11, 1932; *St. Louis Post-Dispatch,* November 9, 10, 1932.

55. *Official Manual, 1933–1934,* 214, 217, 375; *St. Louis Globe-Democrat,* November 9, 10, 1932; *St. Louis Post-Dispatch,* November 9, 10, 1932.

56. *Official Manual, 1933–1934,* 287; *Kansas City Journal-Post,* November 9, 1932.

57. *Official Manual, 1933–1934,* 104, 107, 215, 217–22; Morran D. Harris, "Political Trends in Missouri, 1900–1954," unpublished Master's thesis, University of Missouri, 30. The seven counties that returned majorities for Hoover were Douglas, Gasconade, Hickory, Ozark, Putnam, Taney, and Warren.

58. *St. Louis Argus,* November 11, 1932.

59. *St. Louis Post-Dispatch,* November 9, 10, 1932; *Official Manual, 1933–1934,* 375. The *St. Louis Argus* is in error concerning which four wards of the city had more Negro than white registered voters. In its October 14, 1932, issue the Negro newspaper included the Fourth and excluded the Twenty-third from its list. However, this list does not agree with published reports of the 1928 registration figures, nor does it agree with the 1933 reports. Hence, the *Post-Dispatch's* designation of Wards 5, 6, 19, and 23 as the four major Negro wards appears to be correct. See the *St. Louis Star,* October 9, 1928, and the *St. Louis Argus,* April 7, 1933; unfortunately, the lack of registration data and precinct returns prevents a more refined analysis of the Negro vote in St. Louis. Harry Leitz, St. Louis Director of Elections, to author, February 26, 1964.

60. *Kansas City Journal-Post,* November 9, 1932; *Kansas City American,* February 27, November 10, 1932.

61. *Kansas City American,* November 17, 1932; Meredith Lee to Guy B. Park, June 1, 1933, Guy B. Park Papers (Western Historical Manuscripts Col-

lection, University of Missouri); Hayti *Missouri Herald*, November 11, 1932. Precinct 2, Little Prairie Township of Pemiscot County, identified by the *Herald* as a Negro precinct, went for Roosevelt over Hoover 990 to 282. An editorial in the same issue suggests that Negroes suspected of having sold their votes to Republicans were turned away from the polls by Democratic law officials; *Official Manual, 1933–1934*, 324.

62. Editorial, *St. Louis Argus*, November 11, 1932.

63. Arthur M. Schlesinger, Jr., "Sources of the New Deal," *Columbia University Forum*, 2 (Fall, 1959), 4–12.

CONCLUSION AND EPILOGUE

1. Duane Meyer, *The Heritage of Missouri: A History*, 638–44.

2. Meyer, *Heritage of Missouri*, 626–38.

3. Lyle W. Dorsett, "Kansas City Politics: A Study of Boss Pendergast's Machine," *Arizona and the West*, 8 (Summer, 1966), 116–17.

4. Dorsett, "Kansas City Politics," 116–17.

5. Dorsett, "Kansas City Politics," 116; Franklin D. Mitchell, "Who is Judge Truman?: The Truman-for-Governor Movement of 1931," *Midcontinent American Studies Journal*, 7 (Fall, 1966), 3–15; Gene Schmidtlein, "Truman's First Senatorial Election," *Missouri Historical Review*, 57 (January, 1963), 128–55.

6. James F. Watts, Jr., "The Public Life of Breckinridge Long," unpublished doctoral dissertation, University of Missouri, 73–78; Bernard M. Garfinkel, "The Political Career of Charles Martin Hay," unpublished Master's thesis, University of Missouri, Chap. 7; Mitchell's tenure as Assistant Secretary of Commerce was brief, due to his disagreement with policies of the department. See his *"Kicked In and Kicked Out of the President's Little Cabinet,"* passim.

7. Meyer, *Heritage of Missouri*, 626.

8. Meyer, *Heritage of Missouri*, 626; George Wolfskill, *The Revolt of the Conservatives: A History of the American Liberty League, 1934–1940*, 108–9, 112, 149, 182–83, 185, 196–97, 220, 232.

9. Meyer, *Heritage of Missouri*, 617–23, 642, 650–55; Dorsett, "Kansas City Politics," 117.

10. Meyer, *Heritage of Missouri*, 669–72, 706; John H. Fenton, *Politics in the Border States*, 139–42.

11. Meyer, *Heritage of Missouri*, 694–706, 709; Svend Peterson, *A Statistical History of the American Presidential Elections*, 103, 106, 109.

12. John P. Davis, ed., *The American Negro Reference Book*, 440.

13. Davis, *The American Negro Reference Book*, 119; Samuel Lubell, *The Future of American Politics*, 98; Ernest Kirschten, *Catfish and Crystal: The Bicentenary Edition of the St. Louis Story*, 449.

BIBLIOGRAPHY

A. *Manuscripts*

Jesse W. Barrett Papers. Western Historical Manuscripts Collection, University of Missouri, Columbia.

Bronaugh-Bushnell Papers. Western Historical Manuscripts Collection, University of Missouri, Columbia.

John W. Davis Papers. Yale University Library, New Haven, Connecticut.

Democratic National Committee Papers. Franklin D. Roosevelt Library, Hyde Park, New York.

David R. Francis Papers. Missouri Historical Society, St. Louis.

Edward F. Goltra Papers. Missouri Historical Society, St. Louis.

Charles M. Hay Papers. Western Historical Manuscripts Collection, University of Missouri, Columbia.

William Hirth Papers. Western Historical Manuscripts Collection, University of Missouri, Columbia.

Edward M. House Papers. Yale University Library, New Haven, Connecticut.

Louis McHenry Howe Papers. Franklin D. Roosevelt Library, Hyde Park, New York.

Arthur M. Hyde Papers. Western Historical Manuscripts Collection, University of Missouri, Columbia.

Breckinridge Long Papers. Library of Congress, Washington, D. C.

Ralph L. Lozier Papers. Western Historical Manuscripts Collection, University of Missouri, Columbia.

William G. McAdoo Papers. Library of Congress, Washington, D. C.

Ewing Young Mitchell Papers. Western Historical Manuscripts Collection, University of Missouri, Columbia.

Guy B. Park Papers. Western Historical Manuscripts Collection, University of Missouri, Columbia.

Roscoe C. Patterson Papers. Western Historical Manuscripts Collection, University of Missouri, Columbia.

James A. Reed Papers. Residence of Mrs. James A. Reed, Kansas City, Missouri.

Franklin D. Roosevelt Papers. Franklin D. Roosevelt Library, Hyde Park, New York.

Joseph P. Tumulty Papers. Library of Congress, Washington, D. C.

Frank P. Walsh Papers. New York Public Library, New York City.

Francis M. Wilson Papers. Western Historical Manuscripts Collection, University of Missouri, Columbia.

Woodrow Wilson Papers. Library of Congress, Washington, D. C.

Lloyd E. Worner, Jr., Letters. Western Historical Manuscripts Collection, University of Missouri, Columbia.

B. *Government Documents*

Federal Reserve Bank of Kansas City. *The Monthly Review of Agricultural, Industrial, Trade and Financial Conditions in the Tenth Federal Reserve District: Kansas City, 1929–1932.* n.p., n.d.

Federal Reserve Bank of St. Louis. *The Monthly Review of Agricultural, Industrial, Trade and Financial Conditions in the Eighth Federal Reserve District: St. Louis, 1929–1932,* n.p., n.d.

Rossiter, William S. *Increase of Population in the United States, 1910–1920,* Census Monographs, Vol. I. Washington: Government Printing Office, 1922.

State of Missouri. *Biennial Report of the Missouri Negro Industrial Commission: 1923–1924, 1925–1926.* Jefferson City: The Hugh Stephens Press, n.d.

———. *Fiftieth, Fifty-first, and Fifty-second Annual Reports of the Missouri Industrial and Labor Inspection Commission: 1929–1931.* Jefferson City: Botz Printing and Stationery Company, n.d.

———. *Journal of the House of Representatives,* Fifty-sixth General Assembly (1931). Jefferson City: Botz Printing and Stationery Company, n.d.

———. *Journal of the Senate,* Fifty-sixth General Assembly (1931). Jefferson City: Botz Printing and Stationery Company, n.d.

———. *Official Manual for Years 1919–1920,* John L. Sullivan, Secretary of State, editor. Jefferson City: The Hugh Stephens Company, n.d.

———. *Official Manual for Years 1921–1922, 1923–1924, 1925–1926, 1927–1928,* Charles U. Becker, Secretary of State, editor. Jefferson City: The Hugh Stephens Press, n.d.

———. *Official Manual for Years 1929–1930.* Charles U. Becker,

Secretary of State, editor. Jefferson City: Botz-Hugh Stephens Press, n.d.

————. *Official Manual for Years 1931–1932*, Charles U. Becker, Secretary of State, editor. Jefferson City: Botz Printing and Stationery Company, n.d.

————. *Official Manual for Years 1933–34*, Dwight H. Brown, Secretary of State, editor. Jefferson City: Midland Publishing Company, n.d.

United States, Bureau of the Census. *Abstract of the Fourteenth Census of the United States: 1920.* Washington: Government Printing Office, 1923.

————. *Fourteenth Census of the United States (State Compendium, Missouri).* Washington: Government Printing Office, 1921.

————. *Fifteenth Census of the United States, 1930. Population*, Vol. III. Washington: Government Printing Office, 1932.

————. *Negro Population: 1790–1915.* Washington: Government Printing Office, 1918.

————. *Negroes in the United States: 1920–1932.* Washington: Government Printing Office, 1935.

————. *Religious Bodies: 1926.* Vol. I. Washington: Government Printing Office, 1930.

United States, Congress. *Biographical Director of the American Congress, 1774–1961.* Washington: 1961.

————. *Congressional Record.* 65th Congress, 1st Session (1917). Washington: Government Printing Office.

————. *Congressional Record.* 68th Congress, 2d Session (1925). Washington: Government Printing Office.

————. *Congressional Record.* 69th Congress, 1st Session (1926). Washington: Government Printing Office.

————. *Congressional Record.* 71st Congress, 2d Session (1931). Washington: Government Printing Office.

C. *Official Reports*

Missouri Women's Christian Temperance Union. *Thirty-sixth to Forty-ninth Annual Reports, 1918–1931.* Mexico: Mexico Printing Company, n.d.

Official Report of the Proceedings of the Democractic National Convention of 1924. Indianapolis, n.d.

Official Report of the Proceedings of the Democratic National Convention of 1932. n.p., n.d.

D. *Personal Correspondence*

Louis J. Gualdoni, St. Louis, Missouri, *c.* June 11, 1964.
Austin Hill, Deputy Secretary of State of Missouri, March 4, 1964.
Harry Leitz, Director of Elections, City of St. Louis, February 26, 1964.
Joseph L. McLemore, New York City, New York, March 3, 1966.

E. *Newspapers*

Unless otherwise indicated, all newspapers listed below are on file in the State Historical Society of Missouri, Columbia, Missouri.

Caruthersville Democrat-Argus, October, 1923–November, 1926; August, October–November, 1928; October–November, 1930; October–November, 1932.
Charleston Enterprise-Courier, October, 1923–November, 1926; October–November, 1928; October–November, 1930; October–November, 1932.
Columbia Missourian, October–November, 1932.
Hayti Missouri Herald, November 11, 1932.
Houston Herald, May–June, 1931.
Independence Examiner, April–November, 1920; October 1, 1928; June, 1931.
Jefferson City Daily Capital-News, March, 1919; March 1, 1927.
Jefferson City Democrat-Tribune, May, 1922.
Kansas City American, June 21, 1928–January 12, 1933.
Kansas City Call, January 7, 1922–December, 1926. Microfilm of issues for the years 1925–1926 was obtained by loan from the Kansas City Public Library, Kansas City, Missouri.
Kansas City Journal-Post, July, 1928–December, 1932.
Kansas City Post, February, 1920.
Kansas City Star (Times), 1919–1932.
Kansas City Sun, 1920–June 7, 1924.
Missouri Democrat (Kansas City), October, 1925–December, 1932.
Missouri Farm Bureau News (Jefferson City), October 29, 1926.
Missouri Farmer (Columbia), 1920–1932.
Missouri Herald (Hayti), October–November, 1932.
Missouri Klan Kourier (St. Louis), July, 1923–December, 1924.
Missouri Ruralist (Columbia), 1920–1932.
Odessa Democrat, November, 1930.
St. Joseph Missouri Valley Independent, January, 1923–November, 1927.
St. Joseph News-Press, January, November, 1930; November, 1932.

St. Joseph Observer, 1932.
St. Louis Argus, 1920–1932.
St. Louis Globe-Democrat, 1919–1932.
St. Louis Labor, November, 1924.
St. Louis Post-Dispatch, 1919–1932.
St. Louis Republic, June, 1917–December, 1919.
St. Louis Star, January, 1919–June 22, 1932.
St. Louis Star and Times, June 23, 1932–December, 1932.
Sedalia Democrat, October–November, 1928; October–November, 1932.
Springfield Press, May, 1931.

F. Unpublished Studies

Bain, Jack M., "A Rhetorical Criticism of the Speeches of James A. Reed." Doctoral dissertation, University of Missouri, 1953.
Blackmore, Charles P., "Joseph B. Shannon, Political Boss and Twentieth Century 'Jefferson.'" Doctoral dissertation, Columbia University, 1953.
Brigham, Robert Irving, "The Education of the Negro in Missouri." Doctoral dissertation, University of Missouri, 1946.
Carter, Proctor Neal, "Lynch Law and the Press of Missouri." Master's thesis, University of Missouri, 1933.
Dishman, Robert B., "Machine Politics — Kansas City Model." Master's thesis, University of Missouri, 1940.
Dorsett, Lyle W., "Alderman Jim Pendergast." Master's thesis, University of Kansas City, 1960.
Garfinkel, Bernard M., "The Political Career of Charles Martin Hay." Master's thesis, University of Missouri, 1956.
Harris, Morran D., "Political Trends in Missouri, 1900–1954." Master's thesis, University of Missouri, 1956.
Large, John Judson, Jr., "The 'Invisible' Empire and Missouri Politics: The Influence of the Revived Ku Klux Klan in the Election of 1924 as Reported in Missouri Newspapers." Master's thesis, University of Missouri, 1954.
Mitchell, Franklin D., "Embattled Democracy: Missouri Democratic Politics, 1918–1932." Doctoral dissertation, University of Missouri, 1964.
Smith, Bert A., "The Senatorial Career of James A. Reed." Master's thesis, University of Missouri, 1950.
Towne, Ruth, "The Public Career of William Joel Stone." Doctoral dissertation, University of Missouri, 1953.

Watts, James F., Jr., "The Public Life of Breckinridge Long." Doctoral dissertation, University of Missouri, 1964.

Worner, Lloyd E., Jr., "Missouri and the National Election of 1920." Master's thesis, University of Missouri, 1943.

G. Books

Bagby, Wesley M., *The Road to Normalcy: The Presidential Campaign and Election of 1920.* The Johns Hopkins University Studies in Historical and Political Science, Vol. LXXX. Baltimore, The Johns Hopkins Press, 1962.

Bailey, Thomas A., *Woodrow Wilson and the Great Betrayal.* New York, The Macmillan Company, 1945.

Blum, John M., *Joe Tumulty and the Wilson Era.* Boston, Houghton Mifflin Company, 1951.

Burns, James MacGregor, *The Deadlock of Democracy: Four-Party Politics in America.* Englewood Cliffs, N.J., Prentice-Hall, Inc., 1963.

Coben, Stanley, *A. Mitchell Palmer: Politician.* New York, Columbia University Press, 1963.

Cox, James M., *Journey Through My Years.* New York, Simon and Schuster, Inc., 1946.

Cramer, Clarence H., *Newton D. Baker: A Biography.* Cleveland, Ohio, The World Publishing Company, 1961.

Cronon, Edmund David, "Woodrow Wilson," in *America's Ten Greatest Presidents,* Morton Borden, ed. Chicago, Rand McNally & Company, 1961. 207–31.

Daniels, Jonathan W., *The Man of Independence.* Philadelphia, J. B. Lippincott Company, 1950.

Davis, John P., ed., *The American Negro Reference Book.* Englewood Cliffs, N.J., Prentice-Hall, Inc., 1966.

Farley, James A., *Behind the Ballots: The Personal History of a Politician.* New York, Harcourt, Brace and Company, 1938.

Fenton, John H., *Politics in the Border States: A Study of Patterns of Political Organization, and Political Change, Common to the Border States — Maryland, West Virginia, Kentucky and Missouri.* New Orleans, The Hauser Press, 1957.

Freidel, Frank, *Franklin D. Roosevelt,* Vol. II, *The Ordeal,* and Vol. III, *The Triumph.* Boston, Little, Brown and Company, 1954, 1956. 3 vols.

Geiger, Louis G., *Joseph W. Folk of Missouri.* The University of Missouri Studies Series, Vol. XXV, No. 2. Columbia, Missouri, University of Missouri Press, 1953.

Grantham, Dewey W., Jr., *The Democratic South*. Athens, The University of Georgia Press, 1963.

Hicks, John D., *Republican Ascendancy, 1921–1933*. The New American Nation Series, Henry Steele Commager and Richard Brandon Morris, eds. New York, Harper and Brothers, 1960.

Higham, John, *Strangers in the Land: Patterns of American Nativism, 1860–1925*. New Brunswick, N.J., Rutgers University Press, 1955.

Huthmacher, J. Joseph, *Massachusetts People and Politics, 1919–1933*. Cambridge, Mass., The Belknap Press of Harvard University Press, 1959.

Israel, Fred L., *Nevada's Key Pittman*. Lincoln, University of Nebraska Press, 1963.

Jackson, William Rufus, *Missouri Democracy: A History of the Party and Its Representative Members — Past and Present*. Chicago, S. J. Clarke Publishing Company, 1935. 3 vols.

Kent, Frank R., *Political Behavior*. New York, William Morrow and Company, Inc., 1928.

Key, V. O., Jr., *American State Politics: An Introduction*. New York, Alfred A. Knopf, Inc., 1956.

———. *Politics, Parties, and Pressure Groups*. 4th ed. New York, Thomas Y. Crowell Company, 1958.

———. *Southern Politics in State and Nation*. New York, Alfred A. Knopf, Inc., 1949.

Kirschten, Ernest, *Catfish and Crystal: The Bicentenary Edition of the St. Louis Story*. Garden City, N.Y., Doubleday & Company, Inc., 1965.

Leuchtenburg, William E., *Franklin D. Roosevelt and the New Deal, 1932–1940*. The New American Nation Series, Henry Steele Commager and Richard B. Morris, eds. New York, Harper & Row, Publishers, 1963.

———. *The Perils of Prosperity, 1914–1932*. The Chicago History of American Civilization, Daniel J. Boorstin, ed. Chicago, The University of Chicago Press, 1958.

Link, Arthur S., *Wilson the Diplomatist*. Baltimore, The Johns Hopkins Press, 1956.

———. *Wilson*, Vol. II, *The New Freedom*, and Vol. V, *Campaigns for Progressivism and Peace, 1916–1917*. Princeton, N.J., Princeton University Press, 1956–1965. 5 vols.

Lubell, Samuel, *The Future of American Politics*, 2d rev. ed. Garden City, N.Y., Doubleday Anchor Books, 1951.

Meriwether, Lee A., *Jim Reed: "Senatorial Immortal."* Webster Groves, Missouri, International Mark Twain Society, 1948.

Meyer, Duane, *The Heritage of Missouri: A History.* St. Louis, Mo., State Publishing Company, Inc., 1963.

Mitchell, Ewing Young, *"Kicked In and Kicked Out of the President's Little Cabinet."* Washington, D. C., The Andrew Jackson Press, 1936.

Noggle, Burl A., *Teapot Dome: Oil and Politics in the 1920's.* Baton Rouge, La., Louisiana State University Press, 1962.

Ostrander, Gilman M., *The Prohibition Movement in California, 1848–1933.* University of California Publications in History, Vol. LVII, No. 50. Berkeley, California, University of California Press, 1957.

Peterson, Merrill D., *The Jefferson Image in the American Mind.* New York, Oxford University Press, Inc., 1960.

Peterson, Svend, *A Statistical History of the American Presidential Elections.* New York, Frederick Ungar Publishing Co., Inc., 1963.

Puryear, Elmer L., *Democratic Party Dissension in North Carolina, 1928–1936.* The James Sprunt Studies in History and Political Science, Vol. XLIV, No. I. Chapel Hill, North Carolina, The University of North Carolina Press, 1962.

Ranney, Austin, *The Doctrine of Responsible Party Government: Its Origins and Present State.* Illinois Studies in the Social Sciences, Vol. XXXIV, No. 3. Urbana, Illinois, The University of Illinois Press, 1954.

Reddig, William M., *Tom's Town: Kansas City and the Pendergast Legend.* Philadelphia, J. B. Lippincott Company, 1947.

Rollins, Alfred B., Jr., *Roosevelt and Howe.* New York, Alfred A. Knopf, Inc., 1962.

Schlesinger, Arthur M., Jr., *The Age of Roosevelt,* Vol. I, *The Crisis of the Old Order, 1919–1933,* and Vol. II, *The Coming of the New Deal.* Boston, Houghton Mifflin Company, 1957–1959. 3 vols.

Shannon, David A., *Between the Wars: America, 1919–1941.* Boston, Houghton Mifflin Company, 1965.

Shoemaker, Floyd C., *History of Missouri and Missourians.* Columbia, Missouri, The Walter Ridgway Publishing Company, 1922.

————, *Missouri and Missourians: Land of Contrasts and People of Achievement.* Chicago: Lewis Publishing Company, 1943. 5 vols.

Sinclair, Andrew, *Prohibition: The Era of Excess.* Boston, Little, Brown and Company, 1962.

Smith, Gene, *When the Cheering Stopped: The Last Years of Woodrow Wilson.* New York, William Morrow and Company, Inc., 1964.

Tatum, Elbert Lee, *The Changed Political Thought of the Negro, 1915–1940.* New York, Exposition Press, 1951.

Taylor, Henry, Jr., and W. A. Bingham, *A General History of Shelby County, Missouri.* Chicago, Henry Taylor and Company, 1911.

Truman, Harry S, *Memoirs*, Vol. I, *Year of Decisions.* Garden City, N.Y., Doubleday & Company, Inc., 1955. 2 vols.

Williams, Walter B., and Floyd C. Shoemaker, eds., *Missouri, Mother of the West: Missouri Biography.* Vol. I, Chicago, American Historical Society, Inc., 1930. 5 vols.

Williams, Walter B., *The State of Missouri: An Autobiography.* Columbia, Missouri, E. W. Stephens, 1904.

Wolfskill, George, *The Revolt of the Conservatives: A History of the American Liberty League, 1934–1940.* Boston, Houghton Mifflin Company, 1962.

H. *Articles*

Allen, Lee N., "The McAdoo Campaign for the Presidential Nomination in 1924." *Journal of Southern History*, 29 (May, 1963), 211–28.

————, "The Underwood Presidential Movement of 1924." *Alabama Review*, 15 (April, 1958), 83–93.

"Arthur Mastick Hyde," *National Cyclopedia of Biography*, B, 182–83.

Astorino, Samuel J., "The Contested Senate Election of William Scott Vare." *Pennsylvania History*, 28 (April, 1961), 187–201.

Burner, David B., "The Breakup of the Wilson Coalition of 1916." *Mid-America*, 45 (January, 1963), 18–35.

————, "The Brown Derby Campaign." *New York History*, 46 (October, 1965), 356–80.

————, "The Democratic Party in the Election of 1924." *Mid-America*, 46 (April, 1964), 92–113.

Carleton, William G., "The Politics of the Twenties." *Current History*, 47 (October, 1964), 210–15, 242.

Carter, Paul A., "The Campaign of 1928 Re-examined: A Study in Political Folklore." *Wisconsin Magazine of History*, 46 (Summer, 1963), 263–72.

————, "The Other Catholic Candidate: The 1928 Presidential Bid of Thomas J. Walsh." *Pacific Northwest Quarterly*, 55 (January, 1964), 1–8.

Clevenger, Homer, "Missouri Becomes a Doubtful State." *Mississippi Valley Historical Review*, 39 (March, 1943), 541–56.

Crisler, Robert M., "Missouri's 'Little Dixie'." *Missouri Historical Review*, 42 (January, 1948), 130–39.

Degler, Carl N., "American Political Parties and the Rise of the City: An Interpretation." *Journal of American History*, 51 (June, 1964), 41–59.

Diamond, William, "Urban and Rural Voting in 1896." *American Historical Review*, 46 (January, 1941), 281–305.

Dorsett, Lyle W., "Alderman Jim Pendergast." *Bulletin of the Missouri Historical Society*, 20 (October, 1964), 3–16.

———, "Kansas City Politics: A Study of Boss Pendergast's Machine." *Arizona and the West*, 8 (Summer, 1966), 107–18.

Eldersveld, Samuel J., "Influence of Metropolitan Party Pluralities on Presidential Elections Since 1920." *American Political Science Review*, 43 (December, 1949), 1189–1206.

Friedman, Robert P., "The Candidate Speaks: Arthur M. Hyde." *Missouri Historical Review*, 61 (October, 1966), 51–61.

Grady, J. C., "Missouri Farm Prices Since 1910." *Missouri Agricultural Experiment Station Research Bulletin*, No. 508 (September, 1952), 3–32.

Hennings, Robert E., "California Democratic Politics in the Period of Republican Ascendancy." *Pacific Historical Review*, 31 (August, 1962), 267–80.

Hicks, John D., "Research Opportunities in the 1920's." *The Historian*, 25 (November, 1962), 1–13.

Hofstadter, Richard, "Could a Protestant Have Beaten Hoover in 1928?" *The Reporter*, 22 (March 17, 1960), 31–33.

Huthmacher, J. Joseph, "Urban Liberalism and the Age of Reform." *Mississippi Valley Historical Review*, 64 (September, 1962), 231–41.

"It Won't Be Reed." *Outlook*, 159 (October 7, 1931), 165–66.

"James A. Reed." *National Cyclopaedia of Biography*, 34, 9–11.

"'Jim' Reed's Opening Blast." *Literary Digest*, 93 (October 29, 1927), 10–11.

Kent, Frank R., "Senator 'Jim' Reed." *Forum*, 78 (July, 1927), 62–70.

Link, Arthur S., "What Happened to Progressivism in the 1920's?" *American Historical Review*, 64 (July, 1959), 833–51.

Mitchell, Franklin D., "The Re-election of Irreconcilable James A. Reed." *Missouri Historical Review*, 60 (July, 1966), 416–35.

———, "Who Is Judge Truman?: The Truman-for-Governor Movement of 1931." *Midcontinent American Studies Journal*, 7 (Fall, 1966), 3–15.

"Nation-Wide Press Poll on the League of Nations." *Literary Digest*, 61 (April 5, 1919), 13–16.

Neal, Nevin E., "The Smith-Robinson Arkansas Campaign of 1928." *Arkansas Historical Quarterly*, 19 (Spring, 1960), 3–11.

Noggle, Burl, "The Twenties: A New Historiographical Frontier." *Journal of American History*, 53 (September, 1966), 299–314.

Patterson, James T., "F.D.R. and the Democratic Triumph." *Current History*, 47 (October, 1964), 216–20, 243–44.

Ross, Charles G., "Reed of Missouri." *Scribner's*, 83 (February, 1928), 151–62.

Schlesinger, Arthur M., Jr., "Sources of the New Deal." *Columbia University Forum*, 2 (Fall, 1959), 4–12.

Schmidtlein, Gene, "Truman's First Senatorial Election." *Missouri Historical Review*, 57 (January, 1963), 128–55.

Sellers, Charles G., Jr., "Who Were the Southern Whigs?" *American Historical Review*, 59 (January, 1954), 335–46.

"Senator 'Jim' Reed as Presidential Timber." *Literary Digest*, 92 (February 5, 1927), 12–13.

Soule, George, "Concerning Senator Reed." *The New Republic*, 14 (March 23, 1918), 237.

Stone, Ralph A., "Two Illinois Senators Among the Irreconcilables." *Mississippi Valley Historical Review*, 50 (December, 1963), 443–65.

Stratton, David H., "Splattered With Oil: William G. McAdoo and the 1924 Presidential Nomination." *Southwestern Social Science Quarterly*, 44 (June, 1963), 62–75.

Watson, Richard A., "Religion and Politics in Mid-America: Presidential Voting in Missouri, 1928 and 1960." *Midcontinent American Studies Journal*, 5 (Spring, 1964), 33–55.

Watson, Richard L., Jr., "A Political Leader Bolts – F. M. Simmons in the Presidential Election of 1928." *North Carolina Historical Review*, 37 (October, 1960), 516–43.

———, "The Defeat of Judge Parker: A Study in Pressure Groups and Politics." *Mississippi Valley Historical Review*, 50 (September, 1963), 213–34.

———, "Woodrow Wilson and His Interpreters." *Mississippi Valley Historical Review*, 44 (September, 1957), 207–36.

"Why 'Lone Wolf' Reed Came Back." *Literary Digest*, 74 (August, 1922), 15–16.

INDEX

Anheuser-Busch Brewery, 114, 115, 149–50, 153
Anti-Saloon League: and 1922 senatorial campaign, 55–57; and 1926 senatorial campaign, 91, 92; and prohibition repeal, 94–95; and Reed, 105; and progressivism, 113, 186n31; and 1928 senatorial candidates, 113; and August A. Busch, 114; opposes Al Smith in 1928, 118; and 1930 congressional candidates, 133
Antilynching bill: as Negro legislative goal, 125; Democratic sponsorship of, 136–37, 138, 190–91n43; and Republicans, 136, 138, 191n45. *See also* Federal antilynching bill
Association Against the Eighteenth Amendment, 95, 114, 149

Bailey, Ralph E., 101
Bailey, Thomas, 34
Baker, Sam A.: background, 14; elected governor, 77–80, 126, 162; and Negroes, 87, 88, 125–26
Barnett, Peter, 27
Barrett, Jesse W., 178n52
Barton, William, 151–52
Becker, Charles U., 128–31, 138, 193–94n47
Bogy, Bernard, 81
Bolling, John R., 178n60
Bossism, 151, 153, 154, 156, 193–94n47, 194n48
Bourk, Gil, 136, 137
Brewster, R. R., 55, 59, 60–61
Briggs, Frank P., 165–66
Burger, Nelle, 91–92, 94, 95, 108, 118, 121, 188n61
Burke, Edmund, 172n7

Burkean philosophy, 45, 46, 58
Burner, David, 175n32
Busch, August A., 114, 115, 149
Busch, Mrs. Augustus, 97–98
Busch family, 97
Butler, Edward, 7–8

Cannon, Clarence, 11, 152
Catholics: clash with Protestant values, xii; in Missouri, 5–6, 7; of St. Louis, 7, 113–14; of Kansas City, 8; and American Protective Association, 10; German, 13, 114; and rural Protestants, 67; and Ku Klux Klan, 67–68, 77–78; and Al Smith, 109, 112, 113–14
Caulfield, Henry S.: as governor, 7, 111, 119, 123; and Negroes, 123, 126–27, 127, 137–38; and antilynching bill, 137–38, 191n45
Chambers, Jordan, 87, 130, 189n19
Chorn, Walter K., 69
Citizens Organization Opposed to Proposition Number 4, 94–95
Clark, Bennett Champ: voting formula of, 71; plea for harmony, 85; on Pendergast, 146; political philosophy of, 147, 155, 164; campaign of 1932, 148–57, 164, 171n19, 181n38; and prohibition issue, 149, 161–62; and Roosevelt, 164; mentioned, 8, 75, 147, 148, 151
Clark, Champ, 11, 16, 20, 41
Clark, Crittenden E., 124, 130, 189n19
Cochran, John, 189n21
Cockrell, Ewing, 91–92, 93, 96
Colby, Bainbridge, 25
Collet, James, 109–11
Communist party, 194n54

Ellis, Edgar C., 133
Ethnic groups. *See* Foreign-born voters; German-Americans; Irish-Americans; Italian-Americans; Negroes; New immigrants; Old-stock Americans

Fair Deal, 166
Fall, Albert, 107
Farm prices: in 1926, 101; in 1929–30, 134
Farm relief legislation: in 1926 campaign, 101–2, 112, 117, 160, 184n16. *See also* McNary-Haugen bill
Farris, Frank H.: life and career, 12; pro-League, 21; abandons McAdoo, 72
Federal antilynching bill, 81, 99. *See also* Antilynching bill
Federal Farm Board, 155–56
Folk, Joseph, 7–8, 84
Fordyce, Sam, 74, 181n34
Foreign-born voters, 4–6, 171n10. *See also* Ethnic groups
Foster, William Z., 194n54
Francis, David R., 28, 173n10
Franklin, C. A.: and Negro voters, 65–66; and *Kansas City Call*, 65, 100, 191n45
Freidel, Frank, xi, 83, 143, 175n32
Friends of Irish Freedom societies, 26, 27, 29, 41
Fulbright, James F., 72, 81, 101, 151–52

Gardner, Frederick D.: as Democratic leader, 8, 45; and harmony movement, 68–69
Garner, John Nance, 143, 145
Garner, Silas E., 130
George, Walter, 109
German-Americans: of Missouri, 2, 3, 13; and political parties, 5, 7, 13, 28, 31, 54–55, 58, 70; in St. Louis, 7, 86, 97–98, 100, 114, 119–20, 153, 161, 175n32, 189n18; against prohibition, 13, 54–55, 97–98, 101, 115; oppose League, 26–27, 28, 29, 31; for

Reed, 54, 58; for Al Smith, 114–15, 122
Glass, Carter, 76, 106
Glenn, Ed, 75, 181n38
Goat Democrats. *See* Pendergast organization
Gold Star Mothers, Negro, 127–28
Goltra, Edward J.: as National Committeeman, 8; pro-League scheme, 26; on Reed, 28, 141; and Roosevelt, 141
Good Roads movement, 84
Graham, Christine, 33
Great Depression: economic impact of, 133–34, 139, 140; political effect, 139, 140, 154–59, 163
Greenwade, Charles, 192n21
Gualdoni, Louis J., 145, 146, 192n22

Hadley, Herbert S., 4
Harding, Warren G., xi, 4, 40, 41
Hawes, Harry B.: early career, 8, 84–85; congressional campaign of 1920, 40–41, 176n33; of 1924, 78, 79, 81; on Klan, 76, 78, 81, 84–85; and Negroes, 81, 98; and good roads movement, 84; Jeffersonian revival, 84–85; harmony movement of, 84–104 *passim*; on League of Nations, 84; and World Court, 89, 90; farm relief, 92, 93, 96; senatorial campaign of 1926, 85, 88–89 *passim*, 100, 102; and prohibition, 92, 94, 95, 97, 142, 161; against Parker nomination, 128; role in Roosevelt's nomination in 1932, 142–43, 192n12
Hay, Charles M.: pro-League advocate, 23, 24, 42; and Reed, 23–24, 44, 59, 72, 102–4, 110–11, 148; and prohibition, 23, 89, 90, 96, 111–12, 140, 142, 149–54 *passim*, 161, 188n61; and 1920 senatorial primary campaign, 37–38; role in 1922 senatorial campaign, 45, 59; supports McAdoo in 1924, 72–73; supports

tion to Negro defections to Democratic party, 131; opposition to bosses, 131; support for John Wesson, 132; on antilynching bill, 137

Kansas City Democracy. *See* Pendergast organization; Joseph B. Shannon; Casimer J. Welch

Kansas City Star, 72, 93, 121–22, 131, 151

Kansas City Times, 118

Kem, James P., 165

Kemper, William T., 44

Kent, Frank R., 105

Key, V. O., Jr., 15

Kiel, Henry W., 152–53, 155–57, 162

Kinney, Michael J., 8, 127, 136–38, 189n7, 190–91n43

Knox, L. Amasa, 124–25

Knox County, 36

Ku Klux Klan: and Negroes, 64–65, 80, 86–87, 115, 183n9; nature of, 67–68; strength of, 67–68, 180n14; and 1924 state convention, 75; and Reed-McAdoo contest, 75, 181n38; and 1924 national convention, 76; and 1924 gubernatorial campaign, 77–80, 181n44, n46; and congressional contests, 81; in Kansas City area, 79–80, 182n52; in St. Louis, 86–87, 183n9; effect upon Democracy, 160; and Truman, 182n52

La Follette, Robert, 19, 79, 182n50

Landon, Alfred M., 165

League of Loyal Democrats, 58, 59, 178n56, n60

League of Nations: as political issue, xii, 15, 16–31, 67, 71, 160–61; and Wilson, 17, 29–30; pro-League sentiment in Missouri, 20–22, 30–31, 66–67, 173n15; diminished Democratic support for, 66–67, 180n12. *See also* Harry B. Hawes; Thomas J. Pendergast; James A. Reed; Joseph B. Shannon; Woodrow Wilson

Lee, Charles E., 100

Lemp, Charles, 192n22

Leuchtenburg, William E., 121

Liberal Republicans, 59

Liberalism. *See* Progressivism

Liberty League, 164–65

Lincoln, Abraham, 131

Lincoln Day, 180n25

Lincoln Republicanism, 124, 128, 131

Lincoln University, 87–88, 125–27

Link, Arthur S., xi, 17, 169n1, 169n2, 177n23

Little Dixie, 11–12, 119, 138, 187–n52

Lodge, Henry Cabot, 30

Long, Breckinridge: on League, 30–31, 38–39, 42, 49–50; early life and career, 32–33; senatorial campaign of 1920, 32–39, 40, 41, 45; senatorial campaign of 1922, 44–58 *passim*; and Wilson in 1922, 44–49 *passim*, 52, 54, 55, 57–60 *passim*, 62, 177n17, 178n54; and Wilson doctrine, 45, 46, 51–52, 57–58, 183n55; and 1922 election results, 60–61, 178n52; and Negro voters, 65; and Wilson in 1924, 72; McAdoo campaign of 1924, 72–74, 180n27; Ambassador to Italy, 164. *See also* James A. Reed; Woodrow Wilson

Long, Edward V., 165

Lozier, Ralph, 152

Lubell, Samuel, 115

Lynching, 135–36

McAdoo, William G.: supporters of, 1, 30; as potential presidential candidate in 1924, 69–74, 180n27; convention support for, 74–76; analysis of Democratic party leadership, 105–6; withdrawal from 1927 presidential race in 1927, 106

McCawley, Alfred M., 111

McDaniel, Lawrence, 8, 165, 189-n18

McLemore, Joseph L., 116, 122, 126, 162, 188n64

ABOUT THE AUTHOR

FRANKLIN D. MITCHELL, a native of Iowa, holds degrees from Iowa State University (B.S., 1956), and the University of Missouri (M.A., 1959, and Ph.D., 1964). He served two years with the United States Army, from 1953 to 1955.

In addition to the present work, Professor Mitchell has written articles on Missouri history for scholarly journals. He is now an assistant professor of history at Washburn University of Topeka, Topeka, Kansas.

54581

DATE DUE